MW01485646

ONE OFF

THE ROADS, THE RACES, THE AUTOMOBILES
OF
TOLY ARUTUNOFF

ANATOLY A. ARUTUNOFF

Published by Beeman Jorgensen, Inc.
7510 Allisonville Road, Suite 125, Indianapolis, IN 46250 U.S.A.

Printed and bound in the Slovak Republic
Cover design by Llew Kinst, Cupertino, California
Layout by Brett Johnson

First Printing, September 2008

This book is dedicated to those who start smiling and then grinning, when they approach an interesting car. There are others, also involved with cars, who don't. You know who you are.

Anyone who drives slower than you is an idiot, and anyone who drives faster than you is a maniac.

George Carlin

Contents

My Heroes

The people who inspire me, who've done and do it right: Satch Carlson, Jesse Coleman, Lella and Pete Coltrin, Larry Crane, Tony Crook, Dad, Charles von der Essing, Steve Earle, Art Eastman, Chris Economaki, Peter Egan, Philip Finch, Allan Girdler, Edward Gorey, Ed Henning, Ed Hugus, William Jeanes, Jesus, Delmo Johnson, Charles Lucas, Count Giovanni Lurani, Leon Mandel, Denise McCluggage, Mom, Tom Newcomer, Gil Nickel, Paul Newman, P. J. O'Rourke, Sandy Orttewell, Pastor Bill, S. J. Perelman, Brian Redman, L.J.K. Setright, Trace Sheehan, Bob Snodgrass, Danny Sullivan, Bob Sutherland, Myron Vernis, Bill Warner, Wife, Mason Williams, Brock Yates and _____ (and your name, dear reader, if it's not here and you think it should be).

Foreword

You can't imagine how happy I am that Toly finally put many of his life experiences to pen and paper. Perhaps, as we drift off tonight, I won't have to say, "It's time to stop talking, dear, and go to sleep." Could he actually be talked out? I sincerely doubt it, but then that's part of his charm.

After you hear something long enough your memory fools you into thinking you were there, and that's how Toly's book feels to me. But since I'm *much* younger that simply couldn't be. However, the one story that pretty much sums up our twenty-year partnership and ten-year marriage is one not found on these pages. It's really not about racing and probably too recent in his mind to be considered worthy of discussion, which is just another way of saying he hasn't told it countless times in the pits at Laguna Seca or to the boys in the British Car Club of Arkansas. Regardless, it is an amalgamation of what life with Toly is like.

Shortly after our son, Trace, moved to New York to pursue an acting career, we decided to get one of the new Hondas from the dealership and drive up from Oklahoma to see him. Normal people would fly, especially in the winter, when the Pennsylvania Turnpike has the added feature of being icy, which in some way is a lot more interesting than being just plain mind-numbing boring.

In the evening about halfway into the two-day adventure in southern Illinois at 75mph, we narrowly escaped hitting a deer. As I breathed a sigh of relief, we hit the second deer. The poor thing went sailing into the median with the front end of the brand new Honda attached to some part of its anatomy. We pulled off at the first available exit to survey the damage. In addition to having a missing grill and front bumper there were numerous black plastic ventilation parts co-mingled with deer remains hanging down and around our not-so-lovely new car. As I never leave home without jewelry and duct tape, Toly was able to make the necessary repairs, while adding to the ambiance of the vehicle. Thus, when we arrived the next night in New York, we cut quite a swath!

Trace had made a reservation for us at the ever so *chi-chi* Gansevoort, which if you haven't tried it is worth the show. I would have to say, the night we arrived, we were the headliners.

It had been snowing all day in New York City and by midnight the converging streets of the Meat-Packing District around the Gansevoort were a mix of ice, slush, stretch limos, Maybachs etc. The beautiful people were standing in line in 15 degree weather to the curb to be allowed entrance to the *direct to the rooftop bar* elevator to look at other beautiful people. And then there were the *Joads* – that would be us arriving with the only legit reservation in the place in our bright shiny, newly duct-taped deer fur and flesh decorated Honda with Oklahoma plates. Where is a doorman when you need one?

To say we were ignored doesn't begin to describe the looks of disdain being shot at us from every direction. I doubt if anyone in line had ever read *Grapes of Wrath*, but we were enacting the 21st century East Coast version with aplomb. Determined to check in with some small bit of dignity, I told Toly to stay with the car, while I threw on some jewelry and headed for the lobby (you always get better service with good jewelry).

The bellman wasn't exactly kicking and screaming, as I dragged him into the cold to our car, but you could see in his eyes he was thinking about it. As he held the big glass and chrome door for me, making sure that no one from the line darted through to the bar before their shoes were approved, I caught sight of Toly, who had exited the car and was now having a conversation with someone in a $300K automobile, pointing out that the duct tape on our car had the appearance of a tribute to Frank Gehry.

Why should this surprise me? The surprise was the ball cap he had donned from the floor of the backseat. The cap wasn't one of those things you deliberately pack, but when you need a ball cap you need a ball cap. The problem was, this ball cap said "Wish You Were Hair."

Truly, this completed the pictorial of our arrival at The Gansevoort. I began to snicker, then laugh out loud, then became hysterical with laughter, tears and all! You had to have been there to see the story of my life with Toly unfolding before my eyes in this one little vignette.

I was with the man I love, but he was wearing a baseball cap that said, "Wish You Were Hair." We were at The Gansevoort, but no one would check us in, much less stand too near, for fear some Oklahoma crud might mix with New York City slush and cause an epidemic of men wearing baseball caps that you'll never find on the second floor of Barney's. We had driven up in a car from a dealership Toly had been inspired to begin, except it was covered in duct tape and deer guts. But the fact of the matter is, we were not hurt, there are plenty more Hondas where that one came from and we've stayed in the finest hotels on the planet in pursuit of cars and races and rallies and car friends.

The world should be so lucky to live the life I have lived with Toly. Oh, how I love that man of mine and look forward to the day that all you who read this book can join me in saying, "We've heard that one before."

Karen Arutunoff

Introduction

I f one pursues most any hobby for the duration of one's adult life, there will be lots of stories to tell, but if you're a woodcarver there won't be much of a crowd. Car stories generally tend toward the other end of the popularity spectrum.

So, here are the tales of a bunch of things that happened when I was in cars, near cars or sometimes, just thinking about cars. Many kind people through the years have told me I should write a book and I began to have little brain-stirrings that I could be a *writer* based on the fun had by all with my dozen or so columns in *Vintage Motorsport* and my MA in English Lit. Then I read all P. J. O'Rourke's books in one week and realized I'm certainly not a writer. I'm a talker who can type.

I wish all you guys and I were together as I write and you read this thing. And don't get P.C. on me – *guys* describes people who like cars and especially those who like to drive cars, never mind what sex you are and there's no such thing as fender-gender.

There is absolutely no question that any form of organized automotive competition used to be more fun. Why? I tend to think it is due to Mr. and Ms. Money and Modifications. When Eisenhower was President, practically all racing was "showroom stock" racing. Somewhere I've got a tape of a NASCAR race and in the intro inspectors are shown, as the voice-over states, "making absolutely sure that the parts in these cars are exactly the same as the ones on the car in your driveway."

You could put a straight pipe on your SCCA racer and also remove the air cleaner, but that was about it. If you bought a sports-racing car from a European manufacturer it was built to FIA specs, which meant when you rolled it out of the crate it had headlights, probably turn signals, two seats of equal size, a specified luggage space, spare tire and, most of the time, a license plate mount with cute little lights. Sure, you could fool with it as long as you didn't increase the displacement over the class limit; otherwise you put in seatbelts, taped the lights and went racing.

Some folks street-licensed their racecars and kept the revs down to avoid stirring up the fuzz. Lotus XIs and bobtail Coopers were fast class winning cars often driven, not trailered, to Le Mans. In America, in the late 1950s you'd have to put a rollbar in, but its acceptability was determined by your friendly local tech inspector, not specs from Headquarters. *Non-rollbar GT racing* went on in Europe until the 1971 season.

Examples of all of the above: In 1967, if the cargo ship hadn't been late I would've picked up a Lamborghini Miura at the New Orleans docks, driven it to Bonneville, installed belts and a harness and taken the 4.2 liter sports car class record (wasn't it nice that the SCTA set a limit at 4.2 liters so the latest E-Type Jags could run) from its 140-something mph record to something approaching 160. In 1968 I'd have had to put in a rollcage and all that kind of thing.

And 4 ½ years earlier, if another ship hadn't been late, I'd have picked up the 2.5 liter Lancia Flaminia Zagato 3C, driven through Nashville to pick up my co-driver Bill Pryor and zipped down to Sebring, where we were entered in the 12-hour race. As an FIA race, we didn't need a rollbar in GT Class 11, nor in any other class for that matter, and we'd both sent in our $5 and bought our FIA Competition licenses. Car, drivers, no spares; hey, Lancias may not be many things, but they are rugged.

I took delivery of the car on a Thursday morning, the Thursday when the first day, and only night, practice session was held. New York, Nashville, Sebring – impossible in one day and barely possible in two. That would have meant arriving at Sebring the night before the race. Rats!

I was feeling sorry for myself in the traffic jam leading into the Lincoln Tunnel, making the final decision to head for Oklahoma and not Sebring. Several cars ahead, the driver bailed out and ran back to me. "A Lancia Flaminia Zagato!" he exclaimed. "You are one lucky guy!" As he trotted back to his car, I had to agree with him, Sebring or not.

A few years ago I was told by somebody in a position to know, that if I'd gotten to Sebring an hour before the start, I could have run the race. "Hell," he said, "it was a sport then! You knew Alec Ullman and Chief Starter Jesse Coleman. It would've made a great story – they'd let you drive a reconnaissance lap or two – maybe even in whatever the preliminary little support race there was – while Art Peck or Chris Economaki said over the P.A. 'And with no qualifying time, gridded last, Toly Arutunoff and Bill Pryor in the Lancia that arrived an hour ago from New York. Give 'em a big hand, folks!'" Rats again.

In the SCCA, I ran the stock Miura twice as an A Sports Racer. It had competition belts and harness and an extinguisher bolted to the floor in front of the passenger seat. No additional rollbar. I ran Savannah and Huntsville airport races (at Huntsville I was in ASR with the Howmet turbine car – good times!) and took the car to the Montgomery, AL street race, where the brake fade that showed up mid-race in the first two events came on big time on my third lap of practice – pedal to the floor and lots of downshifting. Since I had to drive the car back to Nashville, I retired from the weekend's sport and half an hour after I'd pulled into the pits the pedal felt normal. It never occurred to me to bleed the brakes, but I did check to see that I had most of the pads left.

The Miura also got me acquainted with the wonderful late Mr. Leon Mandel, under what to me were mildly confusing circumstances. Gary Ford and I went to the '67 F1 race at Watkins Glen and got invited to what I think was the *Car & Driver* party at a private home. We got to park the Miura pretty much in front of the door and shortly thereafter a well-dressed man walked up to me and said acerbically, "Is that your car? Well, make it do something!"

I figured this character for an automotive illiterate, so I carefully explained to him exactly what the car was and what it could do, and at the moment I would make it do nothing, because I was going to get myself a drink. He then informed me that he had a

Corvair in his driveway that hadn't run for years, and walked away. To paraphrase a famous movie line, this was the beginning of a beautiful friendship.

The year before, I'd qualified for the SCCA runoffs (then called the American Road Race of Champions) at Riverside by racing my 427/425 hp Corvette at Courtland, Alabama's airport. Although the car was geared so long that I only used fourth gear on the mile-long straight (my cornering speed was limited by the stock Vette knockoff wheels and Pirelli Cinturato street tires), two of the three 427 Cobras also entered in the A Production class broke down, thereby giving me 6 points and third place in the Southeast Division and a runoffs invitation.

I had the dealer's chassis cutaway drawings to show the Alabama Region's tech inspector, and after he compared all the steel and fiberglass in my coupe's roof with the simple rollbars in the open Cobras and B Prod. Vettes he rationally agreed that my rollover protection was at least their equal.

I put the fire extinguisher in the glove compartment, hooked the competition belts to the standard attachments and sailed through tech. I must say that later Don Yenko told me I shouldn't race on the stock knockoffs, as the ribs could begin cracking and the wheel might collapse in a lap or two.

I'd race a car that way today and so would a good many of you, if you weren't subliminally stimulated into thinking that the more safety equipment you have on your car, the more of a racing driver you are. This is the mechanical/psychological equivalent to walking around all day in your driver's suit. Yes, I walk around all day in my driver's suit too, but it's because (a) I'm too lazy to change clothes and (b) I'd rather not get my regular clothes all sweaty.

Even Indy in those days was a kind of stock. All those Offys were pretty much alike, and just how much suspension tuning could you do to a couple live axles back then? To counter this argument, one could claim that Champ Car Racing is now *Millionaire's Formula Ford* and that the IRL is a similar spec. class, and I wouldn't disagree.

Remember that this collection of words was composed by someone responsible for rules changes in both SCCA and IMSA, after being disqualified in both clubs. Anybody want to back me in an IRL effort? NASCAR wouldn't be any fun, because they change the rules constantly anyway. Yep, people have messed with me and then quietly fixed things and rearranged this and that so the next character won't have to put up with the same stuff. I regard the fixes as kind of an apology.

So let me take you back with some astigmatic and faded glimpses of a time that is no more. It'd be nice if we could include a few little packets of Castrol Racing R (like those ketchup portions at the drive-in). You'd put a few drops in an old pan on the stove, turn all the lights off except for your little reading lamp and slowly, or maybe suddenly – well, let's just get on with it.

Youth: Capers, Frivolities and Other Gambols

More than once, people have accused me of living in the past. That's plain impossible, but sometimes I'd like to. Once someone said, "Toly was nostalgic when he was seven years old, I bet!" and I surprised him by agreeing with him. That's what comes of spending summers, and sometimes autumns, in a magnificent house in southern California, and then returning home to cold rain, Bartlesville, Oklahoma, and school.

Not that I minded school – I had friends accessible to me, while in California they were always a half hour drive away. In Oklahoma I had a bicycle, which I was not permitted to have in L.A. Out west we had the Russian film colony and others of that profession dropping by the house from time to time and of course, coming for parties; Akim Tamiroff, Ivan Lebedeff and his *smack slobber drool pant pant* wife (my reaction, not hers) Vera Engels. I don't know how many hormones six to ten-year olds are supposed to have, but I had at least that many.

Then there was Johnny Weissmuller, Alan Mowbray, I think Arthur Treacher came by as someone's guest once. Unless you're ripe or a film nut you may be asking, "Who the hell are these people?"

My brother-in-law Ralph and my sister Anait were buddies with Robert and Dorothy Mitchum and the Mitchums came by pleasantly often – neat people. Fred Astaire's son and I were great friends for awhile until our nurses got into a fight and then he didn't visit me any more.

Erich von Stroheim had a drink or two at our house. Mom and

Dad had a fight once because one or the other of them didn't want Ayn Rand to pay a visit.

My brother Sergei's pals were the Dead End Kids, genuinely scary types to an overprotected little esthete from the Great Plains such as moi. The Deadend Kids, if you haven't seen any of their movies, defined and were the sole practitioners of a *young hood-lum/noir* genre. The Bowery Boys were their comic spinoff.

The family had a house in California partially because Mom wanted one and partially because Dad built oil pumps and there was quite a lot of oil under California. Trouble was, the sand in the fluid ate up the centrifugal impellers and the seals. So we sold the house. Doggone it! Not only did we have the biggest swimming pool in the L.A. residential area, 25' x 50' and 9' at its deepest point with a yard-square underwater observation window, but there was a girls' school about 150 yards over the hill behind us. I knew I was making plans, lots of plans, but being twelve years old I wasn't completely sure what those plans were. They most certainly involved the girls' school and the pool, though. I was quite sure of that.

Of course the minute we sold that fantastic house (ask me about it sometime. It won't be quick) Dad figured out a new design for the pump so sand didn't bother it. I wish you'd thought about a year faster, Dad.

Capturing the Moment

I still have the memories, but why didn't I keep the pictures? Yes, pictures of your old, and especially old wrecked cars, bring back even more memories and often they can freeze your thoughts into what was going on at the moment the photo was taken.

Think about your old photos for a minute. When someone takes your picture, time stops for a few seconds. You hold the sparkplug you were changing, turn around or look up, put your arm around your pal and freeze; then the picture is taken. When you look at that photo much later, however, the time investment expands. Yep, those new plugs cured the problem. I think I might still have those shoes. I wonder where old so-and-so is today. Gosh, that was a great/lousy/forgotten summer. It's worth every second you spend gazing at that old photo – and, of course, you were oh, so much younger then.

Smells are at least as evocative, but car-wise they're going to be a lot less common. Say "Castrol Racing R" everyone. Oh, and new leather interiors. A diary is a jewel, but for a shock I recommend sounds: 30 years ago I got two cassettes of old radio commercials – old even then. That's a lot of commercials and I bet, if you heard just one or two, you'd think "Hey! About that time I remember…" Hearing one after another after another picked me up and shook me and threw me down time's stairwells. I remembered this and that. I remembered dropping things. I remembered clouds. I remembered socks, of all things! Do I need professional help? Hell, I probably need amateur help.

There's been a recent discovery that spinach and blueberries help the brain retain memory, so I plan to eat more of both, if I can remember….

Smells! Yes, new car smell, among others. If you've accumulated a few years, you can remember how the smells of new cars have changed – expensive British cars smell pretty much like they once did, but many cars full of leather don't smell like leather used to; i.e. like leather should.

Some students of that indistinct area between the rational and the sensory say that the sense of smell is the closest sense to whatever ESP may be – that it is more complicated than sight. Seems to me that it would be less troubling to lose one's sense of smell than to be blind, but save the extremely particular smell of the aforementioned Castrol Racing R, which only takes me back to my very young adulthood; movie theater odors are by far the most evocative.

I saw the movie *Bird* for the fourth or fifth time the other night. Dexter Gordon's sax took me back to the loveliest music I ever heard, and it didn't seem to have a melody. You see, when you drive and listen to music, you can select your music to match your mood, the car, the road, all of these things. The just-right match-up can truly make the moment.

I must admit that I've hardly heard of, let alone listened to, the music that various automotive journalists mention as their favorite driving tunes. I like a zippy version of *Stagger Lee* (or its copy, *Goin' to Kansas City*) or just about anything by Buddy Rich or Woody Herman, but nothing, repeat nothing, was more wonderful than lying in bed, about age 3 or 4, windows open on a perfect summer night, listening to rehearsal notes floating in from the music teacher's house, a hundred yards away across a vacant lot.

Nothing on my mind (what can you expect at 3 or 4?), but to have my sleepy attention focused on those soft notes. And in the silence, through the windows on the other side of the room, the distant bark of the Hemsel's cocker spaniel, a block and a half away.

So, when I was an infant, I delighted in dropping off to sleep listening to the pretty, but disorganized notes floating through the evening air from the music man's house.

Pleasant enough, but for a really cheerful awakening, consider this. In the Oklahoma autumn, when I was at home in my own room, I'd sleep with the windows open in nice weather. Not two blocks away, the high school marching band would rehearse, marching from the school toward my house. I hope you don't have to be my age to imagine the fun of college fight songs and the occasional Sousa march soaring in through your windows. Bands didn't play rock and roll in those days and thankfully rap had not yet been invented.

I guess, all things considered, the most special way to awaken is with a Ferrari sports racer's exhaust stuck into your window; but in a larger life context, the marching band has everything else covered. You probably need to have the whole scene for it to work properly: the band, crisp autumn air, slanting sunlight through maroon, red and yellow leaves. As we float away from this thought, being from Oklahoma I thought autumn meant those colors. Well, maybe orange, too.

When I got out of the car at Watkins Glen one October before the Fl race, I saw a grove of trees: lavender, mauve, heliotrope, puce, magenta, lilac etc. I guess you couldn't expect a classy state like New York to have plain old orange and yellow leaves.

There are other fondly remembered sounds, especially for any of you old enough and from oil country. Those tall teeter-totter looking walking beam oil pumps, now driven by an electric motor right there on the pad, were once operated by a long system of rods driven by a gas engine in a powerhouse in the center of the oilfield. I mean gas, not gasoline. These things had, oh, seems like 8' diameter flywheels and turned about 50rpm or less. They operated with natural gas and, for whatever reason, only fired maybe two times out of every five revolutions. With young ears, one or two miles away in junior high school with the windows open in spring and with the wind just right, they were perceptible with their almost subsonic thumps. When I was little, we kids were told they were Indian drums, and late at night (say 9 PM) it was easy to imagine distant figures dancing around a campfire to the regular, but intermittent drumbeat.

But – a band marching past my front door by the time I got some coffee and stepped out onto my front porch – meaningless fun maybe, but *fan-damn-tastic*. Try remembering sounds you haven't heard for awhile. It will make you feel younger for a moment or two - or maybe you don't need that as much as I do.

In 1950s America we had some pretty strange people. They were only seen occasionally, but consistently, way back then. Around Bartlesville we had a funny one and a scary one. Yes, they were mental cases and needed help, but we kids simply took them as interesting scenery. The funny one was a big guy in an overcoat - summer and winter – who walked the highway shoulders for a few miles in every direction. He carried a large sack; the word gunnysack comes to mind, though I haven't heard that word in decades. You'd slow down as you passed and ask, "What ya got in the sack?" and he would lean away from you and defiantly proclaim, "My sack!" Of course, we called him Mysack.

The scary one, actually two, were identical Down syndrome twins, the long-faced kind, not the round-faced ones, which seem to be the majority. These two youngish guys (though some thought they were female) walked through the town, giggling quietly and nudging each other. This was just before and during my bicycle days, and all of us were warned by our parents to stay on the opposite side of the street when we saw them coming, and be prepared to run. They had tortured several small animals. They disappeared in a few years and I hope they got the help they needed. Let me tell you, riding a bike alone in the country and suddenly realizing that on this deserted road you were approaching the twins was a thrill I don't want to repeat. I managed a nonchalant u-turn and pedaled away, but I did look over my shoulder and give a friendly wave - and checked that they weren't gaining on me.

Hormones

Seeing and hearing the *Movietone News* titles even on the TCM channel today, enriched by the stentorian tones of announcer Ed Herlihy, brings back the smells of the theater - the movies, that is. We went to *movies* in Bartlesville, not to *the theater* – and for damn sure never *the cinema*. The wonderful popcorn smell (no, it doesn't smell the same nowadays), and then out the west-facing door of the Osage Theater, squinting in the light and heat of the 1951 Oklahoma summer afternoon.

Then it was onto our motorbikes: Don on the 4-stroke 2½ hp Whizzer in a Schwinn frame. Eddie on the 125cc 2-stroke James, with the 3-speed shift lever on the right side of the tank – 3½ hp. Conrad on the 6hp Salisbury streamlined scooter, something like Bill's Cushman, but with 2 more horsepower – and voluptuous modern styling. The school tennis champion, Dave, had a Marmon Twin - a longitudinally opposed 2-stroke twin in a Monark frame from Oklahoma Tire and Supply. When Dave wound that twin out, it sounded like a four-decades-later F1 car!

I leaped onto the kick-starter of my Powell (flathead single, piston and valves from a Ford 6, oil tank in frame, exterior valve springs 8hp) and Keith lit off his Mustang (9½ hp with 20" disc wheels like the Powell), but where I had a centrifugal clutch he had 3 speeds and an exotic foot shift.

All these sounds, 2-stroke oily exhaust with the resonant metallic thrum of the Mustang, the blatty throb of the Powell and the repressed hysteria of the Marmon combined with the green smell of summer, as we reached the elm-wrapped streets of the residential district six blocks south. The vibrations through my handlebars playing against the gentle bob of the big foam-covered seat. Real close friends were riding ahead, behind and beside, and just pals soon filling in the other spots in our 50-foot phalanx as some others joined our little parade. Nothing to do but go for a 40mph cruise with school way off in the past and the future. The folks will be home and dinner will eventually be ready, but I won't be late because we've timed the ride just right. And wow look – two girls in shorts walking along. They're strangers. Dare we wave? We dare! Wow! One even waves back!

Since it will be sunny even after dinner, we might go for a blast out on the new concrete highway, as brilliant as whitewash, wide and straight for ten miles. Before that, there's the big band jazz show on TV, and there might be something as keen as the King Guion band with two big swingin' black drummers, one at each side of the stage. Were they twins?

With the jazz program over, I put my head down, lying on the floor and smelling the wool of the old Persian carpet. As I dozed, a solitary two-stroke went by, heading downtown on Cherokee. Half a minute later, the oily aroma of the exhaust spread through the room, faint and drifting in through the little open windows flanking the fireplace. Home smell. Bike smell. This was now. This was it, and finally the confused jumble of tiny cylinders, as my group comes by to enlist me in the evening's ride.

So none of us were old enough to have a driver's license. So what? Sure, from time to time the police would seem to have a campaign against us, as we snuck down alleys and took side streets to avoid a lecture by Preacher John on his Harley 3-wheeler. "What you're doing is completely illegal, you know. So, just ride that thing home and park it until you have a license."

"Yes sir. Sorry sir." No one ever got a ticket. No parents were ever lectured. *The Law* had its say and that took care of things for another little while.

The most magical ride of all was one full-moon night. After the last movie was over at about 10:30, a big group of us headed out to the new highway. With the roadside vegetation reflecting the moonlight, the whiteness of the pavement made it look like a big neon tube stretching south to the horizon. There was no traffic, so we rode handlebar to handlebar across both lanes, and then turned our puny headlights off. It made no difference – we could still see the road perfectly.

I think eventually somebody had to give Foster Doornbos a ride back, when his 125cc 2-stroke Harley (built by incompetents somewhere in Europe – BSA?) conked out. The few souls who rode those BSAs removed the mufflers, making them uncomfortably loud and probably messing up their cylinder scavenging, since they seemed to be prone to fouling plugs at cruising speed. The James crowd only discovered a fouled plug, when they tried to restart after a cruise around town, most likely looking for more girls in shorts. We could do an instantaneous leg analysis at more than 50 yards. Ah, young eyes and hormones.

Reckless Abandon

Evaluating my youth as I now, er, approach middle age makes me think that kids probably have a better intuitive appreciation and application of the actual probabilities of harm from dangerous acts; neuroses grow in adulthood. In nature's curious way, this is counterbalanced by a young person's greater-than-adult tendency to really put himself in harm's way. It is an extension of the natural desire for learning, which is a characteristic of the young.

Therefore in the early '50s in Oklahoma we ran our cars full throttle (the term *flat out* was decades away for us) for miles on the many straight roads in the vicinity (a few with less than optimum sight lines over hills) and stood up in convertibles (my Lincoln and my Mom's Caribbean) with the top down at over 100mph. That is to be recommended for a great face and upper-body massage. Even tight young skin turns to vibrating corduroy at 100.

We also tanned on trips to Tulsa by lying down on beach towels on the trunk with the top down. I wish we'd compared aerodynamic effects by once leaving the top up and crawling out through the unzipped rear window –- top down probably gave us as much windburn as suntan. By the way, if you gotta go, do *not* try it out of the unzipped rear window, turbulence, uh, *distributes* stuff around the back seat area.

Biggest thrill was lying on the trunk going over Dody's Dumps, as the dirt road to the Rocking D Ranch was called. At 60mph, over the 4 little hills, the wheels of the car would just leave the surface for perhaps two seconds per hillcrest, so lying on the trunk meant you'd go weightless and the wind would catch you so you had to pull yourself forward and back down. Don't think we weren't safety conscious, besides checking the road looking for stray cattle, we'd post guys at each end to flag down any traffic until we were through with our pass.

There was one tragedy years later. Although there was a good long flat stretch to slow down before the t-intersection with the highway, one night a few kids crashed heavily into the berm on the other side of the main road. Alcohol was suspected, but in our time and at our age that sort of thing was almost never done – except at my house on New Year's Eve, when any visitor was given a glass of champagne. I think if you were young enough to have arrived by bicycle you only got a sip, though; my folks were really cool.

In a few years, "beer, because my folks are out of town" was a not totally unknown occurrence at friends' houses, but it didn't catch on too widely, because you can easily imagine what a 16-year-old with three beers and a motor scooter is liable to do after midnight. Police were never involved, of course, but there were several parental questions of the "whatever happened to all our gauze bandages and mercurochrome?" variety.

One autumn afternoon in 1953, gray and cold, the late Eddie Turner, Helen Smith, Sydney Grant and I put the top down on my Lincoln and drove down to Tulsa. In the full flush of teenage energy, we saw *The Robe*, went shopping, saw *Mogambo* and went to a football game that freezing night. We beat Houston 17 – 14; now ask me to remember something important.

The big moment came in mid-afternoon, though, when we saw two Mexican-Road-Race Oldsmobile coupes tearing down a main barely-suburban street about 80mph. We agreed they must be heading for the Turner Turnpike south toward Oklahoma City, and we were right. When we arrived at the gate the Mexican crews were in animated conversation with a couple of carloads of Oklahoma State Troopers, who, I'm happy to say, were laughing at the whole situation. Nobody seemed to be getting a ticket, but I wonder, based on their performance through town, just how fast they drove the 86 miles toward Oklahoma City.

It was just a few years later that a German national, delivering the first 300SL to the Oklahoma City dealership, figured that a toll road logically wouldn't have a speed limit. Now you see the short *American* axle ratio meant he was topped out at about 146mph, but anyway he arrived at the southern tollgate to find it blocked by a collection of patrol cars and crews with guns drawn.

A reporter on the scene told me it was quite amusing to watch the cops trying to figure out how to open the gullwing door while the poor alien inside, quite old enough to have been in the Wehrmacht, seemed to be trembling in fear about what might've finally showed up on his war record.

He was bailed out of jail by the German attaché who flew up from Dallas that evening. There was a photo of the car in the paper, too. Good advertising.

I tore it out of the paper and put it in my drawer full of car brochures and similar stuff and one day, for no reason, I threw it all away, along with a slightly leaking oil-damaged acceleration and braking meter made in W. Germany. 8" across – must have weighed 5 pounds. Worth its weight in silver now I bet.

Convertibles were great gun platforms in the winter. You had the guys with the strongest arms sit up on the folded convertible top and the front seat passenger (the "loader") made a couple dozen perfect snowballs. Next you drove down deserted streets at a constant speed while the gunners practiced to figure out how far to lead a stationary target – a bush right by a sidewalk was best. Then you went looking for prey. Thirty miles an hour gave a pretty good extra kick to a snowball fired from a good arm who'd had target practice.

Of course one doesn't need a car to have fun with snowballs: some evenings we'd hide behind a ridge at the edge of the McKinley school playground, and figure the proper angle to lob a snowball blindly over the fence so it'd land in a lane of traffic. After timing the flight of a few snowballs, an immobile lookout would peek over the edge and when he gave us the sign we'd launch our frosty mortar rounds. *Whomp! Whomp!*

Sometimes we'd hear nasty curses, but even if the car stopped there was no one visible under the streetlights, no footprints in the snow, and we were behind a long chainlink fence anyway. It was probably a good thing we hadn't discovered beer yet.

Cars were so slow in my youth that we used to race to Tulsa; sometimes to make a movie at the last minute, other times just for the heck of it. The '51 Bel Air would just touch 100 on my uncorrected speedometer, with a hint of a following wind. Performance was no different after a factory recall, of all things, in early 1952 for some sort of carb work.

The car was pretty ineffective in any sort of drag race, especially when most of the cars in town had stick shifts. Powerglide's low range was permissible up to 40mph, so I'd floor it in low (never thought to wind it up against the torque converter) and, with my hand at the ready, slap the lever up from L to D as the speedo needle touched 40. It would hit an indicated 60 in 14 seconds.

It's funny that I can't remember checking the speedometer over a measured mile since they were so convenient. There sure was a lot I didn't know, didn't do and didn't think about.

Our impromptu road races, which if you think of it, were quite closely related to the early developments of road racing worldwide, in both philosophy and execution. We always kept in mind that traffic might show up at any time, so we pretty much kept in our lane unless down road visibility was excellent. We also relied on using the tar strip down the center seam to either lean the tire against on the right-hand turns, or hook the tread over on left-hand turns. Suspensions of the day were such that you could actually feel it holding the car on line.

I learned how to use the slipstream in the longest close race of my highway career, against a 4-door '50 Ford sedan and a girl fully the equal to any sexy woman in the world. Let me say right now that there were a couple more girls in Bartlesville who fit into that category – in life, once you reach a certain level of intensity in whatever the category is, you just can't assign a ranking. Nothing's better than anything else in the top 10.

Anyway, Jean Ann and her girl pal, La Vey, driving a stick shift, obviously pulled out a lead over Don and me in my Powerglide '51

Bel Air in a standing start down new U.S. 75, just south of Johnston's Drive-In. It was about 10pm on a weeknight in summer.
Maybe she slowed down just a little to let us catch up; I'd heard
she might've been kind of a sport, if you get my drift.

In about four miles we were in her slipstream (gee, she had a
lovely slipstream). I got a great tow as I closed up to the Ford's
bumper and pulled out to pass, but the bow wake off the Ford was
enough of an air-wall that I was hung out there, pretty much side
by side. We'd used up all of the nine miles of straight, and there
was a bend to the left coming up that I'd taken wide open in the
Chevy a few times before. Jean Ann may or may not have had similar experiences, but she wasn't going to lift either. I'd kept my
eyes peeled for a sign of headlights in the distance (in Oklahoma
there's almost always enough dust in the air for you to see a faint
halo a long, long way down the road). So, I stayed out in the left
lane and as the road curved my little shortcut put the Chevy in the
lead. The road got narrow, rough, and twisty after that, so we both
turned around and, I guess, went our separate ways. No trophies of
any sort were distributed. Darn!

Jean Anne with her exquisite figure, not that she was aware of
her build; she had a red sweater with a piano keyboard across the
upper front, her exotic Osage/Anglo features, her soft voice, her
creamy skin the color of old piano keys and smoother than velvet.
At least it looked smoother than velvet. I never touched it. Honest!
Would I ever lie to you – unless I had to?

Once I accidentally customized the right side of that Chevy by
turning into an unseen, shoebox-sized rock out in a field where
we'd been firing our .22s. By the time I heard the noise and
stopped, the rock had folded the trailing edge of the front wheel
cutout neatly back inside the inner fender. No cracked paint, no
nothin'. The left side of the car was standard, but the right front
definitely had a sleek Vignale treatment.

Everybody had guns and went shooting in those days, not necessarily hunting anything. We even had a 2-man shootout on our high
school stage in a Sadie Hawkins Day skit, using real guns with
blanks and with teacher's oversight and permission, of course. If
we could legally drive David Crutchfield's Austin Bantam down

the school hallway en route to the assembly, thanks to permission from our beloved Principal, Carl "Itchy" Ransbarger, what's a little shootout?

European Conversion

It'd been a dozen years since the end of the war and mom, dad, sis and brother-in-law thought it would be fun to take a trip to Europe. We planned on looking at the hospital in Berlin, where my sister was born. We found the address – a vacant lot, well plowed, though.

Dad's business also had a developing contact in Celle, Germany, so while sis and I wandered around Berlin, brother-in-law Ralph went off to see the head of the Itag company. The German family was quite hospitable and they had converted an outbuilding or guest house on their property for their home, as their mansion had been partially destroyed, and there were just the two of them. The great hall of the main house had been converted into a memorial for their only son, a Luftwaffe fighter pilot, who had been killed in action: regimental banners, larger-than-life portrait of him leaning cheerfully on his plane, letters from his airbase, framed medals on the walls, stuff like that. That was where Ralph was entertained for dinner the same evening.

All of us had flown from Mexico City and had been met by a Spanish-speaking German interpreter - he spoke excellent English, too. That was why Ralph's welcome was so warm. Mexico was neutral in WW2 and so the Baron said to Ralph "Ah, you were fortunate to have such a calm life a dozen years ago, being a Mexican citizen and such."

To which Ralph blurted back "No sir, I'm American, and was in the 12th Air Force." Things were still cordial after that exchange, Ralph said, but nowhere near as chummy as they had been.

We stayed in Lisbon and Madrid for a few days to get acclimated, as even without jet planes people still got *time-zone change lag*. Then we went north into France.

Ever have one of those days? Not one where everything goes right, or when everything goes wrong, but where everything goes weird? I had a really tasty one on that trip to Europe in 1957. I left my sister and her husband in Paris, and took a Sunday day trip to London.

I wanted to see those live stark-naked girls at the Windmill Theater. Nudity is most everywhere these days, all over the world. At that time in England, though, an interesting interpretation of the law yielded the situation where nudity was acceptable, as long as nobody moved. Not the audience, of course, but the girls on stage. So they'd have a dance number, the curtains would swoosh closed, the curtains would swoosh open, and there they'd all be, sans clothing. Nobody told me that the Windmill was closed on Sunday. Appropriate enough, I guess.

So I walked around the general area, up and down the empty side streets near Piccadilly Circus. The day had turned gray: plenty of light, but no shadows. Down the deserted street toward me came a lad of about twelve, schlepping his shoeshine equipment in a big box with a leather strap over his shoulder. He approached me and asked, "Stajeera sguffered, sir?"

I asked him to repeat himself. Same sounds piped out. "I'm sorry, I can't help you," I replied, and he walked on.

I strolled down to the Circus, and after half a lap around the circle, I realized that what with the huge drapery over the statue in the middle, the kid was asking, "Is the statue of Eros covered, sir?" Okay, that would've cut down his potential business from folks sitting on the steps around the love god, but there did still seem to be a lot of foot traffic. Hmmm, and the boy had only been a hundred yards or so from Piccadilly. Well, spindly youth and heavy box.

I was mulling this over when a well-manicured hand descended on my shoulder with about fifty pounds of force. I half-turned and was face to face with a Roger Moore double in a tan tweed plus-four (knickers, to us) suit with matching cap. "Regent Street!" he exclaimed.

My zippy reply; "Wha?"

"Regent Street!" he cheerfully bellowed again, maybe a foot from my ear.

"Er, I'm sorry – I'm a stranger here myself," I said.

He pivoted on his right heel and strode off. Okay, this is it, I decided. The next odd thing that someone says to me, I'm going to tell them to take me to their leader.

I walked slowly, very slowly, to the Piccadilly Hotel to give agent #3 a chance at me. Nothing. Before I went to bed I wanted to write to some girl or another on the hotel stationery, which bore the legend: *Piccadilly Circus-the Hub of the World.* The concierge, excuse me, Hall Porter, tried to explain how to get to the writing room, but eventually gave up and led me to it by a perplexing network of stairs which had to be the model for the stair-maze library in *The Name of the Rose.*

Next day, flying out of London City Airport on a Vickers Viscount I commented to the stewardess that I'd never experienced a series of 80° banks in a departure pattern. "The Captain is a Battle of Britain Spitfire pilot!" she told me with a smile as she handed me a mini bottle of champagne, which was warm to the touch. I'd had enough experience with *champers* even at the age of 20 to know not to open it warm, and especially at altitude. In the next few moments there were two or three loud pops followed by wonderfully British upper-class expletives before the rest of the passengers figured out what not to do.

I guess I'll never know if I would have blushed at the Windmill girls. Well, blush maybe, look away – never!

Meanwhile, back in France, we bought a Renault Fregate, and drove via the French Riviera (so many lovely girls on the beach) to Italy. One afternoon we came to a country intersection we couldn't cross – *Carabinieri* everywhere. What's going on? Why, *Signori,* the *Mille Miglia!* And at that very instant two cars zipped by less than a yard from where we were standing. I took movies of Portago going by, just several miles before his crash, which stopped the Mille forever. My conversion, though, from drag racer to road racer started immediately on that May afternoon in Italy, 1957.

Cars: They Tell Me My Very First Word was "Car"

C ar was the first word I ever said, or so I am told canceling the little bet between my parents as to whether it would be Mama or Dada. I even remember the first sports car I ever noticed at the age of three or four. Walking with my beloved nurse, Kathryn Jordan, near one of those hugely wide 6-way inter-sections near the Beverly Hills Hotel, I heard an unusual exhaust note and then something low and red, windscreen folded down, flew across the open space and disappeared toward the hotel. The driver wore what folks later called a *sports car cap* and sunglasses. I like to think he had a mellow briar pipe clenched in his teeth, but that's fantasy. It wasn't a particularly small car – SS Jag maybe? Low-chassis Invicta? I've never forgotten it.

The Family's Cars

The family had a couple pairs of interesting cars, back at and just before the limits of my youthful memory. I can vaguely recall the 2 Cords – 1 blue, 1 champagne – that the folks took to the Cad dealer and traded in on Monday, December 8, 1941. The Cords weren't really making it through peacetime and darn sure would not have lasted through the war.

My brother and father went through a short series of Lincoln Zephyr coupes and sedans, and my sister had a maroon Zephyr convertible that was just about perfect. In September of 1939, Mom and Dad took my sister Anait to dinner at the Beverly Hills Hotel on her birthday (in '39, not an unfamiliar place, since we'd all lived in a bungalow there until the recent purchase of our wonderful house). As they went down the steps after dinner, parked under the porte-cochere was that Zephyr convertible with a bunch of roses in the driver's seat and a note under the windshield wiper. My folks told my sister it looked like a present to some movie star, and to go steal a peek at the name on the note. It was hers, of course. What a lovely moment that must've been. A few hours earlier, Warsaw surrendered to the Nazis; depends on where you are....

At this time my brother and several of his friends at USC had Zephyr coupes, some with two-speed rear ends and multiple carb intake manifolds. Roaming through our parking lot at a party, I figured out that the earlier cars had the floor shift snaking out from under the dash on what looked like heavy flex cable – was that a cover on an ordinary shaft? A couple Zephyrs had what could well be the first humorous decal on cars, even earlier than the well-known Lady Luck on many rods or gow jobs of the forties (and still available today); it was a takeoff on the stubble-jawed, parallelogram-faced cartoon character promoting Hastings piston rings. The face was an exact copy (in those litigation-free days), but with black and white prison stripes instead of the mechanic's cap and apron, with the words "Sing Sing" on either side of the friendly visage. There were the occasional USC and UCLA decals low in the center of the rear windows of some other cars; this must've been near the beginning of such things.

There was one *Real Fifties Moment* car-wise at our house in Oklahoma. Here I came on a beautiful summer's day, top down in my '53 black Lincoln convertible, sun glinting off the all-chrome continental kit with the exhausts exiting through the step in the extension above the rear bumper, rumbling sonorously (the exhausts, you understand, not me). As I wheeled into our drive (people did a lot of wheeling into drives in those days), there gleaming in the sun were my sister's pale metallic blue '53 Buick Skylark and mom's '54 white and jade green Packard Caribbean. There we all were with new and newish American glamormobiles; no performance heritage; no competition heritage; just aesthetic expressions of a particular time by three different automobile companies, each secure in its own niche in America. If Mrs. Adams, wife of the President of Phillips Petroleum, had dropped by with her '53 Cadillac Eldorado convertible with its secret formula pink paint – way before Mary Kay – the situation would've been oh so close to over the top that I would've sat on the wall and just grinned for much longer than I actually did.

My sister's limited edition Skylark with those keen cut-down doors was the absolute stocker of the bunch. It seemed like the best handling, too, and the quietest. Mom's Packard had been tricked up a bit while she was out of town; although she'd gotten rid of the split-manifold dual exhaust (thank you, J. C. Whitney) because the second pipe occasionally clanked against the car's underside. She thought the finned Offenhauser flathead (the original head was aluminum too!) looked good. I eventually had to tell her the reason that the car was a bit peppier, but bucked just before the Ultramatic's direct-drive clutch released when coming to a stop, was because of the Harman-Collins ¾ race cam that'd been slipped in one afternoon. It was back to the stock bumpstick soon afterwards.

Then there was my Lincoln with Chet Herbert roller-tappet cam and headers. It was so cramped under the hood that the left-side header went up and forward and then down and back, to clear the power steering apparatus. There were also factory-cut holes in the wheel wells so the plugs could be changed after the car was jacked up to let the front suspension drop the wheel out of the way.

It had Octa-Gane water/alcohol injection that worked off a pressure tap in the header, not by vacuum from the intake manifold. A Marvel Inverse Oiler somehow fed Marvel Mystery Oil into the intake for upper-cylinder lubrication. The Mallory Magspark ignition had advance manually controlled by a t-handle at the lower edge of the dash and the McCulloch supercharger had a variable pulley to cut parasitic drag and a maximum output of 5psi. A Sun 90° tach hung beneath the dash, too.

J. C. Whitney sold all sorts of fun stuff long ago – that's where I found the big German-made accelerometer. They had the world's teensiest air conditioner: it was a roll of that stuff that makes up the sides of a cardboard box, in a little metal box that was installed into the ventilation duct. You disconnected one of your windshield washer hoses and hooked it up to the nipple on the little box, and when you hit your windshield washer button you'd get about ten seconds of cool damp air out of your vent.

Then there was the 20-pound weight in a five inch thick, four foot long metal tube, which you installed crossways in your trunk or in front of your rear bumper. The idea was that when the rear of your car started to skid out, the spring(s), which hold the weight in the center of the tube would unload 20 pounds from the rear mass of your car, so the tires can take hold again. I never installed it.

Mom loved the little tapered ashtray with the suction cup that stuck to the inside of the wind wing (remember those?). When you tapped in your cigarette ash, it was immediately swept out of the window - assuming it was open.

There was a big clunky device that worked quite well: you pushed a rod down, which pushed on the top of the accelerator pedal, and then it stayed there, held by a ratchet. Another lump of metal went under the brake pedal, so when you tapped the brake, it disengaged the ratchet and the accelerator came up. Quite a simple cruise control on generally flat terrain.

Of course, there were those new Hudson engines for a bit over $200, a little refrigerator that worked from an oscillating valve you hooked into a vacuum line and there were all those wonderful hub caps and driving lights. How about a sports car cap with hard stuff in it to serve as the most minimal sort of helmet? I guess it was supposed to stay on your head without a strap, if you rolled your car.

Then there were carb idle screws with the little passage drilled down their centers, which probably helped vaporize the fuel in the idle circuit, not that I could tell much difference. In fact, only last year I bought some patented sparkplugs that had a small hole drilled in the side electrode just over the tip of the center electrode to help let the explosion get into the center of the combustion chamber faster.

I still have a load of those engine overhaul pills, apparently wax and lead and such, that you put into the cylinders through the plug holes. Then you drive 45mph for a couple hundred miles and your rings and cylinder walls are coated. I haven't used any of that stuff since Restore came onto the market.

Naturally, I had one of those sintered bronze oil filters that you could wash and reuse, but I didn't want to go through the trouble of installing one of those oil re-refiners that ran exhaust gas around the filter housing to evaporate all the impurities, allowing you to use toilet paper rolls for the filter medium and never change your oil again, just add oil as the level dropped. I guess you could have used a sintered bronze filter instead of toilet paper.

Cop-Sil-Loy brake lining paint-on coating really worked on the Studebaker GT Hawk at Sebring in '64. You could even buy an adapter to bolt a 4-barrel carburetor onto your 2-barrel intake manifold. It probably helped the breathing a bit, like those throttle body raising spacers you can buy today that claim to noticeably improve performance.

But, the biggest bang for the buck came when we put their *Big Bore* exhausts on our new 1970 Siata Springs for about $25 including shipping, why not? The Siatas were on the 817cc Fiat chassis (817cc was the maximum size not having to meet emission regulations for a few years in the late '60s). The replacement exhaust yielded an increase of almost 50% horsepower at the rear wheels! Why did Fiat put such a strangulated system on their cars?

A couple years later we thought a racing Alfa Veloce had pulled into our service drive, but it was only a guy with a first-generation Honda Civic who had holed a muffler on a rock on a New Mexico highway. He'd stopped at the next town and had the local muffler shop put on a glasspack and straight pipe. Besides the lovely sound, he said his mileage went from 32 to 35mpg. Does anyone know the reason for those convoluted systems that were put on, way back in those pre-catalyst days?

How many of you guys remember the brief and wonderful time of Atlas Bucron tires, sold at your nearest Esso service station? It was the first time *high hysteresis* was used in an ad, and probably also the last time. I think there was a TV commercial where the nattily uniformed station attendant - yes, they really existed - held a tire off the ground with each hand and let them go.

The standard tire bounced. The Bucron tire just sorta flopped. These were great tires. They were the first tires that didn't squeal under high cornering loads; they just sort of swooshed. On top of that, they had a great mileage guarantee and they really stuck to the road. So you bought a set for your sports car, see, by bringing just the wheels to the station to have them mounted. Then after a couple of race weekends, you brought them back and said they really wore out fast, and got another set - free. Some of the cheekier people actually drove the car in. Who noticed tape residue on the headlights and who knew what a rollbar was anyway? Or you could take fifteen minutes and just unbolt that device, so no one would suspect a thing.

Anyway, that particular guarantee went away real soon. It never mentioned any ban on being used in competition, and heck, it didn't cost the dealer anything. Free racing tires for a couple months. Those really were the days.

But I digress; in the late summer of '53 there was some unrest at Reda Pump Company (at which my dad was founder and president). Some people wanted to unionize. Some people didn't. According to the local papers, a picket line was due to be set up at all the gates the next day. I'd just got my Lincoln convertible back from having the supercharger installed and the continental kit added. The car gleamed black and chrome as I pulled into the parking lot at Murphy's Steak House on the west side of town.

As teenager me got out of my shining chariot in the midst of pickups and dust-scoured sedans someone yelled at me. "Hey!" I turned to see a rangy feller of middle age (maybe 30) loping toward me, clutching something metallic in his hand. "You that Arutunoff kid, aren't cha?" he asked.

I started figuring out escape routes, and had to admit that, yes, I was the youngest scion of the family. He raised his hand to his face level, displaying a Stag beer can as though he were saluting. "You tell your Daddy that tomorrow Ashworth's goin' through that line!" He suddenly looked like a Knight of the Round Table. "You got that? Ashworth's goin' through that picket line! Tell your Daddy he gave me a good job. I'm goin' through that line!"

I held out my hand. He switched the beer to his left hand. We shook. Made my evening. I should've invited him in for a burger and fries, but I only realized that just now. Murphy's is still there, and if anyone knows Mr. Ashworth, tell him I'll take him out to a proper dinner

The only time I got into something approximating a road race, as opposed to those long straightaway runs on the New Tulsa Road, was with Hal Price and his '54 Corvette. I could steam away from him down the straights of whatever back road it was, but he'd close right up through the turns. Being out-cornered by a first-edition Corvette is all you need to know about the handling capabilities of the Lincoln, but remember I was unaware that I should have ordered the *export suspension* (aka Mexican Road Race setup), when I ordered the car. I also scrupulously set the tire pressures according to the owner's manual: 24psi cold. Tore the tread off several of those Double Eagles on 100° days at 120mph and I wasn't alone – many others got free replacement D.E.s with a new rib tread instead of the original individual little diamond pattern.

Next up was my '56 Studebaker Golden Hawk. The pebbled vinyl yellow and white seats were comfy. There was a lot of wind noise and just like the '62 GT Hawk I raced in the '64 Sebring 2-hour race, the un-powered steering felt like the steering shaft was cast iron running in sandstone bushings.

But the power! Even before I put the blower on, the 352 c.i./275hp engine gave the car what the radio ads said was "the highest power-to-weight ratio of any car sold in America." I'll bet it weighed under 3000 lbs., and I'd love to know what the engine output was after I hung the 5psi McCulloch centrifugal supercharger on it. Stock, the car would run an indicated 145mph or so with 3.31 diff. ratio and .8 overdrive. Without the blower it took about ⅚ of full throttle to maintain that speed; with the blower it needed, honest, only about ¾. Oh, if I'd only had those brakes fixed… I must say it was very stable at high speed. Tom McCahill said it had the weight distribution of a blackjack, about 60% front, 40% rear.

The Hawk had twin antennas on the tailfins and reception was awful, unless I either touched one or hooked a jumper cable to it and let it hang on the ground - rather impractical at speed.

When I took the blower off the Lincoln and put it on the Hawk, using the kit supplied by McCulloch, all the tolerances were off in the same direction, thereby requiring a 5" long oval cutout in the hood. I put a rubber grommet around the edge and a small white pinstripe decal behind the hole. With the bright red flange protruding up into the air stream, the effect was menacingly mysterious.

One night at Johnston's Drive-In I got tired of the murmurings of how the Hawk, being a Studebaker, even with a blower, couldn't be all that fast. So I put three representative doubters in the passenger seats and headed south down that nine-mile concrete straightaway. In those days I believed that the power peak was equivalent to maximum permitted revs, so when the tach got to 4,500 rpm and the speedometer was a bit over 145mph the guys were convinced. Then I slowed to 4,000rpm and floored it and we still got a shove in the back. At 145mph I was running maybe ¾ throttle. I guess I still miss that car, even though it kind of tried to kill me once (more about that later). No power steering. No power brakes. Just power.

A fellow student at Tulsa U. talked his parents into ordering a Hawk, and their enthusiastic dealer talked them into super-special ordering the Packard Caribbean engine. I guess they were so desperate to sell cars you could order just about anything. It had the same stroke but ⅛" wider bore (I used to know the exact displacement, but you know how that stuff goes). The car was also delivered with dual four-barrel carbs as befitted the Caribbean, but for some reason the thing came with an Ultramatic transmission, so while I got about 18mpg at 70mph, he got maybe 14. Automatic or not, it was no slug, but we never ran against each other, doggone it.

And while *special order* is in mind, many years ago in *Hemmings*, for under $2,000 (that'll give you an idea how long ago it was) a Packard service manager's estate in New England was offering a very interesting machine: A '54 Clipper coupe, a bit smaller and lighter than the Patrician/Caribbean lineup, but carrying the 359 c.i. Patrician engine, aluminum flathead and all, with a 3-speed overdrive stick shift. That car, boys and girls, can be called a Carrera Panamericana Replica – a car with those very specs beat out a stick shift Buick Century (another rarity) for seventh place in the sedan category in the last Mexican Road Race.

That was a swell straight-eight motor: nine main bearings, 116 lb crank – which had been buffed with powdered walnut shells – and water jacketing around each cylinder. The early '54 Packard catalog claimed it was the most highly developed straight-eight in the world, but left that phrase out of later catalogs when the Bugatti club complained, with good reason.

The average American used to notice, smile, and point at our funny foreign cars because they were smaller than the U.S. land yachts, but once Americans made smaller cars for a while the distinction was lost. The late and revered Mr. Leon Mandel took this as the explanation for no one giving the spanking new TR7 he was driving from Florida to the north a second look. Odd shape alone did not catch Joe Sixpack's eye, just differences in size.

It must've been comparative size on the road and not on TV, because when I was driving my new Lotus 7A from L.A. to Oklahoma two nice bluehairs in an Imperial, noticing my little white car, asked if I was one of those cute boys from the *Route 66* show. The car was white like the Vette on the telly, but what probably threw them was that at the time I had as much hair as George Maharis. At the time. This was the summer of '61, when just plain folks would point at your radial tires and say, "You got a buncha flats, boy," and your super-trick Marchal headlights with their sharply cutoff low beams prompted them to continue, "And why are them headlights half-full of water?" Of course, if you had a British car with right-hand drive they were struck dumb and just pointed.

I hadn't always been a fan of foreign cars. When I had my supercharged Lincoln, it didn't impress me to look at a road test of a black and yellow Fiat with portholes like a Buick, of all things, and read that its two-way average top speed was 87.4mph. Ferraris, Maseratis, okay, but who had one of those?

Then I got thrown in at the deep end by stumbling across my first sports car race: the '57 Mille Miglia. Wow! Not only was it four thousand times longer than a drag race, but you could take a friend and the food was infinitely better!

Came home, ordered a Jag XKSS. Factory fire; no more cars. Then I got a price dipsy-doodle on a new 300SL, when Studebaker took over distribution and raised the price from $8,300 to $10,300.

Settled for a Porsche Carrera Speedster GS, which was only $5300. Speedsters with the normal pushrod engines started at $3300. Golly, things were tough. Porsche guys out there, please answer me this. S stands for Sport. T stands for Touring. So, why is the GT the hotter car?

A question for the older guys: when you had to slip the clutch in your new 356 Porsche during an uphill start, did it smell like shrimp frying? My Carrera sure did.

Since I truly loved my '56 Studebaker Hawk, I suppose it was only normal that a few cars later I got a '62 GT Hawk. Same keen dash, but only 289 c.i. It had four on the floor, a limited-slip diff and the radio actually worked. A/C too! I used it as a tow car for my Lotus 7A until, while returning from the Jim Bowie airport races near Bossier City, LA, the retractable trailer hitch retracted on the highway. I threw the trailer away and sold the remains of the Lotus to Allan Girdler, that magnificently Jesuitical thinker and car and bike writer. He rebuilt it, and on a cold evening, when he decided to test the car, he put on his helmet to keep his ears warm. That helped a whole lot when he spun in front of a pickup truck and wound up in intensive care for awhile; he'd be dead and fondly remembered otherwise.

Allan flew from Los Angeles to Sicily to run the last-ever Targa Florio in 1973 in my Lotus Europa. I had re-jetted the Stromberg carbs, removed the heater in the intake manifold, put on a European-spec distributor and headers. Amazingly, with only those mods it ran an honest 145mph!

Anyway, Allan told me that he felt quite the *international racing driver* as he settled into the seat in the Boeing 707 and placed his helmet bag between his toes under the seat in front of him. His seatmate eyed the bag. "Here comes the question," Allan thought to himself, "Act international."

"Oh," said his fellow passenger. "Do you sell Bell helmets?" Not the sort of question Allan was expecting...

Back to the Hawk; I put a ten-pound rollbar that I'd had in my '61 Corvair Monza coupe (also a tow car) into the Stude and ran a few SCCA races with it. In those more rational days the club had a category called GT, which covered everything that wasn't mentioned in other regs. For example at Green Valley Raceway near Dallas, my class included a 3.8 Jag sedan and Snuffy Smith's Renault R8 with Weber carbs. You brung it, you got to run it. How sensible!

Just before Nader (ach! pfui!) plopped upon the scene there was a blossoming of neat car stuff sprouting out of Detroit's foggy attempts to get on the European small car bandwagon. Spanning a few years we had that cute little Oldsmobile with the aluminum V8, if you preferred, a turbocharger with water/alcohol injection for the momentary octane boost; the zippy turbo Corvair; the Pontiac Tempest with its slant-four made by cutting off a bank of the V8- and it had a rear transaxle with its IRS - and a rope driveshaft, that actually drooped in the middle requiring no center driveshaft support. Don't forget the Plymouth Barracuda with, so what, a slant six engine. Well, if you wanted, you could order the engine with an aluminum block - for a while.

Oh, those wonderful compact car races. Plymouth offered a kit with a hot cam and multiple carbs. Webers, I think! Still had drum brakes, of course. Ran the Daytona road course, with no stupid chicane in the backstretch. Top speed 136mph.

It might have been in *Sports Car Graphic*, where an anonymous Plymouth techie, when asked what he told the drivers to do when they encountered the inevitable brake fade, said, "Hit something cheap." There was also a moment of alarm as the TV network covering this new small car event did a rehearsal during practice. "For the luvva Pete, when the cars leave the oval for the infield, quit calling it the transition from the outer course to the inner course!"

I wonder if the car companies today have any semi-hidden books of options like I stumbled on when mom was ordering her '68 Cadillac? We sat in the dealer's office and things were pretty simple: black, blue cloth upholstery, tilt wheel, but no cruise control (because mom was afraid of it), non-tinted glass (because we liked to see natural colors – it was the only Caddy in the zone not ordered with tinted glass), optional front disc brakes – they were standard next year and optional limited-slip differential (useful for auto-crossing). Then the nice man handed me a vinyl-bound book. "Hey, Toly, you're a car nut. Mebbe you'd like to check this stuff out, before I send in the order."

Mom didn't want any of it, but included: any steering wheel on any car, like an Eldo wheel in your limousine; or, for that matter, a limo wheel in your Eldorado. You could also get your upholstery stitched with any color thread for under $40 and lots of other trim stuff.

And yet a few years later GM only let you have red, white or black upholstery in a black car (now you can get your choice of taupe, taupe, taupe or taupe, it seems). You could even order a Dodge with orange paint and green upholstery, or vice versa. My '68 silver 383 Dart GTS convertible with all striping deleted and dark green interior and top looked so good that folks thought it was a subtle custom. During assembly, a UAW drone erred and put a black sunvisor on the driver's side. I saved Chrysler Corp.'s bacon by telling whoever noticed that it was an antiglare safety feature.

Art Eastman once wrote that nobody would buy a new MGB or Alfa Giulia these days, because we all expect more creature comforts. Art, you're so very rarely wrong. We can't talk manufacturers into building more of these, but can't we please have the old standby, the *delete option*? Buy your car with rollup windows, stark interior, manual top and no power steering. If my 120 lb mother could drive her 1954 Packard Caribbean for two years after the power steering hose broke and never bothered to have it fixed, you could certainly horse your BMW Z4 around all by your precious little self.

Getting back to mom's '68 Cadillac, allow me to tell you how to make a car like that handle. Now, class, we have a factory installed limited-slip differential, which, if anything, might add a touch of understeer to the already understeering design. So, simply get a rear sway bar from Addco and bolt it on. Easy job. That helps.

And now for the *piece de resistance*, radial tires on the front wheels only! It's an illegal setup in European countries and parts of the U.S., but let me assure you, when you gave that Caddy's wheel a jerk, the front end leaped in that direction – and believe it or not the car was an eventual understeerer, even prepped like that! It did not understeer much, though, and boy was it fun running up on the bumpers of MGs and Alfas on long sweeping freeway onramps.

Delivery: Italian Style

When you took delivery of your high-performance car in Italy, you used to be unable to escape the dreaded *Check Ride with the Pre-Delivery Mechanic*. This likely didn't happen if an actual Italian bought a car, but who's to say, because your American purchase was a moment for Guido or Vito or whoever to demonstrate that it was, you bet, possible to hit 130kph in city traffic!

The new owner/passenger's fear for life and limb was switched back and forth from personal to mechanical focus, because while Aldo was holding down the horn button as he aimed for a microscopic gap between two baby strollers, he was repeatedly missing his shift – up, down, who could tell – with a resultant intermittent noise like Paul Bunyan's bicycle with 4' x 8' plywood sheets in the spokes.

If you spend enough on your new car these days, you get to go to a lovely test track somewhere and ride along while charming young men make your new purchase do video game things, minus all the leaping, crashing and stuff. Know what I like about Italy? Take a piece of paper and number from one to a hundred. No, I mean in this particular instance; just because you're on a track doesn't necessarily mean you have to wear a helmet! They figure it's your car now, and you're going to drive like this occasionally on a regular road, and here there is not only no Alpine cliff to drive off of, there's not even oncoming traffic! Contrast this to those car test shows on TV where the driver is wearing a helmet while he tests a puny minivan on a drag strip.

I picked up a new Alfa Junior Zagato 1300 in 1971 at the dealership in Modena. Boy, were they ever hot to sell me one of the Montreals they had in stock, but I wasn't having any of that. So they phoned the dealer in Bologna, who had a pale yellow Z, which they brought up immediately.

After taking delivery in Modena I had one more day to kill before setting out for Genova to put self and car on the *Michelangelo* and sail to New York. It didn't take much time to pack, so following a drink in the Hotel Canalgrande's bar, I watched a bit of television before dinner. There were early '30s American cartoons, produced and/or directed by Ub Iwerks, my second favorite name to baseball pitcher Van Lingle Mungo.

Cut to the chase – cartoon hero Bosco, in his open-cockpit two-seat racing airplane, has picked up a hitchhiking angel off a cloud. Our villain had passed the angel (halo, bald-headed, big ears, long beard), who was thumbing a ride, and as the villain swooped by, the angel gave him the finger. That sort of woke me up out of a light doze - I must have imagined it. So the angel, now in Bosco's plane, gestures *blessingly*, I guess you could call it, and Bosco's plane picks up speed and passes the bad guy. The angel, with a smile, stands up in the cockpit, turns around and gives the villain the finger again. Five fingers per hand - none of that four-fingered Disney stuff.

So, we have a middle finger in the air in a kid's cartoon. Can some sociologist tell us when that gesture went from cartoon acceptability to *really not nice*? I was a protected child, so I only saw it in real life for the first time just before the Korean War.

Anyway, I drove the little darling to Genova to put it on the boat, scrupulously observing the break-in revs in the owner's manual. Then, while shipboard, I computed the average speed the car must have been driven to get to Modena in the elapsed time between the phone call and its arrival at the dealer and realized the Alfa was pretty well broken in by the first time I saw it.

During the summer of 1976 I went by Scaglietti to say hi, and noticed a heavy wire rusty metal shape out back. It was the buck for the 206SP – possibly the competition show car from the Torino Salone in 1965. How much you guys want for that? I thought it would look great on a pylon in front of our dealership. I mentioned I'm a dealer. "Oh, you're a Ferrari dealer? Well, you can just take it away." Isn't that nice. I told them I'd get some padding for the roof of the rental Volvo sedan and be back tomorrow. Next day? "Well, we'd better keep it." Aw, shucks....

On the same trip, I went by Abarth in Torino, looking for transmission parts for my 3000P hillclimb car. They said everything was at Osella, but I was invited to prowl around their storeroom for anything else I might need. They were eager to sell me a crate, which measured about a cubic yard, of new Weber 58DCOEs. I didn't want any. I find a meter-square of expanded metal, nicely framed, of every Abarth badge I had ever seen, and several new to me. Can I have these two? "Sure!" They were slightly rusted in place, "Go ahead and take the whole thing."

With all our luggage and stuff, there was little available space (we were also carrying niece Kyra's extensive wardrobe to the boat in several suitcases). "Thanks," I say. "I'll pick it up next year." Next year it wasn't there, but you knew that already.

In 1983 I bought a factory-fresh Lancia 037 from the same Torino dealership that had sold us the Stratos in '76. The 037 (which actually has more Abarth logos on it than Lancia ones) was delivered with a huge range of suspension adjustment, but set up at the factory to feel like a '50 Buick, i.e. maximum understeer settings at both ends. Everything is so accessible, though, it takes less than an hour to put the car into full *yee-haw* mode.

I knew it'd be the last *homologation* special that would ever be on the market for $26K. Heck, Lancia was trying to unload the stock Stratos in 1977 for $12K or please make offer. Oops. Rats! I've occasionally made some good moves, so you really don't have to feel all that sorry for me. Still, I should have bought a couple more.

In late 1969 I'd topped that by turning down an offer of two Abarth Carrera Porsches for $12,000, or my choice for $6,500. Let's not talk about it. How about the 2-liter Ferrari championship replica hillclimb car and Serenissima F1 car $8K a piece or both for 15? But like Dad used to tell me, "Let some other people have fun, too."

Just another mistake – I'd bought a 365BB, which was not legal to sell in America. As a Ferrari dealer, I thought that it would be clever to have it sit on the showroom floor to let folks see something our government was saving us from. Well, we got in some trouble with the Feds – they tried to entrap us for two days – and while that was being churned through the legal system, I got a letter from Ferrari, offering me what Pete Coltrin said was the first Ferrari F1 offered to a private citizen. Pete had told them I could be trusted not to make *The Organizzazione* look bad by haring around the streets or blowing it up in front of crowds – things that would have been pretty unavoidable in Italy.

Asking price: $40,000... Hmmm. I've got these legal bills to pay (though we eventually won our case and eventually I actually made a profit on the car) and it's probably Merzario's car anyway, so I wouldn't even be able to get my shins past the steering wheel. It'd look pretty swell in the garage, though, but I let the deal go by. I've got their offer letter framed in black in my garage.

$2500: The Going Rate

You *really* need to hear the story about how I flat gave away an alloy-bodied SWB Berlinetta – that Targa Florio car, the *factory hotrod* on the cover of a recent auction catalog – I'll just have to tell you that tale in person. Come by for a drink sometime.

At least I made a pitiful few bucks on the alloy Pegaso spyder, the two Le Mans Pipers and the 3-liter Abarth. The most fun to drive was the 7-liter, twin turbo, four-wheel-drive McKee Cro-Sal Olds Can-Am car - perfect condition and under $10K. Albert Way has it now. I hear he gently pranged it at the last Nassau race. I wish he'd run it again. LJK Setright came and looked at it once. It's about a foot bigger than a McLaren in every dimension. He walked around it in silence for several minutes. "Rather a good example of the law of diminishing returns," he said.

I'll report elsewhere on the ladies I missed out on; here are some cars in the same category. There was the F1 Ferrari in 1974, and the "cheaper next year" BMW 507 and the SWB Ferrari I gave away. They all involved a decent level of finance, but once I was after a car that was inexpensive.

Inexpensive? In the early '70s almost any old car that wasn't a Ferrari was $2,500. My first classic, that neat little Cooper-MG for 850 British pounds plus shipping was my first encounter with the mystical figure of $2,500. A guy comes by with an alloy-bodied Pegaso spider on a trailer, missing only one side curtain and, er, the twin Weber four-barrel carburetors. Do I want it for $2,500? Heck, why not? He's already delivered it. A Cooper-MG *barchetta*, also $2,500 but the shipping costs took it a hair over that amount.

In the Serenissima garage in Modena accompanied by the late

wonderful journalist, Pete Coltrin, was Alf Francis' road car: The tub of the Lola GT prototype and a Serenissima Fl engine, minus carbs, manifold and rear bodywork. They asked $2,500 and were surprised when I said okay.

One time a guy pulled into our showroom drive with a nicely running 1900 Alfa coupe, 4 on the tree, plastic windows and magneto ignition. Surprise! A buck per cc: $1,900. It even had a photocopy of the complete owner's manual.

Then there was an odd Cooper-Ford MKIV Sports, again from England. At about $3,000, it was obviously the cosmic way to get my average per-car expenditure back to about $2,500.

Yet another Cooper-MG, this one much bigger than mine, but good grief, they wanted $4,500 for it! A month later I said I'll take it, but it was gone by then. Stuff went up after that. I paid about $9k each for the Abarth 3000P and the McKee Cro-Sal twin-turbo 454 Olds-powered four-wheel drive Can-Am. It all sure was fun at the time.

I think $7,500 must be my *bad* number, as compared to $2,500 being my *good* number. I had an opportunity to buy a fine Alfa Romeo 2600 Zagato with a rebuilt engine and a blown clutch master cylinder for $7,500. I tried to talk the owner down to seven flat, but failed. Actually, if the flatness of the side windows hadn't contrasted quite so much with the roundness of the rest of the car, I'd have gone for it.

Then in Denver, an auto shop teacher at a high school had a Devin-Chevrolet for the same figure. It had to be the longest body Devin ever made and looked a bit swaybacked, because it carried a flawless '56 Corvette wraparound windshield (I figured that by removing the windshield and selling it I could recoup a good portion of the car's price). It ran a little rough, but that was to be repaired. I tried for a $500 discount there, too; no luck.

Here's the fun part that should have given me a clue. That was in 1988, and a week or so later I was in southern California at some car event. I mentioned that I'd been dickering for the car *at around seventy-five.* "Oh, that's way too much," said a local collector. "Maybe forty-five, or fifty thousand max!" Why didn't that factor of ten send me scrambling back to Denver? Well, now we both know why, don't we?

So I'd been after my wonderful buddy Pete Coltrin to go by the Osi warehouse in Modena and see if they would like to sell their Alfa Romeo Scarabeo. This wasn't the Bertone Carabo of much greater fame, kind of scaly and dark green. The Scarabeo looked like a chopped AMC Gremlin - it was even orange - and had a Giulia Veloce engine sideways across its slabby, stubby rear with a Z-shaped driveline from the end of the tranny to the rear axle.

Pete, Ing. Ferrari's favorite English-speaking journalist, was always busy writing and photographing things. Years came and went. I offered to pay for his time, and that embarrassed him. His wife Lella (the absolute epitome of a Northern Italian or should I say Modenese lady with more enthusiasm than Knute Rockne) was on my side. "Peter! Business is business! Do this business for your friend!"

I went back to America and Pete went to Osi. Some German dude had gotten there two weeks earlier, put a battery in the Scarabeo, looked at the ancient motor oil, aired up the tires, and driven the thing onto his trailer and taken it away - for $2,500. How can I play *2500* in Vegas? Somebody's trying to tell me something.

My Cars, Favorites All

I've had three Corvettes: '65 396/425hp, '66 427/425hp, '71 alloy-head 454; silver, white and white. Interiors were silver leather, black and black. All were ordered with the *rock crusher* c/r gearbox, lowest numerical/highest top speed rear axle ratio, competition suspension and large gas tank. I ordered them just the way I wanted them.

I actually ordered a fourth one in 1970, but a strike prevented it from being finished in time to run the Targa Florio in Sicily, where we almost certainly would have won the over 2 liter GT class. That was the last year you could race without a rollcage.

I converted all of them to the quick-steering ratio by the simple expedient of disconnecting the tie rod ends and swinging them over to the other holes on the steering arm. I also had the dealer do the same on the shift linkage to get the shorter throw of the shift lever. I was told that modification (was it really a *modification,* since it was mentioned in the owner's manual?) would void my warranty.

With the c/r gears, long rear end and the fact that my car was on the upper level of the delivery trailer, the clutch was so far gone on the '65 that I got less than a mile from the dealer before the car quit moving. The dealer claimed I'd been drag racing it in the 20 minutes it took to walk back to the dealership in downtown Nashville.

My only other problem with any of them was that the '71 was missing a lower rear shock bolt. I was told there would be about a month-long backorder on the bolt, so I went to a hardware store with the bolt from the other side and matched it up.

Also the rear panel on the car was rough as sandpaper. Our bodyshop smoothed it out. It also had a tiny leak in the radiator header tank. All that performance from three cars with just those few problems (the clutch problem was fixed under warranty); those people who badmouth Corvettes of that era don't have a clue, period.

I must add that the '65 was a sloppy handler in long high speed turns. One of those two-ply gold stripe Firestones wore out and blew out in Italy, so I replaced them with a set of Pirelli Cinturatos. Fantastic change for the better! I'm aware of Duntov's concern about radials not being able to handle the torque, but he was wrong. The car was photographed in front of Pirelli's headquarters by their official photographer. Never occurred to me to ask for copies of the pictures. I wonder where those photographs are now.

When I took delivery of the '66 Corvette coupe, the sales manager said, "Come over here, reach through the window, and gently feel the headliner." I did, and for a moment I was stunned and confused. "Feels just like a girl wearing panties, doesn't it?" he said. He was absolutely correct - although it was a cool day, it felt just like a warm rump in underwear. "We call it the pantyliner instead of the headliner," he said.

At the time lots of Corvette owners I talked to said, "Oh, sure, everybody knows about feeling up the headliner!" I don't think my '65 had the same material, or the '71 either. Comparative youngsters who own older Vettes I've mentioned this to don't know anything about it. I've never talked to one who owned a '66, though.

I quickly put the knockoffs on it, added headers and a set of those keen Stebro twin-outlet exhausts where one pipe came through the regular hole in the rear panel and the other hung down below.

Other cars through the years: my first car, that '51 Bel Air, '53 Lincoln supercharged convertible, '56 Studebaker Golden Hawk with the old blower off the Lincoln, '57 Porsche Carrera GS Speedster, '59 Alfa spider 2000, '61 Corvair Monza coupe, '61 Lotus 7A, '62 Studebaker GT Hawk (Sebring '64 sedan racer and tow car), the '63 Lancia Flaminia Zagato, '59 Appia Zagato, the '67 National Championship Morgan 4/4, alloy-bodied SWB Ferrari I gave away, '67 Olds 442 convertible - 130mph @ 5000rpm – '68 Dodge Dart 383 GTS - the only silver/green interior and top ever built – '69 Bristol 410 sedan, 2000SP Abarth sports racer, '72 Lotus Europa race car, '73 Europa twincam race car, '76 Lancia Stratos, '61/'71 Zagato Ferrari SWB Spider California, a few Mazda Rx/7s (street and showroom stock), '77 Saab Sonett III - and then 3000P V8 Abarth hillclimb car, two Le Mans Pipers, 3 front-engine Coopers, Abarth 1300 Periscopio coupe, Alfa 1900 coupe, Iso Grifo, Pegaso alloy spider, Studebaker-powered Glaspar Ascot, Bristol 407 Zagato, a different Appia Zagato GTE with Sebring history, MG Savoy art car, my very-own-designed Lapin Agile straight-8 Chrysler-powered art rod, Cunningham C3, the Serenissima GT on the original Lola GT tub, Lancia Flavia Zagato. Stuff like that and several more. "Blessed" says it all. Of course, a fly fisherman wouldn't think so. I drove 'em all. Lots. I washed them. I waxed them. Sometimes. I enjoyed them most all the time. Concours cars they were not, at least not after I had them for a week. I like flawless gleaming cars as well as the next person, but…

Well-known automotive personage Jean Lindamood, editor of *Automobile Magazine,* once referred to formal concours as *Dead Car Shows.* It's a succinct description and is right on the nose. It was inspiring to read that the phrase most despised by the members of the Veteran Sports Car Club in England is "Concours d'Elegance."

A special car of mine was a Pontiac Trans-Am 455 SD I ordered in 1973, but because of EPA certification problems, Pontiac didn't build any until '74. With the usual dearth of GM color choices, I settled on white with tan interior. I also specified automatic transmission (I used it for a tow car), no console, and the shifter on the tree. It was the only one built like that.

I *de-desmogged* it with a different advance curve and different carb needles, a bit too rich, but I left them alone. For about $600 I changed the rear axle ratio from 3.54 (or whatever was compulsory) to a 2.9. I like long-legged cars.

A few months after I took delivery, a bridge on the Indian Nation Turnpike south of Tulsa, shifted, so most of the turnpike was closed except for the northernmost 12-mile stretch. It began a few dozen miles south of Tulsa and was sort of a road to nowhere; there was an exit just before the closed part. The unspeakably foul 55mph limit had come into effect, so every couple weeks I'd drive down to the turnpike, smile at the tollbooth operator, and then gently waft southbound – for about a half-mile. Then I'd floor it and laugh crazily for the six minutes or less until I had to brake for the exit. Better than twenty cups of coffee. I'd exit, stop, check the oil and the tires, and floor it back northbound. I stopped doing this refreshing exercise when I put some cheap-ass wire wheels on the car, which we could never get to be properly round. Of course, not leaving well enough alone, I put a set of Koni shocks on it, too.

After installation, the front end floated like a motorboat. A close look at the Koni catalog revealed that they specified the exact same shock for the 6-cylinder and small block Firebird, as they did for my 454 monster. We adjusted the front shocks to full stiff and they were okay. Koni says the adjustment is to compensate for wear, not for stiffness, but anyway our adjustment worked well enough.

I had an equal amount of joy over a longer period of time, as I used the car to lay out the track at Hallett. What an exquisite feeling! Driving onto my new land and motoring gently around and around, laying out one circuit and another and another, and only occasionally tearing off the front spoiler. Knowing I was creating a new road racing track. Man, it was intoxicating.

My big-government-states friends couldn't believe it when

they'd ask me, "How long did it take to get the permits?" and I'd answer "What permits?" I bought the land, paved a circuit (3 times!) and built a 3-story building. Yep, we had to build a sewage lagoon (I called it Loch Mess), but we never had enough sewage for it; it's still there, but pretty much dry. We had to have the water well drilled and government certified for purity, and that took care of all the necessary bureaucracy.

Driving around and around on a summer afternoon, knowing a road racing circuit was coming into being because of my (Divine, I hope) inspiration – an indescribable feeling. Not too long afterwards, for some unremembered reason, I sold the 454SD (after turning down a spare crated engine for $1,200). The cousin of the new owner (new owner, 15 years old, didn't have his license yet) rolled it into a ball somewhere.

Selling so many of my cars was pretty silly, but not as silly as giving up my Ferrari dealership. Let's just call it all, hmmm, *thoughtless.*

I ordered another neat car once, but never collected it. Dick Irish and I decided to go to Europe to check out the Earls Court and Torino car shows, and I figured that a new AMX would be just the odd machine to blast around in. I ordered a gray car, silver stripes, black leather, *Go* package, big motor, and the highest-speed axle ratio available. I made the proviso, that if it didn't arrive in time to drive it to the Queen Elizabeth, I didn't have to buy it. It was a couple days too late – yet another little problem I seem to have had with cars getting on boats.

So we took Dick's Ferrari GTB-4; not so bad. After the car show in London we made a rapid run down to Modena in the Ferrari to let the factory see how it'd been holding up in America. En route we'd done a few laps of the Nurburgring, Dick driving and me operating the movie camera. We learned that where there were goodly clumps of spectators there was a goodly chance of spinning out on a tricky curve. And this was no race day – people just went to the 'Ring for a day's outing and to watch all the amateurs crash at the best spots. Well, Dick did a very safe spin at one of those places, and I took my finger off the camera button as though if I quit filming, the spin wouldn't happen. The mind is not thoroughly logical; or at least one particular mind isn't.

We were prepared for general road problems, with a mat to lie on, flashlights, the legally-required reflective triangle, and a couple highway flares. We found out they don't really do highway flares in Italy. Since we were flying home the flares were unnecessary, so Dick wrapped them neatly and put them in our hotel room wastebasket.

The police caught up with us as we were having a drink with Alf Francis in the Fini hotel bar. We were courteously asked to accompany them. We thought perhaps a family member had died. We were put in an Alfa sedan and taken to police headquarters by the only Italian I've ever seen who couldn't handle a stick shift. We were taken into a large, well-decorated office, with a large, well-decorated police chief behind a walnut desk. Out of the shadows behind us, an Anthony Quinn look-alike in Quasimodo makeup barred the door. There was silence until the Chief spoke. "Why did you try to blow up the hotel?" he asked us.

Obviously they figured us for a branch of the Tyrolean separatist group that wanted a portion of Italy returned to Austria. Dick and I burst into laughter, which unnerved them for just an instant. We told them that they had found our highway warning flares, and then another man produced them, one flare inside a bomb-blast quenching bag and the other lying on top. Dick said "Look, let's go outside and I'll light one and hold it in my hand," and as he reached for the loose one everybody flinched and one cop drew his gun.

Well, it turns out the cops had read the instructions on the side of the flares, but wanted to check us out in case the flares really were dynamite sticks. The tension wound down from there. They brought in our luggage, which they'd taken from the hotel checkroom and searched. On top of our clothes were a couple *Playboys*, which we'd brought over but never got around to reading. *Playboy Magazine* at that time was illegal in Italy. Dick put them on a corner of the desk, saying "Here's some fun sexy stuff from the States I guess you don't have over here," and as we repacked we noticed a couple detectives sidling toward the desk to seize the booty – no pun intended – as soon as we left. We shook hands all round, complimented the Chief on their efficient work, Quasimodo retreated to the shadows, and we were driven back to the Fini. And that cop still couldn't find third gear.

Since Dick had ordered his car personally from the factory, and had raced Ferraris in the early '50s for people like Tony Parravano, the factory was familiar with him and asked him to leave the car with them, so they could tear it down to see how things were going. They shipped it to him a month or so later. Some months later, a fluctuation in the oil pressure made Dick think it had spun a bearing (which it had) and he eventually sold it for a multiple of his purchase price.

The new owner took it to Bob Wallace in Arizona and when he tore down the engine it was revealed the factory had installed special rods, pistons, cams, or something like that, very, very special. The last Dick updated me, decades ago, the car was a trailer queen concours item. How sad.

Anyway, that AMX was still on the dealer's lot when we got back several weeks later. The zone rep for American Motors wanted to take it for his get-around car, but the factory told him it was so special it had to be sold. I wonder where it went. That was the same dealership where I traded in my '67 442 convertible on the '68 Dart 383 GTS convertible, and the salesman then came up to me and said he'd figured the deal wrong and could I please give him $50, so I did.

Once they gave me one of those raunchy SCRamblers for an afternoon's test drive, but it was stark and harsh. I eventually ordered a Dodge coupe from them in whatever year Ricardo Montalban was promoting their "fine Corinthian leather" interiors, and they refused to take a deposit. I wanted to use it as a tow car, but it turned out they were going bankrupt and I never got that car. Oh well, one outta three ain't bad.

I really must tell you about my wonderful Abarth 1300 Periscopio. I thought I was buying an Ogle Mini Cooper S – that neat egg-shaped fiberglass body with 10" Minilites, Dunlop green spot racing tires with 20,000 miles on the clock, for $800 at a Tennessee estate sale. Due to a mix-up, however, with my friend/agent, I wound up getting this lovely Periscopio for $8,000.

He drove it on his trailer and dropped it off in Oklahoma for me.

Over the next year or two I tried starting that car two dozen times. It had fuel. It had spark. It wouldn't do more than occasionally kick over.

Okay, I thought. I'll take it to Sebring for the vintage race before the 12-hour, where we'd entered the Stratos. The crew brought both cars down. I decided to sleep in and miss my demo drive in the Abarth, so Gene Baker took it out. Fired it up, ran a few laps, came in, put it on the trailer. Got it back to Bartlesville in my garage. Couldn't start it. I finally sold it – it won a class award after restoration at Pebble Beach a few years ago. I wasn't at home when the buyer arrived, who hopped in, fired it up, and drove it on his trailer and took it away. If I had known the power of prayer at that time, I'd have exorcised my personal little mechanical demon and probably still have that lovely car.

It was an old used red racecar, naturally, $8900 plus shipping. It had been checked out by the factory. They said it was a hillclimb car, which did 132 at 8K in fifth. Oh, the poor way I treated that Abarth 3000P. I didn't hit anything, and I made sure that whoever checked the fluids didn't repeat the error of filling it up to an inspection hole, a couple inches below the fill hole. That was done on the transmission of our 2000SP (Ed Swart has it now) and the tranny held together for a couple dozen hours!

I got down to the garage after the 3000P was delivered and heard it idling from the front door. Its 3 liter four-cam V8 was Abarth's cancelled attempt at an F1 engine. It sounded a bit a rough, as it also did when I revved it up, but my crew chief at the time (oh, what those various guys put me through - and it was all my fault!) told me it was because the car had a flat-plane crank.

I raced it in ASR at Ponca City and somewhere in Texas. It was about as fast as a Corvette; I was a bit disappointed, but I figured it was because I was keeping it 1,500rpm below the redline. Then I took it to the second Monterey Historics in '75. I decided to have a look at the plugs. 3 of them were fouled beyond belief. I cleaned them and headed out for my practice session. I barely touched the throttle and nearly spun in pit lane! *Quel difference!*

The reason I decided to check the plugs and look the whole car over very closely was that in the previous session I felt a chill on

my back. Seems one of the fuel banjos on a front Weber had
backed all the way out and I was getting gas down my spine. At
least all the parts and gaskets were right there, by my neck. So, on
the first lap with all that power the transmission broke; but, by
golly, it wasn't low on oil!

Modern Cars

In the early days of postwar imports, a traveler to Europe would
be told, "Oh, you lucky Americans! The only models we can buy
here have small engines and low horsepower. You get all the fast
models!" Before things got pretty well equalized worldwide
though, we went through a dearth of imported hot stuff. Mercedes
had to send us 450SLs to get the same performance as European
350SLs; they even labeled some 450s as 350s to keep the European customers from craving the additional displacement, which
was necessary to get back performance lost to emission regulations. We couldn't get AMG Mercs and Alpina BMWs.

Americans, with their notorious worldwide reputation of not
knowing how to drive well, combined with our reputation of suing
everyone in sight, got *chassis condescension*, too. To wit: There
was a time in the early '70s when lightly used Panteras were numerous and cheap. The local dealer told me all the doctors and
lawyers, who bought the cars as country club eye candy, got tired
of the exercise required to get in and out and soon traded them in
on Lincolns. We got a jellybean green Pantera with 6,000 miles on
it for about $6,000. Like new. My shop checked it out and I took it
for test drive through a nearby industrial park, as yet undeveloped,
that served as our little test track. It felt like a two-seat Buick. I
asked our staff if they'd taken the trouble to check the tire pressures. "Just what the book says," I was told.

That they were. I checked myself. The tire pressures were printed
on a little piece of tape stuck into the owner's manual. I'm guessing here, but let's say 23 front, 29 rear. I, oh so carefully, peeled off
the tape and underneath (again guessing after all these years): 28
front, 32 rear. Pumped up the tires and I was suddenly driving a delightful GT car. Heaven forbid an American was ever to be sold a

vehicle that didn't grossly understeer at any speed.

It is to be assumed that large scale manufacturers like Porsche had separate owner's manuals printed for the American market. We were Ferrari dealers then and I think they continued the Italian practice of earlier Alfas and Lancias (Morgans did it, too) of giving a range of tire pressures, depending on anticipated driving speeds. We can't really be bothered to make such adjustments these days. How long do you think it will be before there is a lawsuit over failure of one of the tire pressure monitoring systems now becoming available with the claim that an unreported low tire caused an accident? Maybe we should start a betting pool...

When American cars were just barges, there was a lot more use of the phrase fun to drive. Cars are just so much more competent and capable now, but you can feel their bulk, no matter how high their levels of performance in any area you care to name. It was a dozen or so years ago that I last drove a vehicle that made me think, "Hey, this thing is really fun to drive!" It was a Jeep Cherokee.

Karen and I were putting on *Las Millas Encantadas, The Rally of New Mexico*. Chrysler was our sponsor, and they brought along some machinery for us to drive: three of their brand-new Vipers, a Dodge with silver metalflake paint and their first manumatic transmission, and this particular Jeep.

The Mopar staff told us it was equipped with their Australian Police heavy-duty suspension, and it felt just like the world's tallest MGA. Unfortunately it was 4WD, which meant the front axle was burdened with the unsprung weight of the differential - if it had been just rear drive I would have considered stealing it. What a responsive and communicative chassis! I was so taken by the opportunity to fling this creature around the back roads of New Mexico for three days that I didn't have the sense to see what the tires were.

I did seriously think about buying a Jeep (if it were equipped with that lovely suspension) with 2wd and scrapping the body and building a vintage-homage sports car on the chassis. Well, I was told that, of course, the exact suspension calibrations would doubtless be changed for the American market (how many millions are wasted by the incompetents at the major American automobile manufacturers with their compulsive not invented here tic?). That wonderful crispness; the sense of each of the tires rolling on the road (I wonder if live-axle cars have this *handling flavor* in general); that eager six-cylinder engine... okay, so I would've hung three Webers and a header on it. I still can't get over it: a Jeep that was fun to drive!

Let's not bother considering the lower emissions and stickier tires and all the hundreds of pounds of electronic garbage put in cars – which you cannot delete order. That electronic stuff is put in to appeal to people, just a half-generation removed from people today, who think that driving a car sideways with tires smoking, at a pulse-pounding 30mph or so, is a form of motorsport. Jeez! Synchronized swimming with overhead cams!

But back to my subject; cars today are different, and mostly it has to do with weight. There is also in this mix a definite influence of cleverly designed bushings and mounts and the marvelous materials they're made of. If you take two cars, and both pull .85g on the skid pad, the lightweight on 6.70x15" rubber will be more fun to drive than the two-ton *GT* on its u-name-it width 20" tires. The skinny-tired lightweight might even ride better. In general, then, a lower level of technological sophistication makes a car more fun to drive, because the driver gets much more feedback. Some passengers might say, "This car rides kinda rough."

One now historical example: the late '70s brand new Mazda 626 vs. the brand new Honda Civic. Civic: smooth. Mazda: a faint scent of harshness and lots more fun on a winding road. Chocolate and vanilla.

There was a time when you could buy cars in actual colors. Not white, silver, light gray, dark gray, pewter and maroon. Get ahold of some brochures from the late '50s. Red, cream, yellow, light green, dark green, light blue, dark blue, turquoise, gold, even brown. And the interiors were designed to either match or contrast. During the late '60s you could order, in Moparland, any color paint/interior combination they had in the book, although they recommended certain ones.

What do we have now? Car colors today seem to consist of

black, white and various shades of gray. Oh yeah, as a car dealer, I know how happy the sales force is to not to have to offer the customer real choices. "Yes, Mrs. Jones, the silver is lighter than the gray, isn't it? Sorry, we can't order you a metallic green with cream interior. Mrs. Jones, will it be the gray or silver? And the black is rather nice, isn't it?"

The monotony of car colors today! Man, in the mid-'50s there were bronze Oldsmobiles, lipstick red/turquoise/white tri-tone Packard Caribbeans, cream/metallic green Buicks.

International racecars were painted their countries' racing colors (until Chapman pulled that Gold Leaf caper with Lotus), but there was latitude. There never was an official *British Racing Green.* Various Brit builders had pale green, very dark green, bluish green, pea green, but by golly, English cars were green. Lancia's red tended toward Bordeaux – or should I say Chianti – when compared to Ferrari's red, and Maserati's red, if memory serves, was paler.

But nowadays? Black; Taupe; Gray. I have a fondness for that particular red that was available on Chevys in '54 only, Martian cream of tomato soup; or the gunmetal gray of the '53 Packard; and the strong dark spearmint metallic green Dodge offered in '52.

Does anyone have well-preserved color photos of Triumph motorcycles in the late '40s or early '50s? Triumph Thunderbird blue was close to the mid-ocean blue. The Speed Twin came in a dark maroon, which looked old when it was new. Could it be that I was so smitten with the bikes themselves that their colors still resonate in that part of my brain? The deep, liquid-perfume-candy colors of late '50s Chryslers, obviously derived from some of the customs and rods of a decade earlier, are beautiful and you can almost taste them, but they don't grab me deep in my esthetic soul like the Triumphs and the Chevy.

When I rule the world, you'll have to get a doctor's prescription for a gray car and hazelnut-flavored coffee. This has nothing to do with cars, but the sight of a big bunch of yellow marigolds right next to a big bunch of orange ones absolutely hypnotizes me. I even get a buzz from the mental image.

After looking at dozens of paint chip catalogs I figured it out. I want a car painted the color of the full moon. Karen says I need a car painted the color of duct tape.

When I met Karen, she told me about her favorite cars, blue ones, but I detected nascent enthusiasm there. Her Eldo, although not blue, had a full aero kit and Fittipaldi wheels. The lady can drive, as well. She ditched a cop a few years back. She had a head start, as he had to find a hole in the raised median curb to make a u-turn, but she lost him through the town's most fashionable shopping area. She knows those particular streets really well.

How attitudes change! Dozens of years ago I remember when magazines picked on the Shelby Mustang GT 500KR as being another big and fat mutation of an originally nice car. We sporty car drivers shook our heads sympathetically when we saw the driver get out of one of those tanks. At least the hood scoop was real on the KR.

Seems like another Shelby modded Mustang has a fake hood scoop. Fake scoops! In 2007! And a low axle ratio! How about a 3.08 or so diff ratio, with the lower gears set up for acceleration (or will nothing help the mileage of this machine)?

Back in '66-'67 I went to the only Shelby-authorized dealer in Nashville, trying to order a supercharged GT350 convertible. He was never in and never returned my calls, so I got a magnificent Olds 442 convertible: quick-ratio manual steering, limited slip, etc. etc. and 130mph at 5,000rpm (that 3.08 ratio) with the canvas top stretched about 8" above the top bows. I towed my Morgan racecar with it, and, as long as I'm rambling, I sort of regret trading it in on a '68 Dart 383 GTS convertible, again with quick-ratio manual steering, of course. How nice it would be if we could delete power steering like you could in the good old days.

Automotive progress pluses and minuses, Minutiae Division: The cruise control on my '86 RX-7 Turbo II wouldn't work over 92mph. The cruise control on my beloved '94 will engage way on up there.

Some of the new adaptive cruise controls won't let you get within recognition distance of a car ahead – pretty useless unless you're the only car on the road. Then again, some electronics whiz might be able to hook it up so it would instantly respond to jam police radar and then revert to normal mode. Even though your private little hidden switch would convert it to normal operation, you would probably get busted anyway. Well, 'twas worth a thought.

High-end cars get more and more of these automatic gadgets year by year. Let's hope one day they'll have a sensor that won't let the fog lights turn on unless it's actually foggy!

Speaking of lights, you guys have it pretty good driving at night, what with modern headlights. But even in the mid-90s some major manufacturers produced some pretty crummy lights, and they admitted as much – well, off the record, of course. Because lights are so good these days, or more likely, because cars today don't have room and mounting surfaces in the grille area, you miss the fun of driving behind a pair of Cibié Oscars on a deserted road at night. My, could you see way down there - straight ahead, of course.

Then there were people like Dick Irish, who mounted a pair of small aircraft landing lights in his '59 T-Bird. They tended to eat up an occasional generator (no alternators back then), but you could recognize the species of bird trying to sleep on a telephone pole crossbar 50 yards away. They must have had a near conical beam. Trouble was, when you switched to dims for an oncoming car, your eyes told you nothing past twenty feet in front of the car.

I took the chrome and gold V emblem out of the center of my '53 Lincoln's grille and mounted a huge J. C. Whitney driving light there – the kind of light with all sorts of shields and supports for the filament, which was the size of a ballpoint pen spring. As I drove across western Kansas in the very early morning, returning to Bartlesville from Colorado College (and eating No-Doz dry, because I had nothing to drink) a car approached from the far distance. I dipped my lights. He blinked his. I blinked mine. He blinked his again. As we closed on one another, I realized I could see his face in the glare of my forgotten driving light. He had his hand in front of his eyes. Oops! I switched if off, nailed the brakes and pulled way onto the shoulder - at that moment he needed all the road he could get.

Cars are so complex nowadays you probably can't do stuff like this any more; my Porsche Carrera Speedster cracks a distributor cap. Porsche dealer can order one: $22.50 (in 1960!). A friend says to me, is that a Bosch cap? Yes. We drop in at the Nashville Bosch warehouse. They match it up for about $4.

Cam followers for that 6-cylinder Maserati engine in the Citroen SM? Some incredible amount from Citroen; some American piece for $5 fits.

Then there was my Miura with internal chain snatch, doubtless due to a worn sprocket, which kept breaking the $7.50 exterior toothed alternator drive belts, and at around 10,000 miles there was a lot of slop in the half-shaft u-joints. For an outside opinion, one day after lunch I dropped it off at M&M Automotive Electric in Bartlesville, Oklahoma, to be looked at by a friend who was working there. Various trifles occupied my afternoon, and it was near closing when I popped round to see what he thought.

"Your car's ready," he said. Ready? "We took the end cover off and there was a worn out gear in there, so we put in one from a Yazoo mower. And your u-joints were the same as Ford F-100 truck stuff – we had to just polish 'em with emery cloth and they slipped right in."

The Alfa Romeo Owner's Club back in the '60s had a multi-page typewritten (and mimeographed!) list of stuff that fit Alfas; I can only remember that a Giulia and a John Deere tractor had something in common in their water pumps.

So if you want comfort and amenities in your daily life by all means get a nice new car. But you'll never experience the thrill of an oddball fix in your garage or in the middle of nowhere.

This life long like-affair (you can only love people and pets) with cars must be part of my DNA. There has never been a time when all of my senses weren't fully engaged at the sight of a new one speeding through a yellow light, a vintage one passing me in a random locale or the sound of a distant engine that was not yet within view. Sure, the other things of life are important too. I just can't think of what they are.

The Fairer Sex: The Shine on the Glaze on the Cherry on the Frosting on the Cake

There are limits to our appreciation of extremes in many areas. Think of the funniest TV scenes, monologues or Tonight Show bantering that you've seen. You can tell when your personal laugh-meter has pegged. Nothing could be funnier, and it's happened more than once. You have a garage full of hot cars and they can all go over 180? Never mind the exact number; they're all *damn fast*.

Beautiful girls, same thing – except I hope you're not keeping them in the garage, too. The most beautiful, sexy woman I ever saw was in a car and so was I. Not the same car, though. I've had the trans-intellectual hots for Joan Collins since I saw her running up and down a beach in a bikini in *Holiday for Sadie* in 1959.

But before I knew who she was, in January of '58, Don Neptune and I were cruising through a nice Beverly Hills neighborhood in my Carrera Speedster, when we came to a narrowing of the street caused by cars parked on both sides; a party, no doubt. There were Jags, Cadillacs, the usual fare. As we crept through, I was craning my neck to the left to keep maximum room on the right, where a car had pulled out slightly and then stopped to let us through.

I'm doing 2mph and Don keeps saying in a loud whisper, "Toly! Toly!" I look over in exasperation and he's gesturing surreptitiously at the adjacent car. And there, turned sideways in the driver's seat to watch us pass, is Joan Collins. I turned into an Armenian marshmallow. Never before or since, have I seen such transcendental loveliness. We drove on. Or could it have been Dana Wynter?

53

Girls: Appreciation 101

In regards to my appreciation of women, I (and none of my friends that I can recall) never went through that *girl hating* phase that little boys exhibited through most of a century of family-type movies. I might have received a bump start or jumpstart in fondness for females when I was about five, though.

The family had just finished the basement rec. room/rumpus room (anyone still use those terms?) and my 21-year-old brother convinced mom that it should have pinups on its walls. I got to stir paint and wash small brushes as he, mom and sis matted and framed the complete 1941 *Esquire Magazine* Vargas calendar.

I can at this very moment emotionally recall my pre-testosterone feelings as I closely scanned those dozen oh-so-nearly-naked girls, as the pictures slid behind the frame glass. I longed to see a little bit of that or why not just one of those? I'd seen pictures of nude classical sculptures and Old Master paintings, so I had an idea of what was what; but what was that new and formless longing in my little brain when I looked at those Vargas girls? What was the deal with just barely covering everything?

Within the month my friend Jimmy and I started tearing just about any photo of a bare-legged girl out of our families' magazines and keeping them in a growing stack at my house. Mom told me later that if I hadn't been such a fine child in so many ways she'd have worried about me becoming a sex maniac. Well, I didn't, but Jimmy grew up in, shall we say, a different direction altogether. Maybe that was the wrong hobby for him at such a tender age. I can still remember some favorite pictures, though. And as I do, wouldn't it be nice if some 90-year-old woman somewhere suddenly felt that warm feeling you get when you're absolutely certain that someone's thinking of you.

Looking back, don't think the schoolteacher (female) fooling around with a student (male) is just a recent development. Even though I was out of the loop in the general area of physicality in high school, I found out that the really cute blonde Mrs. S., (and my goodness, even a divorcee, I think) left her teaching position in mid-semester because somebody spotted her photo in *Sunshine &*

Health, the nudist/naturist magazine back in the day. Although that magazine featured more airbrushing than a heavily customized panel truck, her face, of course, was *au naturel*.

After she was gone the story got out that you could pay a fee to the actual kid who had her on his paper delivery route, and get to go ring her doorbell to collect for the paper. It seems she liked to answer the door in something transparent and, while she cheerfully fumbled in her purse for the exact change, the door would swing open, slowly and just enough. There was also another rumor that much more had happened on occasion, than anyone would admit to. She left town, too.

This next incident could have happened innocently, but as I examine and re-examine my memories in the age 12 file, I just can't be certain. I was walking to a movie early in summer vacation when a very pretty, trim brunette, who was somehow affiliated with the school and who also represented a summer camp, pulled alongside and beckoned me over to give me another sales pitch. You see I'd recently read some supposedly humorous stories about all the awful things that happen at camp, and holding an unverbalized feeling that the stories must have had some basis in fact, I just plain didn't want to go.

Mrs. D. put on a sweetly coaxing act, but I wasn't too sure of what she was saying, since she was leaning way over from the driver's seat and the top two buttons of her summery white short sleeve blouse were undone. I guess what ultimately scared me off is that the camp's name was the same as the only condom brand I'd ever heard of. Poor kid, I was just scared. So what else is new?

In my early motorcycling days, during the Korean War, when '52/'53 Mercurys were delivered with only their left rear bumper-taillights installed (due to the chrome shortage), sex was infinitely better and that was because there was infinitely less of it. An example here, even a paragon of the embodiment of that thought: Dorothy!

Now, D knows all about this, because I told her years ago. I even told her kids – back when they actually were kids – and, of course, they said, "You mean you're talking about mom?" I've told my wife. Now I'm telling you.

I was keeping Don Hinkle company while he was collecting for his summer paper route. We were riding my Indian Scout; 26.5 c.i. vertical twin, painted a brilliant custard yellow. We climbed the stairs of a garage apartment and knocked on the black screen door, peering into the cool darkness. Our first perception in the distance of the back of the room was a gently swaying pair of trim white shorts approaching us. A few more sways and a watermelon sleeveless blouse materialized atop the shorts. Then, well, Dorothy: slim, tan, languorously cheerful, the epitome of loveliness in a young woman.

Unexpectedly discovering such beauty on a standard school's-out summer day was a blessing almost beyond description. Here she was, living in our smallish town, practically in our very neighborhood and we'd never seen her! Maybe her family had moved in recently.

How I relate all this to sex is that, had I been able to simply hold her in my arms for thirty seconds, I would've perfectly balanced so many levels of hormones, romantic fantasies, companionship, friendship, etc. etc., that I would've become for a short while at least, some sort of *ideal me*. Not even kissing her, mind you – just absorbing some of her loveliness by osmosis would've kept me on that teenage cloud nine for a few days. Didn't get to hold her for months for sure; maybe even years. Better than sex. Heck, just the memory of the imagination is good for great vibes for ten or fifteen minutes right now. Beauty. God-given beauty.

In those hazy days of the early '50s, as real then as today is to you, we teenagers were apparently either much better behaved, inhibited, or both. Carolee Smith came to town, the older sister of a girl, name forgotten, who was also visiting Bartlesville. She rode in on her Indian Warrior, a 30.5 c.i. vertical twin, built several months after my 26.5 c.i. Scout. I wonder why they ever built the smaller engine.

Anyway, I think those extra cubic inches might have given me the first twinge of threatened masculinity solely on the basis of a possession or artifact. Also, Carolee was good-looking, older, self-assured, and said things like — but let me set the scene.

A bunch of us, having a minor picnic up on Kane's Hill overlooking what *Sports Illustrated* had called one of the eighteen most beautiful golf holes in America. Midsummer. Mid-evening. There were a dozen of us, about half girls, all on motorcycles. When it was time to leave, and as we straddle our bikes, our dates sitting behind, Carolee was casually stubbing out her cigarette on the brick wall where she was sitting. One of the girls asked, "Carolee, are you coming?"

Carolee replied, "No, just breathing hard." Sitcom stuff today, almost paralyzingly *outré* then. Was it a gentler time? It is safe to say yes, oh yes.

Of course, there had to be some physical stuff going on then, but it wasn't bragged about or even talked about. Knowledge just seeped out years later. There was this nice guy, just one of the fellas, who told us that the quilts in the trunk of his folks' car were to slide under the vehicle, so he could keep clean while he tried to track down an occasional elusive leak. He was sliding under something, all right.

There was also a brilliant girl, who didn't date much. He didn't date much either. They were never seen together, but if you snuck down a dirt road to a certain small oil well at just the right time of just the right day, you would have seen a couple serious students with their textbook.

Yes, they really had a book: the *Kama Sutra*. While she dressed modestly in school, it was obvious no one had a better body. After graduation they went their separate ways, somewhat better educated than the rest of us, one might suppose.

Girls: Appreciation 201

Considering the mores of the times, exponentially increased by my naiveté, there's not much to report in any "cars and romance" category. Oh sure, *she* and I steamed up the windows quite a few times, but it was just necking. Heard that word lately? In the current culture, things have been so unromantic for so long, that over a quarter-century ago I was told in Los Angeles that if you're not in the sack by the third date, she loves the dinners, but hates your guts! Now it's probably two dates or less.

Once at a drive-in I was feeding Sydney Grant (first girl I ever kissed) an onion ring, when my left thumb and index finger touched her tongue, I felt the shock up to the base of my skull. Well into my teens I'd never eaten an onion ring, or even onion soup. I'd had onions in salads and on burgers, but a fried onion ring was one of those foods I was, for want of a better word, afraid of. Anyway, after the tongue touch, an onion ring became a sort of holy object to me for years, like a cow to a Hindu – an object of reverence and awesome memory. Ah youth.

As a child, I was afraid of ice cream sodas, but I loved sundaes. I was afraid of cotton candy and popcorn and marshmallows and radishes and Tabasco sauce. I suppose I thought they'd taste beyond revolting. My nurse (they're called nannies now) probably told me they tasted horrible and my active imagination took it from there. In fact, even though I was allowed the occasional couple squares of a Hershey, I was spooked by all those weird lumpy candy bars. What could I have thought was lurking under the chocolate coating? Any shrinks out there have any idea what was wrong with me?

Then there was the time in the Packard Caribbean when, although I was hosting a party at my house, I found myself (phrase that avoids responsibility) parked up on Kane's Hill with a certain Sarah (I've dated five Sarahs, all of them exquisite). Anyway, during our conversations or at least my conversation, about college and cars, two or three times Sarah stood on her knees, sideways in the passenger seat, and fell over toward me, her complete collapse halted by my face becoming wedged between, well, you know (I'm writing in this fashion to illustrate my utter *dipness*, as if it were necessary). I drove us back to my party before I developed whiplash. Just a momentary lapse on my part? Not with *old Toly, the consistent.*

I once told Sydney that, while Marcia was a doll and a real *sosh* (socialite, pronounced with a long o), she somehow just didn't do anything for me. Even though Syd and Marcia were friends, it never occurred to me that Syd would tell Marcia.

Shortly thereafter word filtered to me that Marcia would really, really like to go out with me. We went out in mom's '49 Cadillac fastback 2-door on a cold night in which the car's heater, on full blast, made even more intoxicating the results of Marcia's hurrying to be ready when I called. She had dropped and broken a full bottle of Horizon perfume on her vanity table and gotten most of it on her clothes. Intense!

Marcia thought we should go out to several parking spots and go bushwhacking; that's where you pull up next to a familiar car in the dark and say "Hello, Sandy! Hi, Jim!" and then glide off. Nobody was out on this particular night, so I said, "Hunting's not so good tonight," and drove us to Johnston's Drive-In. I would have bet money she wanted me to kiss her, but that chicken feeling was ever present.

After the concept soaked in over the next month or so, we had some good clean fun. I knew that I was a great kisser, because I thoughtfully and analytically practiced various techniques on my arm. Hey! I didn't want to hurt some babe!

I wonder if times have changed. In college (10 years) I was amazed how many girls, especially southern ones, were bad kissers. Sort of *present face* and that was it. I actually was enough of a dork to give several young ladies specific instructions. They seemed to enjoy things more afterward, but if they were offended, I was too dense to notice.

It's wonderful to have parents who're always on your side. I was out with another of the five Sarahs - Sarah Jane this time, and she was just 15, I think, or maybe 16, almost my age. We had the top down on the supercharged Lincoln and it was June and she wanted to drive.

It was after the last movie and getting late, but the more she drove, the more she liked it. We cruised around town for awhile and then went out on the highway, where she made several 0 - 80 runs, getting giddier with each. Then she had me drive her home, while she relaxed with her eyes closed and her long brown hair blowing in the moonlit breeze. Lovely. She was all butterscotch except for the bones.

Meanwhile, her mother got a bit worried, and decided to drive over to my house to find out what might be going on. Late it was, but my mom, a night-owl like most of the family, was still puttering around in the living room; lights on, front door open. Mom looked up to see a strange woman standing in the hall. "What has your son done with my daughter?" demanded the lady.

"What has your daughter done with my son?" replied my mother. They both laughed and had a glass of wine – no, I remember mom told me it was a couple of Millers in those beautiful glasses, all of which our maids eventually broke – and they got along so well that they were still chatting away when I got back.

I've got a real field exercise for you here, with no answer conveniently at the bottom of the page. I was out in the Lincoln with *The Built Girl Who Lived Next Door to Bartlesville Bill,* when she asked to drive. I got out, she slid over, and as I approached the passenger door she drove off. I chuckled, walked up to the car, and she drove off again. This happened several times; she finally let me get in. I was peeved. Nothing further developed. What would you have done? Send me your ideas c/o my publisher. Please. At my age I'm about out of fantasies.

Anyway, back in that Eisenhower administration a close friend of mine had a discussion with his girlfriend. She was leaving with her parents for a couple weeks and he told her that, loyalty aside, he might get on rather well with a new girl in town.

Loyalty aside, girlfriend strongly disagreed. They finally decided on a bet on the subject, but she wasn't about to simply take his word. So, before girlfriend left town, he called the other girl up and asked her out. She accepted.

They went on the date, with some extra cargo – a live turkey under a large cardboard box in the back seat area, which cushion had been removed. You guessed it; it wasn't a turkey under that carton, it was girlfriend. Some grain had been scattered on the floor back there, and girlfriend occasionally scratched and pecked at the inside of the box.

She got her evidence. He got a little something or other, and the new girl never found out a thing. Girlfriend said the hardest part was muffling her giggles from time to time. Quasi-innocent fun.

But hold it just a second. We weren't total goody-goodies in our adolescence. Am I naïve for thinking you might've thought so? Consider this. There's more than one thing you can do in a garage.

Work on cars, of course. Then there are garage bands. Lots of times it turns into a general storage area.

When we built our swimming pool in the early '50s, mom turned one bay into a pair of dressing rooms. Even though the garage was as useful as a garage could be – with a drive-through capability to the back drive with street access; we eventually never used that.

At the time, our little band of brothers was future-tech oriented, reading science-fiction magazines and novels and eagerly awaiting the first cheap helicopter or amphibious motor scooter, as predicted by the cover art on *Mechanix Illustrated* and similar publications. We found out about a bit of then current modern hi-tech, which we could put to nefarious use: the one-way mirror.

With suppressed unease, we approached the local glass company and inquired about such a project with vague references to a science project involving clandestine observation of animal behavior. The ol' boy in the glass shop didn't care one way or the other. He cut us a square foot or so and made sure we knew that it would reflect whichever side had the most light, a fact previously unknown to us, but obviously vital.

Well, we framed the thing, put a hole in the dressing room partition, unscrewed the ceiling bulb on our side (the partition stopped a yard short of the garage ceiling) and put a 150-watter in the socket on the girl's side. It worked like a charm.

We had a clever set of plans involving chatter, dropping shoes, etc., to avert any suspicion that might arise from our side falling silent the instant the first *vict* -er, young lady, whipped off her undies. We'd even josh about getting ready to peek over the top, which once had the serendipitous effect of making a nervous beauty cuddle right up to the mirror for protection. Oh, we were clever.

There was one real babe who was a bit shy – changed in her robe both into and out of her suit. Next time she was in the pool, we guys got into a friendly fight and somehow wound up throwing a couple towels, and, oops, our mistake, *the bathrobe*, into the pool. We concealed our pleasure with the success of our plan with suavity, I like to think, and the remaining minutes of the pool party seemed to drag on like a school day.

It was worth the wait. No bathrobe. *What a bod!* Of course, we'd known she was built, but most of you are probably too old to remember the suits of the day: one-piece, thick nylon and carrying more wire than a suicide bomber.

As an aside, there were two transparent-when-wet suits that appeared on our little scene in the mid-'50s, and they were both Rose Marie Reid's manufacture. Wonder who the friendly perv. in the fabric-purchasing department was?

There'd be a lawsuit today, of course; and there'd certainly be a lawsuit over our behavior today: weird, isn't it? Slut-O-Rama in movies and MTV, but jail for peeking. It actually happened recently around here, but it wasn't us! We were caught too, way back then. I forget how it happened - some guy must've talked, I guess.

Two girls out of some thirty or forty we'd checked out got mad (I'm sure not even a third of our subjects ever knew, since they weren't all close friends) and one of the best-lookers came to me and said, "If you wanted to see us naked, why didn't you just ask?" About twenty years later it dawned on me that she meant it!

In our youth, hormones doing whatever it is that hormones do, we found it interesting that sexual arousal never occurred - the sheer loveliness and general innocence of all concerned gave us guys an attitude of awe and wonder. Bikinis and thongs today – why would anyone bother with a one-way mirror? The good old days: *Girls Gone Tame*.

We guys were a pretty conservative bunch about the female form. Big bazooms were completely unnecessary. Brunettes looked fine. Real blondes were definitely interesting, but we thought redheads whose carpet matched the drapes looked really odd. Picky, picky, picky.

It surprises me how often my thoughts return to my '56 Studebaker Golden Hawk – a model made only that year. That car may have had an unintentional pheromone magnifier in it. On a quietly romantic night, rumbling back to Tulsa in the Hawk, about 50 miles, taking the lovely Sarah K home – Remember the fairy kneeling by the pool on the White Rock Club Soda bottles? Make her a brunette and you've got Sarah.

Anyway, she'd gone to sleep with her head so far up my shoulder that her forehead occasionally brushed my ear. Every several seconds, when her warm moist exhale coincided with my inhale – heck, I don't know what it was, but it was intoxicating, and I had the better part of an hour to enjoy it. I gave up trying to analyze it. What breath. Never anything like it before or since. Cloud nine? Shucks, pardner, I was looking down on cloud nine. Had to be pheromones.

Sarah did something to herself, though. I can remember vividly just where we were sitting in her house, when she decided she did not like the wonderfully delicate little bridge in her nose and decided to have it removed. She didn't have one of those nose job looks afterward, but doggone it, I liked that little bridge. So, when she went off to Lindenwood, I dated her younger sister.

And speaking of doing things, you should have seen what they did to their pale blue Buick Super '53 convertible. It was really dirty and they decided to suds it up all over – with SOS pads. They didn't rinse it off till they were finished. Ever seen a big piece of blue chalk in the shape of a Buick Super convertible?

I didn't interject this aside to gloss over dating her sister. I even dated a sister named Sarah after her older sister went off to Kansas State. I dated a mother and daughter, too, but not at the same time. You knew I was a gentleman.

I also had an unhelpful cocktail of *fear of commitment and your conscience says you're fickle, son* in my psyche. Why did I tend to stop dating the girls I was looniest about?

There I was at the dorm at Lindenwood College near St. Louis, on a beautiful spring night in an Olds my folks had rented for me, since I was only 20. I'm about to pick up the exquisite Sarah K.

I check in with the housemother at the desk (this is the way a proper girls' dorm is operated, kids). Sarah comes out of a sitting room and I practically float off the floor. I open the door for her and we hear a feminine cough. "Just a minute," says Sarah. "Turn around."

Now, this particular dorm had a balcony all the way across the hall's upper level and a staircase curved down along the wall opposite the desk. I turn around and the entire balcony and part of the staircase is lined with girls, checking out this guy who'd come 400 miles for dinner and a movie.

My higher brain centers were stunned, so the remaining centers said, "I'll take that brunette, and that sweet wispy one, and the bright one with the *hoo-hahs*, and…" and then my forebrain kicked back in and said, "Why you bastard! You're not good enough for Sarah with that attitude!" I mean we had a really great time that evening, but I worried about myself.

Late night driving trips and the passengers' attendant relaxation (occasionally helped by a sip of scotch) and the corresponding fatigue brought about a kaleidoscope of conversational topics. Almost every time a new passenger – someone unknown to the others in the car save one – was carried, it was a whole new condensed encyclopedia. One elderly (i.e. thirty-something) guy along for the ride (who was he? Where were we going? Were we towing a race-car or not?) gave us teen-ish/twenty-ish people an education somehow stemming from a discussion of the Founding Fathers, and segueing into Ben Franklin's comments on older women.

We were enlightened and a little apprehensive, as he advised us virgins and near-vees, "Don't knock an opportunity to go off for awhile with a 40-year-old, or even some gal around 50. Nah, it doesn't matter if they're divorced. You can tell if she's got a decent figure. She's probably not getting much action, whether she's married or not, or maybe she's just looking for a change. Guys generally like 'em young and she knows she's not getting any younger. She may have some facial wrinkles, especially if she's the outdoor type. but you get her undressed – hell, she's likely to undress herself *and you* – and you'll find soft skin everywhere important. Remember, ol' Ben said they age from the top down and he's right. And you're likely to get a lot of gratitude. You'll be bringing back memories of her youth, and maybe memories of something she always wanted to try but didn't. Or maybe it'll be the other side of that coin – 'I bet a kid like you never tried this!'"

We guys were a little disturbed, as it was an intimate discussion of *the unknown* and also sounded vaguely Oedipal. The mystery man continued, "Important thing for optimum results – before – after – during - don't just lie there saying 'wow' and 'gee whiz'. Rub her back with a free hand. Massage her feet. Legs. Kiss the back of her neck or behind her knee. Just touch and kiss, but don't make a big deal out of it. She probably won't chase you around the campus next week, but she'll generally be available for awhile, more'n likely."

This got us to talking about a couple good-looking mothers of girls we dated. There was an apocryphal story in my hometown of a mother, a former professional dancer, who seduced her daughter's date when he got to the girl's house after the girl called home to say she'd had car trouble and would be two hours late. She was the best-looking mom and did have an attitude about her, and the daughter, although pretty, was known to be a flake.

Thank heavens none of us guys had attractive moms or my not-to-be-named pal would have gotten in trouble after hearing about the monologue. He was by far the freethinker of our bunch and none of us would have taken kindly to our mother being an object of his attention, even in a philosophical discussion at 60mph at 1 AM.

Anyway, the whole concept made, from then on, occasional eye contact with a trim middle-age waitress while we were far from home, a mildly disturbing and faintly frustrating experience. *The Graduate* must have been the real deal. Eventually, we got used to the idea, I suppose, and one of us even followed the mysterious stranger's advice and told us, well, yes, he'd been pretty much right. The stranger had left out the part about the mood-breaking bit shortly after *the big deal*, when our friend was shooed out of the bed, the shower and the house.

Another of our group extemporized on the lecture and would occasionally cruise (a heterosexual term back then) department stores (remember those?) and supermarkets, claiming that five seconds of expressionless, but intense eye contact meant "into the sack" in the next half hour. I won't tell you what he eventually got his Ph.D in, but you'd hit it in three guesses.

The take home thing about funny, intense indulgences of the flesh is that there are consequences. Being aware of that law of unintended results does not mean going to the extreme of the focal point of the Oblomov movement. This Russian literary character – and with this kind of logic what other nationality could he have been – decided that any action taken by a human being creates innumerable consequences in all directions; and since the devil is the prince of this world, eventually bad things will result from the most benign activity.

So he took to his bed for the rest of his life, inspiring, for a brief period a century ago, a portion of Russian college students to stay in bed for, one imagines, semester after semester, wearing daytime pajamas, the usual sort of nighttime pajamas, entertaining in formal pajamas, and so on. Obviously, school attendance suffered... Who knows if they were expelled or not? The fad lasted a very few years, and whatever notoriety these guys got must have been a real buzz in the butt to the communist cadres coalescing in grubby secrecy at the time.

Hemingway, I think, defined a right action as something – anything – you feel good after, which packages up 99.999% of sexual activity right there. This is the polar opposite of the Russian layabout, and the truth, while somewhere in between, is surely closer to one pole than the other.

I used to think that the Good Book (ah, to heck with that – the *Greatest Book*, to quote Napoleon) was a really good way to play the odds; but after a half-lifetime of experience and observation, I've decided that following it gives the greatest total satisfaction at the moment, in memory and for confidence in the future. So regarding the sexy stories, amusing to recount, but please don't replicate the activity down your particular road. But then should I have recounted them? Should you have enjoyed reading them?

Look, Jack, should all simple moral choices be easy too? Should I apologize to the guy I ever so gently nudged into a spin to win the race (we were in identical cars and there was nary a mark on either in impound)? It's been a quarter century and I still can feel it plain as day. What if he's forgotten it and I bring it up?

What's the gym equivalent to *conscience reps* like this? What about fooling around with someone else's wife? Oh, just that once. Besides simply not doing it, there are no alternatives. And if done, well, repent.

The simplicity of the last word in the last sentence most certainly shouldn't encourage you to do more *bad things*. And regarding atonement, do whatever the spirit moves you to do. In any case, if you're a studied Christian, you know you're covered. Completely. Just don't do it again. End of sermon.

Girls: Appreciation 301

One of those *Didn't Think of the Consequences* moments: Driving to Tulsa one fine afternoon, with well-constructed Texas gal, as a passenger. Had read about females flashing truck drivers (this was just before the 55mph/cb era). Mention this to passenger. "You mean like this?" she asks, and whips bottom edge of sweater up to her eyebrows as a car passes us. I'm quite entertained and very amused at her bravado. Then I realize I'm driving my father's car. Yee gads! Great bravado, though – or should that be bravados?

My late, sorely missed, 17-year-older brother, when he was about twice as old as I was, used to impress me with his offhand comments about dating this movie star or that one. He got to grow up in Hollywood, just before WWII. In the spirit of sibling rivalry, with the deceased no less, let me say, first, that when I saw his girlfriends, they were all in black and white. Then again, he got married at 23, while I waited until I was almost 60; so, big brother, check this out.

I've dated two movie stars, Miss World, Miss Canada, Miss Davidson County, Miss Bartlesville, Miss Tulsa, Miss Wool (oh, clean up your mind!), the last ever Miss Oklahoma Service Station, the late, sweet, deeply philosophical Miss Tennessee Dairy Princess, one of Ray Anthony's Bookends, a deejay and a significant TV personality with really outstanding talents.

Unsure of myself, a regular born-again Woody Allen, I edged away from them with varying degrees of alacrity; the strongest example being the night I was out to dinner with Miss Universe. We were having a wonderfully smooth-flowing semi-personal conversation, and as we agreed on some important point in *life and living*, she gently rested her hand on mine. Momentarily stunned, too good to be true, I jerked my hand away as if a five-legged tarantula had landed on it. Shortly afterward she went to powder her nose (and possibly silently screamed, "Whadda maroon!" in her stall) and I sat, no idea of what to say next, while they boiled our soufflé for dessert – or whatever. Now let's say that I fix you up next Saturday with a beautiful girl, an expense account and a Lamborghini Miura. Does anybody think you wouldn't do exponentially better than I did? I can't remember how much I cringed at the memory of my performance back then, but it couldn't be as much as I'm cringing now.

Anyway, tying together our teenage naughtiness (the girls' dressing room) and my decades later really good, artistic and not the least bit naughty nude photography of lovely figures on and around a Cooper-MG, Serenissima, Piper Le Mans, Alfa 1900, mini-Chaparral H Modified and various cars that were new at the time: a young woman I was dating commented approvingly of my work and said she knew a gymnast/dancer who would be an excellent model, and put us in touch. The photo shoot went very well and she was just a living doll with the sweetest personality imaginable and great sense of humor. We had a late snack (I generally photographed late in the evening at the showroom, since we were on a side street and had smallish windows except for the standard glass double doors.

So the young lady signed the standard release form, and then she said, "I really need to get home since I have a test tomorrow I need to study for."

Dedicated student, I thought to myself, another plus. "You go to Tulsa U. or Junior College?" I asked.

"Oh, I'm a sophomore at (blank) High School," she said as she got into her car. At least she's old enough to have a driver's license, I thought in only a small state of panic. Sixteen – I hope – no wonder her skin was perfect. I wouldn't have been too surprised to get a call from some sort of law enforcement, but it never happened. The pictures are, to this day, really good. I might show them to you some day, but I won't identify which ones they are in my portfolio – unless you can show me something really solid on the statute of limitations. As I write this, she'd be at least 51. She might even like copies, as souvenirs of how lovely she looked. I've always wondered what she told her folks about what she did that evening.

. My first session using the showroom for a studio included two figure models from the University of Kansas art department, chaperoned by my niece, who was a student at K.U. at the time. It was about midnight when I heard a car pull into the parking lot. I was a bit nonplussed, but the models didn't bother to put on their robes - one was leaning on an Iso Grifo (it was yellow and you can see it in black and white in a Mooneyes promotional photo book with yet another nude next to it; was it another type of chick magnet?) The other girl stood at ease next to a Siata Spring. I never saw our visitor, what with the lights on inside and none outside, but I heard a shouted, "God damn!" and a door slammed and whatever it was, peeled out of the parking lot. We wrapped up the shoot in the next few minutes. I'd used up most of my ideas and was concerned our mystery caller might return with a bunch of his friends, but all was calm and uneventful. Thank heavens!

Hey guys, just in case you aren't fully convinced that a swell car doesn't act as a chick magnet, this should convince you. In late 1967, as a party guest I couldn't get to the bar, since every time I tried to leave my Miura more people came up to ask about it. It was soon after a nice newspaper article about my first fashion show, and a pleasant lady, a member of Nashville's social scene, remarked about the esthetic similarities of fashion and automobile design. "Yes," I said. "But what this car needs is some photos of a lovely, sleek nude draped here and there over the bodywork."

"I know just the young lady you should use," she said. "I'll call her tomorrow and mention your plans and that you will be by the TV station where she works to take her out to lunch on Friday, so you can work out all the details."

"How nice," I thought, and Friday at noon I parked the Miura at the foot of the station steps and trotted up to the receptionist. "I'm here to take (Miss X) out to lunch," I said.

"That's me. Let's go." she said. I must mention here that she later married an Oscar winner and was in several movies herself. The upshot of the lunch date – the lady had never called her! And while she wasn't keen on lying bare on the Miura, we still had a lovely time. Yes, as you might have guessed, I was so nonplussed that I never called her again. The nth power of dweeb; I reached that plateau all by myself.

It wasn't like I didn't need help, socially; and it wasn't like I didn't have help, especially from my friend Bill Pryor. I can't count the times - okay, five or six - when there was a knock on my apartment door while I was watching some lame TV show. At the door there was Bill with some luscious, lovely young thing. "Toly, this is JoAnne/ Pat/Connie/Cissy/Katie/Judy. She's yours for the evening." Then he'd take her hand and place it in mine and leave.

As I shifted from one foot to the other, finally remembering to ask her in, the L.L.Y.T. would say, "Gosh Toly, I'm so glad to meet you. Bill's told me ever so much about you and your cars and racing in Europe and stuff!" Doggone if I can remember anything about what happened afterward. Dinner, probably - and once, I do remember - ah, never mind.

Beautiful women, oh my, seeing one every now and then is like coming around a highway curve and – bang! – there's a gorgeous bit of scenery. You don't have to move your eyes as much, though, when looking at a woman, compared to a panorama.

Taking a back road across Mississippi in the early '70s, I crossed a construction area of the Natchez Trace Parkway. I pulled up and stopped next to the person holding the stop sign. She turned to face me and believe me, there is/was no more beautiful woman in the world. Yes, in the total world population of over three billion, half are women - one and a half billion. A third of them are in the age range where great beauty can exist – 500 million. Let's say one in ten thousand is slap-in-the-face stunning. She was one of the equally staggeringly beautiful fifty thousand most beautiful women in the world. See why we all ought to get out and around more?

There were a couple of Elizabeth Taylor at her best waitresses, at cafés fifty miles apart, but they were glum and sullen. They'd been beaten down by the comments of every other man who came in the door; not dirty remarks, just shift-long, day after day, litany of "Gee Merle, lookit her. Ain't she a beauty?" I'll bet each of them had loved it for the first month – or week.

There was an exquisite creature working at my dad's company over forty years ago, when I was there; Dovie Branstetter. She was very demure, because everywhere she walked all men's eyes were upon her and her beauty was beyond the crudity of lechery: pure feminine esthetic.

At this point I'll mention the nude sitting on the hood/bonnet of an Elva Courier. Supposedly, this photo was sent from Eric Broadley to the SCCA board to persuade them to classify the Courier as a production car, which they did – for whatever reason.

Okay, she was great looking, but in this particular philosophical pursuit, you must be aware of the large overlap between beauty and sexiness, because they sure do coexist. Isn't it interesting to occasionally see a beautiful woman who's just not at all sexy one little bit? Kind of like a Maserati Quattroporte on Chevy cop car wheels. I put myself in full Dobie Gillis mode now (the young Dwayne Hickman was my personal Steve McQueen) to state, "Gee, girls are nice to look at!"

At the other emotional extreme, in the mid-'70s, in my sister's Beverly Hills women's-art-only art gallery (the first in the world), a friend of hers dropped by with a friend of hers, named Lois. Now Lois was late 20s, fifteen pounds over optimum and cute. Nowhere near beautiful, just cute. If I'd had one more microgram of testosterone in my system, I'd have dragged her into the utility closet and utilized her. And judging from our eye contact, I think I could've taken her gently by the hand to that closet; but true to form, I didn't even ask her out to dinner.

Bill Pryor and I did do a fine thing after the first Road Atlanta Racing Car Show in, what, 1970? Bill and I had a champagne party afterward, and invited Malcolm Smith (star of *On Any Sunday* and winner of about every off-road bike race in those days) and Gordon Smiley a good road racer, who was killed in Indy qualifying the following year; oh, and every single contestant in the Miss Road Atlanta beauty pageant (and no additional men). Malcolm took his drink, a darling little brunette and some pillows, and they sat under the piano for an hour, deep in conversation. Bill and Gordon and I enjoyed the remaining female/male ratio very much, thank you. All the contestants were students at a local fashion design institute, so the group looked real, real good.

I once knew a luscious young woman who curled up in the car seat next to me. She squealed, whimpered, twitched and salivated when I offered her an almond macaroon. I should have gone home and rubbed a couple dozen all over my body and stowed some more in my clothing before our next date, but you know, I never thought of it until a decade later.

Years later there was one lovely young lady that I simply could not come to grips with; and that is as literal as it sounds. She was very intelligent. She was quite attractive. She had hitchhiked around Europe by herself three times. She was in shape. She had me strike a moderate blow to her midsection and it was hard as a brick wall, whereas my midsection is more like the size of a brick wall.

If we even held hands, though, I had a faint taste in my mouth as if I'd put a penny and a nickel on top of my tongue. We got along great (she also had a magnificent sense of humor), but our auras were incompatible. She was also a Jonah.

We went to an event at the Broadmoor in Colorado Springs. The alternator on my '74 Pontiac Trans-Am 454 Super Duty failed just short of Woodward, Oklahoma. We found an obliging electrician, who delicately soldered something back together. Now, we were hours behind schedule, but without recalling exact details, I knew there was a 24-hour gas station in the midst of our Colorado wilderness route. We slowed, approached it - it was closed.

We ran out of gas a few miles short of the Springs. Another two hours waiting for help (thank God for CB radios). We would've been rescued earlier, except some semi-local was trying to skip his frequency to his girlfriend in Los Angeles, for Pete's sake, and we couldn't get him off the air.

Turns out I was right about the fuel availability. There was a dollar-bill operated gas pump (surely one of the first in the nation) at the place where I didn't stop. Next trip with her: wheel bearing failure on the Bristol 410 in Arkansas. Next trip: an accidentally cancelled hotel reservation. What kind of odd vibes were in play? Weird! And speaking of Jonahs, whatever happened to the lovely Jona Phillips, who lived within rifle shot of the Beverly Hills Hotel in 1954? Heck, she can't have aged a bit. I sure haven't.

The same year Bill Pryor and I started racing those twin $1,700 Morgan 4/4s, I staged a fashion show – the first of a pair – of my ladies' clothing designs. I was keeping company with the luscious

Miss Davidson County (oh Pam, where are you now?) and as we were having a discussion of clothes, she said she not only knew an agency that would put on a show if I had a line to present, she even knew a seamstress who'd build the clothes. So I sketched out a couple dozen outfits and Miss Tomella Robinson made them out of the oddest fabrics I could find.

The night of the show I tried to check out the final fittings going on in the dressing room – heck, isn't that what designers always do? The head of the agency and her secretary, a former Balenciaga model herself, wouldn't let me in. "It's customary, isn't it?" I asked.

"Yes, but it's also customary that the designers are not straight." I was told. Well, rats! – and I'd been so well-behaved up to that point, even feigning imperceptiveness of the rare but occasional leading remarks of this charming young lady or that one, while engaged in one-on-one conversation. I did promise one of the most absolutely charming that I would call her and tell her how we did in the Targa Florio when I got back to town. Then I lost her name and number. If anyone was ever ripe for a personal secretary for such things, it was you-know-who.

Girls Can Be Fun
A Wife, at Least One Like Mine, is Better

I was invited to Karen's New Years Eve party by her hairdresser, a *friend girl* (as opposed *to girl friend*) whom I'd met when she was a teenager; but Karen hadn't really invited her, just mentioned the party! So, friend girl brought me and I stayed for dinner, not knowing I wasn't supposed to - even my horoscope says I'm singularly unperceptive about anything besides myself.

The first date we had I told her she was absolutely not my type, but I liked her anyway; that was in early January 1989. Just a few semesters ago.

A few weeks after I met Karen I went to The Continent, ahem, to do the Monaco-Sestrieres winter rally and then the Coppa delle Alpi. Thanks to the late Sally Clayton-Jones, I also got to sled down the Cresta Run. That's where you go headfirst, which is much more relaxing than the luge where you lie on your back and lift your head up to see where you're going.

When I got back and told Karen about all the fun I'd had (including a cheerful conversation with a former member of the Hitler Youth, who actually regretted not making it into WWII), she decided we had to go over, and soon. I sent in entries for a rally and a race, and in May over we went. Both events had been cancelled. We were in Italy. Karen wanted to go to France. Heck, I'd dragged her all the way over here for nothing. So why not France?

Consequently, we began a couple decades of discovering wonderful little hotels, obscure car museums and equally obscure car events, tasting unknown local wines, avoiding tripe and brain omelets, and finding antiques. Burt Levy has paid me the compliment of looking at my cars and murmuring "You have the weirdest shit!" and the same could easily be said about the ancient things we've dragged out of the barn behind the other barn. Antiques yes, barn-find cars no.

Besides the usual furniture and little art objects, stuff you think of when you hear the word antique, we found some big things: we have the last remaining Aubusson cartouches, some 6' x 9', the full size paintings on heavy paper or canvas that the tapestry makers used as patterns, and the last two hundred-year-old, ten foot long solid copper dye vat that the tapestry yarns were colored in. It was hidden in a basement and escaped both the French and German armies' scavenging for critical materials. You want real scavenging, you send Karen. All the other vats were melted down – many even in WWI – so this is likely the sole survivor. Anyone want to swap for a Grand Prix Delage?

The other member of this small family I've gotten myself attached to is my stepson, Trace (for Robert David Sheehan III). A long time ago a girl said she could never marry me because I'd be unsatisfied with our children. That might have been true, but certainly doesn't apply to Trace. Heck, I've only been toothgrindingly jealous of him, oh, twenty or thirty times.

Let's see – high school football team, basketball team, golf team. Never had a B in his life. Duke grad; within a month of joining Wayne Manor fraternity (and how freaking apropos that name is,) he was their social director and girls were all over the place. He was a Rhodes Scholar nominee from Duke; Water polo goalie; a Lord Rothermere Scholar at Oxford; then Lord Mountbatten Fellow in Business attached to Sainsbury's in London. He ran with the bulls in Pamplona and learned hang gliding.

He attended the Sorbonne in Paris and dated Miss Turkey (a fine Christian girl, a real stunner as you might imagine). She could drink him and his friends under the table, and they broke up because she couldn't believe he wasn't fooling around with the 3 girls he was sharing a huge apartment with. He wasn't, really. Just ask him. Of course it was Karen who found that jewel of an apartment one day while we were taking a break from going into Paris antique shops and snickering at their prices. After she knocked the rent down about 15% the real estate agent went out and got us a bottle of champagne to share. Ah, Paris.

Back in London, Trace, tired of the pub scene, walked into the Royal Academy of Dramatic Arts and was immediately cast in some Shakespeare thing. Naturally nothing else would do but to go to New York and enroll in the New York Academy of Dramatic Arts and win their top awards. At graduation neither Karen nor I knew of any awards, so when Trace's name was called, Karen, in the best Notre Dame fan tradition, leaped to her feet and cheered. All the Yankees sitting around us either averted their eyes or smiled at us in that way Yankees smile.

Trace had his 21st birthday party in a private salon at the Ritz in London, of course. Karen and I rewrote the lyrics to A Nightingale Sang in Berkely Square and serenaded him with piano accompaniment. Embarrassed him; guests loved it: "…How could he know that you were twenty-one? The whole wide world is yours, my son…"

In Paris he had even discovered a little old bar in the Mouffetard student district near the Sorbonne, and made it so popular that not only did we drink free when we went there, the owner's family took Trace along as their guest when they went to Disneyland Paris. He's working in Hollywood now. Look for his name in lights!

Racing in the USA

I f you're writing a thesis on eras of motor racing, I cannot recommend more highly that you consult Chuck Dressing and
Henry Adamson. I have never been able to establish exactly
how these guys got the knowledge they have. Obviously they were
at least as interested in cars as I was. Possibly while I was out frol-
icking on the back roads in a sporty car they were reading all kinds
of books on the subject. I mean at no time was I interested in a
Lorraine-Dietrich, unless in its glove compartment were nude photos of Laraine Day and Marlene Dietrich, and that's a stretch.

Bill Pryor has a similar limited interest, and when I asked him
why we felt the way we did, he said simply that those cars were
before our time; we were much more interested in the immediate
kinesthetics of getting into an MGA or a Porsche Speedster with a
cheerful girl and having a run, and then settling down to read the
latest exploits of Ken Miles and Olivier Gendebien while the girls
brought us iced tea and cheese sandwiches.

D and A may not have written books, but they should. In one of
David Uhlein's registered historic mill buildings near Milwaukee,
where he kept part of his car collection, I looked at Mr. Uhlein's
Lorraine-Dietrich, and Henry said "but that's not the Circuit of
Dieppe Lorraine-Dietrich." And at Daytona, Chuck, hearing the
announcer's voice on the late and sorely missed Bob Snodgrass'
foot-long little animated drag race diorama, immediately identified
the man and told me the years he'd been announcer at the Orange
County strip. These people, genuinely, know too much.

Simpler Times, Simple Pleasures

During my youth, the standard view of the international formula and sports car racing set, pretty much one and the same bunch, was like this: There were steely-eyed Battle of Britain vets and slightly younger Brits who'd built racecars in their garden sheds. There were dashing Latin lotharios with their own or their girlfriend's money. There were other interestingly-cultured Europeans. Finally, there was an American mix of amateur enthusiasts, with each individual a mix of different levels of finance, talent and dedication.

"Do have a go, old chap!"

"Viene a Monza con tutti l'equipaggio!"

"You are of course bringing your two-liter Moggabruzzi to Mugello, *oui*?"

"What is that cloth thing on the Corvette seat there? A belt for the safety? Ah, no, is better jumping out before crash; ask Masten Gregory. But maybe good for the passenger seat to keep Gina in place, if she think you *troppo impulsivo*!"

"Hey, Mac, don't forget. Cocktails at the Contessa's after qualifying!"

While in *Most-Any-Mid-Western-State* USA: "Betty Lou, can you get your hair inside my helmet?"

"Why yes, Billy, I can. Why do you ask?"

"Surprise! I talked to the Chief Steward and told him you knew all the flags and here's your Novice Permit and you're running in the Novice Race today and if you do okay, you'll be in the Ladies' Race tomorrow!"

"Gee wow, Billy!" Big hug and kiss while other crews nudge one another and point. In the mid-'50s I betcha most of a region's membership had run a Novice Race. The lucky ones got to drive a car with the latest hot-setup tires on it: Michelin Xs.

As you will remember, the SCCA kept displacement categories for their *modifieds* when they adopted performance categories for the *production* sports cars around '60. H Modified was up to 750cc, GM 1100, FM 1500, EM 2000, DM 3000, and way back they decided to call everything over 3 liters C Modified and that was that. Production classes ran A to H, home of the Bugeye

Sprite, mainly, except for a particular Morgan and Allemano Abarth spider of blessed memory, oh and the Opel GT 1100.

Then the British sent us the Berkeleys: two-stroke and three cylinders. Okay guys, just for you – I Production. But, what about the two-cylinder, 350cc cars? They'd do maybe 73mph with a following wind, and out of the goodness of the SCCA's place that passes for its heart we got – J Production. Not for long, though.

Nashville's Gene Baker raced one of those hot 3-cylinders, and his crew chief Charlie Mitchell never used a pit board for communication. Charlie would get up a head of steam running along the edge of pit lane and as Gene smoked (literally) past, Charlie would yell "Everything OK?" and Gene might nod or yell, "It's cutting out down the backstretch!" before he pulled out of earshot of the sprinting Charlie. Standing starts were also rather gentle in Berkeleys.

Later the works dropped in Royal Enfield 4-stroke twin motorcycle engines, giving us the B95 and B105, the top speeds of the two stages of tune. I would really like to drive a B105 Berkeley at top speed – and live.

Dr. Phil Porch, Nashville's racing urologist, also had a Berkeley. He sent a club meeting into fits of laughter when he explained how he once overtook a competitor who was slowing with engine trouble on the final straight before the checkered flag. "I put on a burst of speed," he said.

Our own *Dr. Phil* had a clever way of preparing for a concours. He pulled into his assigned spot, threw a tarp over the body, opened the hood, and spray-painted the entire engine compartment silver. Whatever works.

On the way to my first ever competition, the Little Switzerland hill-climb in Eureka Springs, Arkansas, I thought I was making decent time at dusk in my Carrera Speedster. I was going about as fast as feasible with those puny six-volt headlights. In my mirror brighter headlights drew closer and closer through the Ozark road's twists and turns. Right, I thought. It's always easier to follow than lead at night. Now the lights – obviously some kind of super bright European accessories – were right on my bumper, and in the turns I could hear the swooshing sound of the big tires on the sedan right behind me. Enough of this! I signaled and pulled off into a little picnic area, and a '59 Cadillac went by; and it was pulling a race-car on a trailer!

It was Ernie Grimm and he later told me that the tongue weight of the trailer gave the whole rig a neutral kind of slide through the turns when he lifted off the throttle and the trailer pushed the rear of the Cadillac out. Getting there was half the fun!

The event was a real gas for all entrants save one. I don't remember his name, but he'd just bought a sparkling new Lotus XI and less than an hour from the event it had somehow come off the trailer and slid downhill through a grove of saplings upside down. He'd never driven it, except up onto the trailer. We assured him the engine and possibly the tranny were in excellent shape, and maybe most of the suspension pieces, since they hadn't touched the ground much. Didn't cheer him up at all.

And regarding good headlights, J. C. Whitney used to sell Autoroche headlights – the high beams were so focused that I picked out the big reflective Scotchlight panel on a bridge over 2 ½ miles away as I crested a hilltop on the Muskogee Turnpike. Old JC must have lots of fun stuff put away, unless they had to scrap it for tax purposes. Wish I'd bought one of those crated Twin H-Power complete Hudson engines for $259.95!

You've all heard Peter Ustinov's recording of the *Grand Prix of Gibraltar*, right? I first heard it at the party at the first Stuttgart (Arkansas) airport race. Remember those official race parties Saturday night, where you put on a tie and ordered drinks from the bar? This was back before everybody took the easy way out and stayed at the track and drank beer with the corner workers. Hasn't been one at an SCCA race in the last quarter-century of the departed 20th. Imagine trying to make a modern *GP of Gibraltar*. It wouldn't have much to do with racing; it'd be all politics and sponsorship and huge amounts of money. Bah!

Jim Hall was at that inaugural Stuttgart race in '59, and he took a Little Rock TV cameraman for a hot lap in his – I believe – Maserati 300S. Featured on that evening's sports show, we were treated to violently oscillating shots of Jim's profile facing up, then down, then straight ahead, combined with shots of the old airport hangers flying by, often with the horizon vertical. Somebody had a cartoon of Charlie Brown painted on the back of his car, with a balloon enclosing the question, "What's the name of this game?"

I made the first official practice lap of both Stuttgart and Garnett, Kansas that year. You'd have found me at 7AM at pit exit, all belted in and ready to go, heart pounding. I wasn't afraid of being hurt, although my big Studebaker crash was barely a year past. I was worried about looking silly. Stage fright!

I was pitted next to Tommy Allen, his wife Mercedes (!), and his 1500 Super Porsche Speedster. Tommy was a doggone good driver in those showroom stock days. A set of Michelin Xs lasted a racing season. Tommy cleaned his only set of plugs after every session (I think he had a couple spare new ones) and checked his tappet clearances after every weekend. Race gas was free in those days; a local fuel distributor usually sponsored the races. They'd announce Sunday afternoon, "Hey! We've got 20% of the gas we brought remaining in the tanker truck, so if you have a tow car, bring it by and fill it up! Free!" So after springing for a few meals and those $11 per night motel rooms, Tommy raced very well, for very little. Remember, entry fees were $20 or under.

Reminiscing over a glass of lemonade, it's teasingly fun to remember the nearly-valueless old cars we'd see at the races. In the early to mid 1960s there was a pleasant man who used to bring his beautiful-sounding, gently smoking Ferrari Monza to Mid-America Raceway west of St. Louis for a sporting drive around the course near the back of the pack.

Then there was Chuck Nervine and his Maserati 250F running the one-hour race at the Courtland, Alabama airport, on the long course with a pair of nearly mile-long straights. Chuck couldn't get racing tires for the rear wheels, so he substituted truck tires, tires not exactly built with 150mph in mind.

About every ten laps Chuck would come into the pits and his crew would dump buckets of water on the rear tires, and out he'd go again. He said he really wasn't worried about the tires coming apart. What bothered him was that this particular race was open to all entrants, so on the maybe 200'-wide straights Chuck had to deal with FVs and Bugeyes heading for his slipstream, way way before he'd passed them. And he couldn't try to dodge them, since they were aiming for his line from both sides. Chuck probably could have used a shot of Miles Nervine. It wasn't his brother; it was a nerve tonic advertised on the radio back then.

I was an instructor at the first-ever SCCA driver's school; check the date on this, but I think it was the weekend of Feb. 16, 1962. Some group had claimed the world was coming to an end then.

That was an amusing event in those relaxed days, with no *Directive from On High* on how it was to be presented. One of the longest lectures of the first morning was on the expense of racing. You know, you might have to overhaul your engine more than once a year, and probably have to spend a hundred bucks a season on tires. Not to mention those $15 - $25 entry fees, $15-a-night fancy motel rooms and the meals at maybe $3 per person per meal. Then the eager enthusiasts went out for their first drive.

It got interesting fast. The corner workers called in a continuous stream of passes, although the entire course was under a standing yellow flag. Okay, wave those yellows. The dicing continued unabated. Enough of this! Red flag the nitwits! At least some of the drivers acknowledged the red flag with a wave as they flew past start-finish; one or two even pulled into pit lane. Finally, we all more or less joined hands and blocked the course at the S/F line, waving our arms and red and black and checkered flags vigorously. The drivers all warily stopped at a decorous distance.

What had happened? The guy who was supposed to teach the neophytes the flags had never made it to the event, and nobody noticed his absence! "I thought to myself, red, that's a funny color for a flag," testified one of the drivers. Everything went smoothly after a little additional instruction.

A few months later Jesse Coleman invited me to go to Indy qualifying with him, as houseguests of Sil Silverman, the chief tech inspector. A lot of those cars had the most beautiful paint jobs imaginable and the chrome was perfect. The Indy jinx was reinforced that year by a Brit crew with their Connaught with an Alta engine. As I recall, international sports car racer Cliff Allison was the driver. The car showed enough speed in practice, but you see, it was painted dark green, with a light green chassis. It wouldn't start with the outboard starter. There were two large-angle u-joints in the coupling between the starter and the engine and they kept binding up. Rules said they weren't allowed to qualify with a push start. So they would push start the car, roll it back to its pit, kill the engine, and hook up the starter again. It never worked. It couldn't work – the car was green!

Fun at the track and then I had to smother myself with a pillow at night – the Silverman library had a book of the funniest limericks I ever read. Really dirty.

It was a sporting trip. Jesse and I drove up and back in my '61 Corvair Monza coupe with those $20 J.C. Whitney duals and the ten-pound rollbar held in with 6 carriage bolts. People stared at us, as we passed them. We were rocking back and forth with laughter as we planned taking a Corvette to Le Mans in '63. Then I bought the Flaminia Zagato, but the French didn't know who we were and declined our request for entry. They might've let a Corvette in.

In November 2002, the racing world, or that part of it of a certain age and philosophy, lost a neat guy. J. Frank Harrison, Jr., left this world at the age of 72. I thought he was a lot older, but then I used to think everyone was a lot older. He owned Chattanooga Glass and made ever so many disposable Coke bottles; he also owned Dorsey Trailers and supplied the big rigs.

Lloyd Ruby raced Frank's metallic gold/powder blue striped Lotus 18 Climax on the dirt at either Trenton or Langhorne. I have an 8mm movie from Dick Wallen Productions taken with a camera on Lloyd's rollbar. Frank and Smokey (Sierra) Drolet raced his pair of futuristic Lola Formula Juniors in the SEDiv of SCCA. I'd like to have seen a match race between Smokey and Janet Guthrie — although a fraction of a generation apart in racing terms, they both were as good as anyone I've seen.

Frank had an engine dyno, an exotic piece of equipment in those days, to test all his new Coventry Climax engines. He had Jerry Eisert take them completely apart before even starting them. "The English send us all their junk," J. Frank told me, as he showed me various machinings and castings that should've been melted down back in Blighty.

J. Frank called me one evening, summer of '62, and said he really liked the looks of my Lotus 7A. It did look pretty good, since over the original white paint, I'd added a layer of the lovely '53 Packard gunmetal gray, with a center stripe of '52 Dodge dark spearmint green. The white underneath gave a candy-apple effect. Very nice.

J. Frank said that for the Lotus, and about $6,000, he'd give me his just-overhauled 5.7 liter V8 birdcage Maserati, the one with the windshield sloping down almost to the front of the car. He said he wanted me to have it because I was the only guy he knew who wouldn't kill himself in it, and to this day, I'm not quite sure if that was a compliment or not. I'm also not quite sure if in turning down the deal, I revealed myself to be incredibly stupid or just chicken.

He took a chartered DC3 load of mechanics and their wives and girlfriends to Nassau in the autumn of '62 for those glorious Nassau Speed Weeks, and Ruby, who'd never ever even practiced in the rain, led Innes Ireland in an identical Lotus 19 in a steady drizzle until, well, Eisert had set the engine up just a bit too loose. "I like 'em to blow on the cool off lap," Jerry said. "I guess I just miscalculated."

After dinner and one of the every-nightly parties that were included in the Speed Weeks entry, J. Frank and I strolled down the beach. He spoke: "You know, I've spent a lot of money racing sports cars and the USAC circuit this year. About $120,000." Wow! What would that get you today? A Pebble-Beach restoration? Two fairly competitive cars at the SCCA Runoffs? Okay, so allowing for inflation takes it to about $700K in today's money. So, make it three Pebble entries or a couple Speed Challenge cars.

Stuff used to happen all over the place back when staging a race was the equivalent of Mickey Rooney and Judy Garland saying, "Hey, kids! Let's put on a show!" There was the one and only Puerto Rico GP. GP used to mean: *an event looked upon with favor by the local chamber of commerce.*

I missed it, because I was sponsoring the last Petite Prix through the Oklahoma City fairgrounds in late '62. The Oklahoma City Petite Prix ran for 4 or 5 years on a course laid out through the O. C. Fairgrounds. The gentle bend in the backstretch went through a gate in a chain link fence. The light poles, a couple yards from the course on the start-finish straight, were protected by hay bales. Jack Hinkle backed his Birdcage Maserati into one in 1960, I think, and when the pole squashed the gas tank it blew the flip-top gas cap way up into the air. No fire, thank God.

In the 1961 race I lost the left rear wheel on, rather off, my Carrera Speedster going down the backstretch. Naturally, the single-circuit brakes were immediately inoperative. I went through the sawhorses and hay bales and had a fleeting thought that all the stuff flying through the air looked just like it did in movie crash scenes. I held the wheel firmly, ready to counter steer, when the left hindquarters of the car dug into the road, but there was no more than the gentlest drag.

Then I saw what someone meant when they had said about the backstretch, "a couple hundred yards and you are in traffic!" Ahead of me, and approaching at by now what was probably about 70mph was 4-lane May Avenue – with traffic. I can still see the white over blue '55 Buick Super crossing from left to right. A three-wheeler cop was waving his arms, but I didn't want to know how many vehicles he was attempting to stop. Heck, maybe he was trying to stop me.

By now I'd long since cut the ignition and put the car into neutral as I scraped across May Avenue, thumped over the gentle lump of the median, and when I saw what looked like a wall in the lower part of a tall fernlike hedge (after crossing the road), I decided it was time to duck. I'd put a Y shoulder harness in the Porsche and arranged the mounting strap so I could lie down on my right side with the harness maintaining tension, so I grabbed the passenger assist handle and got horizontal. There was a swish as I went through the hedge. The wall was just fallen, dead branches. Then there was a thump as I hit the only tree in the front yard of a house, whose owner was showing prospective buyers of the property her landscaping.

I got out of the car and saw a throng running down the escape road toward me. Momentarily, I thought about staggering around and falling down, but I just waved both arms. Everybody turned around and went back. Eventually, a tow truck showed up, and the old body shop guys in those expert days hammered out the nose just like new, although I still have the horizontal Porsche badge as a souvenir. Oh, I've got the steering wheel too; I'd replaced it with a Nardi in Los Angeles for $110. Golly, that was a lot of money back then.

So the next year the club asked me to sponsor the race. I lost $10,000; most of that was buying TV time to broadcast film of the race and the '62 Sebring race film as a promo. Hmmm. I wonder where that film is.

Anyway, in 1962 we had a Queen for every class and had them kiss not just the winner after the race, but all the drivers on the grid before the race. I had to check out a wee contretemps when I noticed the driver of a beautiful red F2 Cooper-Alfa fighting off the embrace of one of *Our Girls*. Turns out, the driver was the late Edna Sherman of Denver. I must say that with gray curls peeking out around the edges of her helmet, goggled and without makeup, she did bear some resemblance to George S. Kaufman.

I think her car blew up. It was built somewhere on one of those Colorado mountains and we always figured that it had too much compression and/or spark advance to stay together near sea level. Sure looked great, though.

You know how people in major races take their crew around now on a victory lap? In those days winners took their victory laps with the trophy girl. Dave Morgan won FJr. in his Lotus 20, and he talked the trophy girl into straddling the engine cover and holding onto the rollbar, as he drove gently around. Until he got to the back straight, and then he opened the throttle. The young lady dropped the checkered flag she'd been carrying and got her chin right down on the rollbar, her long hair vibrating in the wind. Mouth and eyes wide open, she dismounted at the finish line and bounced up and down in happy panic. I remembered her name for 20 years, and it just might be in a little event program I have in some scrapbook or another. She's probably about 35 years old now, right?

That was the last ever Petite Prix and I really don't know why. Some guy raced Fiat Bianchina (one of those tiny 500cc cars with a one-square-foot canvas sunroof) with the race number ½. He had a cigar in his mouth, unlit. Safety, you know. The late Harry Washburn, a great guy from Louisiana killed in a private plane crash, won the feature race in his Cooper Monaco, as the sun set. I sprang for a champagne and barbecue party at C. S. Trosper's sports car dealership. Rented 400 champagne glasses and 410 were broken that Saturday night. Can't remember how many cases of champagne people drank.

In a gesture of friendliness I invited several girls I'd been dating to be my guests. I was going to go into more detail here, but let's just say that was a big mistake. Then somebody slammed my dad's hand in a car door and I was given a police escort at high speed to the wrong hospital. Remember, that November weekend was the same as the Puerto Rico Grand Prix and I'd really planned on going. Then I got into this sponsorship stuff even though God invented time so everything wouldn't happen all at once!

What, Me Worry?

The sport was more laid-back way back when. A certain southern club of which I was a member had, among other club offices, a club bartender. The same guy won the election for his position year after year, and nobody left the meeting the least bit woozy – or at least no woozier than they were when they got to the meeting. There was also another amusing facet to the meetings. One of the members had a sideline job of copying porno movies for what, I suppose, could have been called the local mob. So while we debated whether or not all our cars should have seatbelts for the owners to be eligible for club membership and should we carry fire extinguishers, off to one side the black and white grainy movies went on and on.

The continuing collection was extensive enough that when *Playboy* concluded their *Sex in the Movies* series in mid-'65, we realized we had seen every movie they mentioned as outstanding examples of "the blue movie" – and they missed quite a few outstanding productions, too. Perhaps their standards were different.

They contrast with today's niche markets becoming nodes of conformity: want a motorcycle? Gotta get a Harley. Got a Harley? Gotta wear a do-rag and leathers. (Do you get a discount at a local tattoo parlor from the dealership when you buy your first Harley)?

*Where's the motor? Don't I get a motor??
(Toly age 1)*

*First car, custom paint, Filipino houseboy in
tow, prototype Renault Racer ala Bartlesville,
Oklahoma, Christmas 1940*

*The Arutunoff family "at home" Christmas Eve 1961. Left to right: Anait Arutunoff Stephens,
Ralph Stephens, Chris Arutunoff, Sergei Arutunoff, Tina Arutunoff, my nephew Rocky Stephens, Dad,
Mom. I took the picture*

Bartlesville, 1955. My mother's Packard Caribbean, jade green and white

The $10K McKee Cro-Sal all wheel drive twin turbo 427 Olds Can Am car. Albert Way has it now in New England

My 3 liter Abarth. You could still get a used 3 liter prototype Abarth for 10 grand in 1974

Cooper MG at the first Monterey Historics, 1974. I miss this car!

course I race my one of a kind Ferrari. Don't you?

Hey Buddy got any pix of a naked girl on a Serenessima?

Stirling Moss' famous mechanic, Alf Francis, in my Serenissma built from the original Lola GT tub, 19

Me and my '66 Corvette at the Gaisberg, Austria Hillclimb 1966

My car that everybody could start and drive – but me. 1300 Periscopio Abarth

course I o raced my e off 407 stol Zagato, uldn't you?

The fabulous Dorothy 195[

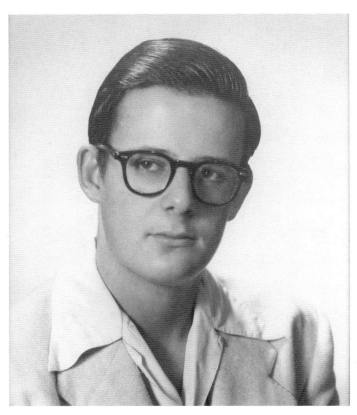

Hair! High School graduation pi[
just turned 15, bright for my age[

My second fashion show. This outfit precipitated what made it onto the national AP/UPI wire as "The Great Nashville Navel Battle", late summer 1967, Bill Preston, The Nashville Tennessean

Karen Arutunoff racing and rallying in Europe

My Porsche Carrera Speedster, 1959

Who needs Nomex? Courtland, AL Airport 1961

Standing start of the 1962 Last Petite Prix through the Oklahoma City Fairgrounds, which I sponsored

ar #29, the Lancia Appia Zagato, Nassau, 1964 – Le Mans start. Me and Dick Irish.
moto Roland Roase, Bahamas Ministry of Tourism

Age 27, number 27, I never really looked this good. Bahamas News Bureau Photo by Roy Newbold, Jr.

Studebaker GT Hawk, Caddo Mills, TX, 1964 Airport race. Roll bar, seat belts equals the then catch-all GT Class of SCCA. Beat John Peach in a Mini

Don't let a well-meaning friend rebuild your perfectly good engine. Blow-up Daytona Continental 1964. At least I brought a suit to wear in the stands

Green Valley north of Dallas mid-1960s. Don't worry; the trees will stop you before you hit anything

Montgomery Alabama Street aces in 1968. he Jaycees egally" closed Federal ighway for the aces by doing naintenance:" ounty prison- s putting avel & a bit of sphalt on the ad shoulders. 'ever, wot?

Daytona Run-offs 1967. We thought we were old then

Kiki at Daytona in 1970. She really is my niece!

"In Good Company" – My Abarth, a 312P Ferrari and a 917 Porsche, Sebring 1971

'72 Daytona 1000kn race, FIA Manufacturer's Championship. Ferrari and Alfa teams and me in my 2 ... er Abarth SP.

Lake Charles, LA Airport 1972. Me and my Morgan 4/4

rack manager, Marty
Marina in my Abarth 3000P
s I celebrate the opening
f Hallett in the summer of
976

hallett
MOTOR
RACING
CIRCUIT

2232 So Nogales
Tulsa, OK 74107
918-583-1134 Fax 583-1136

STEPHENS
RACING
School of High Performance Driving

Aerial view of
Hallett Motor
Racing Circuit
built in 1976

Remember when racetracks had near-nekkid trophy girls? This one had the distinction of having 30 speeding tickets!

The Stratos at our Hallett Trans-Am race, 1978

Porn movies today – how un-sexy can you get? Muscular guy, silicone-bazoomed girls. Clipped, bikini-waxed or scalped. Tattoos, of course. Continuous phony facial expressions of agonized lust – look at the face alone and you would think the young lady was having a splinter removed from the sole of her foot. It wouldn't surprise me if early teen sexual experimentation would be greatly reduced by showing every eleven-year-old two or three hours of these soulless exercises.

But in the old days, wow! We even had an 8mm movie that was supposedly the oldest porn in existence – the cast wore wooden shoes! Seems like it was included in a mailing from the fascinating and short-lived *Aspen* magazine, "the magazine that comes in a box." Each issue included all sorts of inserts, card sets, a movie etc. This was when people thought of a tree when you said *aspen*, not a little town in the Rockies.

And now, back to our movie. There was stuff from the '20s, '40s, and early '50s. Young men, old men, virile men, even the occasional impotent man. Humor in many, if not most. Coy girls, confused girls, the occasional passionate girl and even a couple of gorgeous girls you'd recognize. Clumsy camerawork. Real *cinema verité*. Like the sports cars you raced were real cars, not machines made to a set of rules, equalized in performance and boring. I'd like to overextend and belabor this comparison with some dirty movie equivalent of avoiding full-course yellows, but enough is enough. It just looked like even the business of sex could be a sport sometimes.

There's supposed to be a dirty racing movie out there! It's called *Pit Stop Girls*. No, I haven't seen it or Googled it. It seems that at one of last big races at Riverside, the producers got cooperation from the innocent organizers to have their cast mix and mingle with the drivers and crews. Thus there are scenes, I'm told, of cute girls chatting with *Famous Names*, watching fast cars roar by, all that sort of thing. A few seconds later, said female is accommodating all and sundry. Not the people from the track, understand! If I weren't one of those *born-agains*, I'd have to make this movie the 4 AM feature at our weekend-long car movie festival.

Moving on, standing starts are better than rolling starts unless the vehicles' clutches can't take the strain. They're more uniform, and if safety is a big consideration, make the grid wider, longer, staggered or all three. Truly the best start of all is the Le Mans start. Seems that in the old days at Le Mans, the cars were lined up with tops up, and first you had to drop the top before you could drive off. Or maybe tops were down and had to be erected? But let's forget that part. The absolute best, *swellest* Le Mans start I ever saw was at Nassau in the early '60s. I wish Walter Cronkite could speak these words to you for maximum dramatic effect (he used to race an Austin Healey, you know, and quite possibly my Appia Zagato).

Anyway, there were the cars parked in a line diagonally, of course. There were the drivers, milling around with several minutes to go. There was a pedestrian bridge across the track, with a narrow, higher portion in the middle. Suddenly, quietly, a man toward one end of the bridge held up a *3 minute* sign. The drivers began to take their places in their little circles across the track. Just as silently, the 3-minute guy disappeared and a 2-minute board was raised on the other end. There was no music on the PA. No announcer was hyping it up. It was still. It was silent and dramatic. And when Mr. 2-minute dropped below the railing, suddenly, splendidly, standing almost atop that center piece, Arch James, in patch-bedecked jacket, shirt, tie and cap, stood immobile, with a Union Jack stretched between his hands. What a freakin' moment! He didn't stand there for anything near a minute, but it was such a magnificent sight that no one jumped the start. That was the Michelin 3-rosette, 5-star-general of starts. You should've been there.

I ran the Caddo Mills airport race with my 1962 Hawk - main thing I remember about the track was that if you really lost it on a particular corner, you'd take out the port-a-johns. Therefore, it's probably a good thing that Tulsa's erstwhile budget director, son of Irene Castle, and eventual Bizzarrini Sebring driver, Bill McLaughlin, didn't get carried away at Caddo like he did from time to time. At Stuttgart airport he spun his Vette on the half mile left-hand sweeper and kept his foot in it – just for fun. He must have spun 10 times, flat out all the way. At Greenwood Raceway, a new road course in Iowa, he rolled the Vette partway down a long embankment and then got out in disgust, and with a hefty kick rolled the car down the rest of the slope.

Bill said he wasn't comfy cornering with both hands, so approaching all but the sharpest corners he'd grip the upper door frame with his left hand and steer with only his right. I'll bet you have your little quirks too.

In early March of '64, Jesse Coleman, Sebring's longtime chief starter and SCCA official darn near everywhere, phoned me. "You still got that dinky-ass rollbar in your Studebaker that you took out of your Corvair?" he growled. I replied in the affirmative and he made me a wonderful offer, "Bring that thing down to Sebring and enter it in the 2-hour sedan race." Didn't have to ask me twice.

As the car turned 50,000 miles in Nashville, the u-joints started clunking, just like they'd done at 25k. So I rebuilt them, took the a/c compressor out, Cop-Sil-Loyed the brakes, cut out some big number 2s from contact paper and cut out those phony scoops above the bumper to get a little more air around the cast-iron drums. The car already had a 4-speed and a limited-slip, so I was just about ready to race. New tires would be a good idea, so I got a set of Avon radials with that gummy, high-hysteresis overlay that made the tires look like I'd picked up a layer of fresh tar. They were metric, and when I made the conversion to inches I wound up with tires a teensy size smaller than standard – oh, well; better acceleration!

I sailed through FIA tech – "That your car? Have fun!" – and I was the first car out for practice. Corner workers immediately called in that some yoyo was driving his Studebaker around the track – I knew I should have taken the mufflers off, but then I'd have had to go to the trouble of putting them back on afterwards. To keep the car cool I ran with the heater on, and when I finally put the windows down, I couldn't hear the radio.

This practice session included my first encounter with a Mini-Cooper. I was bedding in the Cop-Sil-Loy coating I'd painted on the brake linings, so I wasn't surprised by the wee vehicle running up behind me approaching the hairpin. As I started down Hangar Straight, he tucked up behind me. "Isn't that cute?" I thought. "He's going to slipstream me down to the Webster Turns." I up-shifted into third and he pulled out and passed me.

The race went okay. I finished and the car ran fine all the way back to Oklahoma. There was a moment of glory at the start; we were gridded Le Mans style, by engine displacement, not lap times (which is why I was car number 2). So, I was between Walt Hansgen's NASCAR-style Galaxie and Augie Pabst's NASCAR-ized Ford Fairlane. They had to go in through the windows, while I'd found out my car would start in first gear without using the clutch.

So I sprinted across the track when Jesse waved the flag, opened the door, hit the ignition (the key was on the left, just like those German cars) and barely got my left foot into the car as the engine fired, slamming me into the seat and slamming the door too! I put my seatbelt on going down the next available straight part of road, like people did in those days. There's a treasured photo from *Competition Press* that shows me leading the race for the first 300' from the start.

Augie lapped me once, drinking a Coke, smiling and waving. I beat Dan Gurney's Lotus Cortina. One of his wheels fell off. I think Jimmy Clark, in the other Cortina, lapped me when I did a splash-and-go fuel stop.

The FIA made some special rules for airport circuits after this race, because the Cortinas, to keep their speed up, would swing way wide approaching the 90° right turn between the two mile-long straights and make a great arc on the outside of the circuit itself, rejoining about a third of the way down the straight behind the pits, never lifting. If I'd realized it was FIA-legal at the time I'd have done it too.

At trophy presentation Sunday morning, Brooks Stevens introduced himself to me and thanked me for proving what he'd always said, that the Hawk was a true GT car. Augie got first in class; I got second – two car class. Hey, the cup looks nice in the trophy case.

I picked up a map of Sebring that year and still have it. There was a housing development at the edge of town with street names like Aston Martin Road, Ferrari Court and so forth. I saw a recent map and those names had all been replaced by names of flowers, for Pete's sake. *Increasing motor racing popularity.* Yeah, right! Maybe as long as folks can sit in one place and watch cars go round and round at wide open throttle. Ridiculous!

I eventually sold the Hawk to Bill Pryor, who used it in 1967 to tow one of our pair of Morgan 4/4s. Then, one day it quit turning left. He had it fixed, but the problem reoccurred, so he parked it in front of his house. One night it was stolen, but he never reported it. He also won a trophy with it once: "Grottiest tow car." There was some grass growing on the dirt in the passenger footwell. See? There used to be all kinds of fun at SCCA races, when the rulebook and tires were both narrow.

And, hey! It was a lot easier to be just a spectator in the good ol' days. Another friend of mine, Bill Gillespie, (who among other things built a motorcycle-powered mini-Chaparral H Modified) was at Sebring in '64 when I ran the Stude GT Hawk in the two-hour Friday sedan race. Saturday morning I gave him my driver's pass, he put on his racing suit (one of those beloved blue Dunlop items) and, carrying his helmet, he climbed over the spectator fences and strolled out to the far corners of the track. He said he'd watch a few laps, picking out one or two cars to study intently, and then nod or shake his head and start back to the pits. It helped that he looked more like a racing driver than most racing drivers of the time – and he did race a little.

Passes were so simple in those days that a couple years before, Chief Starter Jesse Coleman gave our little group a single *go-any-where* pass. Bill Pryor, with Jesse's knowledge, had brought a complete mini sign-making artist's kit. In an hour or so, we all had passes undistinguishable from the real thing. We put on sports jackets, ties and sunglasses, then also hopped fences. We looked like a bunch of auto execs checking out this newish phenomenon of road racing. I could tell you a simple way of sneaking into another of America's premier-racing events – even today. I'll just tease you and tell you I discovered it by accident....

Here's one of my many missed opportunities. It was after the Friday '64 Sebring two-hour sedan race, where I valiantly showed the flag in the GT Hawk. I was having a snack with Sherrie Zuckert (where is she now?), the utterly lovely race photographer and columnist – once referred to by an aerodynamicist as *Miss Frontal Area*. "You know what would be fun next year?" I asked rhetorically. "I recently read where Checker Motors is going to quit using those old Continental engines in their cabs and use Chevy V8s instead. Now, it might not whip those NASCAR-ized Galaxies and Fairlanes – if any show up – but with the right shocks, tires and a 4-speed it'd make a helluva show. Crew in yellow uniforms, all wearing those wicker-banded cabdriver caps."

"Funny you should mention that," said Sherrie. "I'm currently keeping company with some high official at Checker." Our conversation developed from there, with the upshot being that Sherrie's boyfriend agreed that it was a wonderful concept.

Checker Motors would loan me the car, I'd race prep it, and after the race I'd pay to restore it to excellent condition. Everybody on the CM board loved the plan; who wouldn't?

The company lawyer, who else? He painted a lurid picture of an American version of Le Mans 1955, with the Checker, already a ball of flame, cart-wheeling into the area reserved for the All-Florida Kindergarten outing. Whole scheme nixed.

Years later, someone asked me why I didn't just buy a Checker and, after racing it, make it my tow car. Why didn't I think of that?

My same dead-end brain syndrome surfaced twenty years later, when I requested that Peter Morgan sell me a bare Fiat-powered Morgan chassis. Morgan used Fiats for awhile to shame Ford into building a small engine for north-south use from Ford's all-front wheel drive designs. See, Zagato, my favorite *carrozzeria*, was in the doldrums, and I'd talked to them about building a body, quite like the usual Mog, but Italian in character, and having Abarth modify the engine. Thus, I would have the only Fiat-Abarth Zagato Morgan in the galaxy! I was surprised that Peter was incensed, but, I guess, rightly so. What is a Morgan really, but its body? I could have bought a wrecked or used Fiat-Mog. Never thought of it.

The phrase *lose* a race has more than one meaning. Back in 1964 the SCCA got the use of Enid AFB for a race weekend. This was in the earlier days of drivers' schools for novice racers, and the instructor actually rode along with the racing student. The payoff for the frights this incurred was that the instructor got to drive the student's car and show him the right way to do things.

The base commander had a Jag XK140MC and he drove it enthusiastically whenever he had the chance. With the long straights and standard brakes on the Jag, he went sailing off the end of the start-finish straight onto the hard-packed sod about every third lap. He and his instructor would come roaring back onto the track laughing and punching each other on the shoulder. This detail comes to you because I was the observer on turn 1.

The weekend went well. My friend Bryan Crow drove my *ex-Sebring* Studebaker GT Hawk and a marvelous talent showed up driving a black Corvette coupe. The latter spun under braking for turn 1, pulled a 20-years-before-Danny-Sullivan-at-Indy 360° spin, and still managed the correct line through the turn. I can't recall his name. He built drag cars and engines somewhere in Arkansas; and while he loved the experience, he told his many new fans he thought it best that he stay in the quarter mile business. Rats! The guy was really good. He even beat the chief instructor, Dave Dooley, in the school race.

This was the first year of driver logbooks for beginning drivers in which the instructors would put their comments and criticisms, to be read by the instructor at the next race weekend. The event was such a success that late in the afternoon the base commander pointed out that he had several thousand bleacher seats stored in one hangar and he was looking forward to making races at Enid AFB the "Sebring of the Midwest." Great! Until....

I think the Chief Steward of the event was a Navy ex-carrier pilot. He was occasionally truculent. I'd known him for years.

At any rate, the base commander showed up at the post-race desk to collect his new logbook. Now, the way I've always understood it was that even if you flipped your car leaving the false grid for your first training session, you got your logbook. Of course, it would say, "Flipped car leaving grid. Watch this guy!" or something similar. But the Chief Steward said, "You went off course too many times. You don't get a logbook."

To which the base commander replied, "Get off my airbase. *Now!*" When Dooley heard about this, maybe 30 seconds after it happened, he took off at a dead run to plead our case, but it was too late.

Talk about shooting yourself in the foot, and several hundred drivers and fans in the ass. Just another case, however prevalent or rare, of the attitude "Just because you can do us a tremendous favor, don't think I'm gonna look like I'm being nice to you." Who knows what the Enid race could have become? Grandstands at an airport race were pretty much unheard of, after the SAC races backed by General Curtis LeMay. It coulda been a contender.

Awhile back, I saw where Alan Markelson was racing a vintage car in Europe. Although I never met him he's in my second rank of heroes. The way I heard this story is that about a half-century ago Alan was racing a Corvette back East. He exhibited too much enthusiasm in one form or another, so he was disqualified from any further participation that weekend. The feature race starts, and from somewhere in the paddock, Alan roars out onto the track. He gets black-flagged, but he doesn't stop. I'm unclear whether he finished the race and drove away, or whether the race was red-flagged and he was rudely escorted off the premises, but I like his attitude.

Reminds one of the Mustang II at the Runoffs at Road Atlanta, the one that ran with a 5-foot-tall Wiley Coyote strapped into the passenger seat. He tore a front fender, so it stuck out about a foot or two to the side, but he kept going. He was meat-balled. He kept going. He was black-flagged. He kept going. Don't know what happened afterward; SCCA officials don't like to think racing is too much of a sport, after all, so it probably wasn't pretty.

In Opelousas, Louisiana, during the summer of 1965, I can still remember the blatty engine note from what I'll bet was the last MGTC ever to win H Production at an SCCA race. He beat several Bugeyes. Admittedly, he was running 16" wheels by grace of the SCCA, since the original 19" rims weren't deemed trustworthy by that time. You should have seen that TC when he came in! It took *Britishness* to its extreme – oil everywhere: puddles underneath, dripping off the joint between running board and rear fender, running out from under one of the doors. The owner/driver said, "I guess it's time to retire her, what with actually winning this race."

Also in the race were one each, red, white and blue Alfa Giulia Sprint coupes. How good all the cars looked in the days before fender flares. You sell the teensiest part of a car's soul when you make it look like an actual racecar. As some said long ago in the dispute over making rollbars mandatory in 1958: "I don't drive a racecar. I race a sports car." The argument failed.

A couple more old race stories just for fun. One time a real Caspar Milquetoast type of driver won his class at Courtland, Alabama. At the dinner and trophy presentation Saturday night, the race queen was handing out the cups and kissing the participants. When our Caspar stood up to get his, his wife leaped out of her chair and said, "Just where do you think you are going?" She wasn't joking. He sat down and someone passed him the trophy.

Another time a fella was on the grid (standing starts, remember) with his Ferrari or Maserati 300S, or whatever, and his wife, known to all as being, er, kinda disturbed, fell on her knees before Jesse Coleman. "Don't let my husband race!" she begged and pleaded.

"Your husband will be just fine," said Jesse, at which point she strolled away, picked up someone's knockoff hammer, sidled up to hubby's car, and bashed those beautiful Weber carbs into junk. I suppose they could've salvaged the jets. Maybe.

There might be an amusing photo out there (amusing to us insensitive types). There were a couple road races on the Selma, Alabama airport in the mid-to-late sixties, at the time of the racial unpleasantness that went on then. Some Tennessee Region SCCA member had a picture of a violent situation involving minorities, authorities, dogs and fire hose spray, with the whole scene taking place in front of a store with a sign in the window that said, Welcome Race Fans. I guess you had not to be there to extract the humor from that. It is, of course, most truly unfortunate, but, doggone it, to me it's funny.

Bewitched, Bothered and Bewildered

What a lousy team manager I was – large motel bills often revealed crew had brought girlfriends and fed and wined them well. I never knew. If I had a suggestion and someone didn't completely agree, hey, I'd back down. Didn't want to throw my weight around, just because I owned the car!

In 1965, who was it who took our only spare head gasket for our

Sprint Veloce behind the Daytona garage to spray it with recommended Alfa Romeo gasket cement and dropped the sticky item in
the dirt? Me. We brought a factory-trained technician with us to see
that all the mechanical bits on the Giulia were in fine fettle. So,
after we'd scrubbed the gasket down and re-stickumed it, we got
the car buttoned up with about five minutes to go before the end of
qualifying. The expert then twisted the distributor around to what
he took to be a good enough position and the car melted a piston as
qualifying ended.

Then of course the car wasn't tied down securely in the truck
going home, so the front was messed up a little when the truck did
some heavy braking down Monteagle Mountain.

I was almost a big-time racer once, though I can't really remember how it began. The first thing I recall is sitting on Bill Pryor's
living room floor talking to Rino Argento. I was in Nashville and
he was somewhere in the east. Somehow, I was going to drive a
Grifo at Sebring that year, 1965. No joke. Who put me on to calling Rino? Or was Rino the guy I called by mistake, while trying to
find the real connection to the Bizzarrini drive, who kept me on the
phone for an hour asking about all the details relating to racing
sports cars? No payment either way was ever brought up. The
above is all that I can remember, period.

So I got down to Sebring that March, happily reminiscing over
my fine performance in the Studebaker GT Hawk the year before,
and went to the garage where the Grifos were being prepared. I
walked in, walked around a car and walked back out. They looked
like they were made of cardboard cartons and *papier mâché* and
painted with toothbrushes. I later found out they had crashed at
Monza and been put back together in a hurry. Hmmm, but there
was no major race at Monza that early in the season, was there?

After that, I might have seen the cars in the paddock for a moment, but that was that. Nobody called my home or Bill's house. I
think I'd told them I was staying at the Kenilworth; anyway, nobody called me there, either.

That was the year it rained so hard the Sprites were lapping the
GT40s. The new pit wall had no holes in it, so the river of water it
contained had tires floating down the pit road. These days, the

wusses who run road racing would red flag the thing for a couple hours, but after all, in 1965 the race was an *endurance* race. I think it was Phil Hill, who opened the door of his Chaparral and water poured out from the inside of the car.

Early on, one of the Grifos spun on the main straight and cut itself in two on the base of the Inver House bridge. Bizzarrini himself might have been driving; he was listed as one of the drivers in *Time and Two Seats*.

And that was all there was of another brush with the big time – interesting phone conversations, high-rolling anticipation and then zip. Yeah, I should have talked to someone in the garage about the condition of the cars and what arrangements we would mutually make regarding me driving and stuff like that. In those days, though, I felt that asking about the cars might be considered insulting.

At Sebring in '64 or '65 (it was the year Paddy Hopkirk rolled a British roadster, big Healey, I think) a couple of guys were camping in their sleeping bags next to the car they had driven down to Sebring: pontoon-fendered Testa Rossa. Who were they? This was about the time that *Road & Driver Graphic* (our collective name for the most popular sporty car magazines of the day) had a couple guys drive a birdcage Maserati from New York to Daytona or Sebring. Wasn't it swell when those cars were simply neat old basic machines to travel in? Discomfort was in exact proportion to raffishness and rakishness. If Errol Flynn had been a car nut, he'd have been doggone near perfect.

Whenever I see, or saw, an XK120 or 140 on the road, it always looks like the driver's head is tilted back, rakishly, just a little – but in an XK150 the driver is just driving.

Back when the old racecar market began to take off, there was a surge in interest in the car's provenance way out of proportion to its relationship to the car's price, when compared to today. At a drinks party in Europe someone suggested a ghoulish idea: deceased drivers' whereabouts are generally known – remember, at one time there were several notable funerals per year in the racing community. So to top someone who says, "I've got Gerhardt Mitter's Formula Junior," someone else might whisper, "I've got Mitter's Porsche 906 *and* Gerhardt Mitter." Joke, of course. Corn on the macabre.

Once I loaned a rare vintage car to a guy who kept it for a year or two, raced it several times, and returned it to me with a bill for $1,100 for putting tires and a rollbar on it. Don't think I'd pay that bill today, but I paid it then.

Back to the '60s: there was the Ecuadorean GP, won, as were most of the races south of Texas, by Freddy Van Buren in his GT350. The race was on a road around a lake, near a town un-findable in any world atlas. The races continued into the darkness with the course delineated by the white-clad locals standing on the edge of the road – not because of a desire to be of service, but just to get nearer the action.

When mom heard that the drivers were supposed to fly down with the cars in chartered Ecuadorean war-surplus flying boxcars to some dirt strip near a technically nonexistent town, she fast forwarded her imagination and visualized number two son's shrunken head showing up on a keychain or in a tropical flea market and forbade me to go. I'll bet somebody somewhere has movies of these wing-dings. Wouldn't you love to see them on Speed instead of another ho-hum mid-80s oval drone?

About that same time, in the States, there was *Las Ocho Millas*, an SCCA race through Bottomless Lakes State Park in New Mexico. Eight, count 'em, eight miles per lap! First practice sessions were familiarization runs with drivers riding in the back of trucks. You can drive around it today. To slightly alter an old Brit racing adage, "Don't worry, the rocks will stop you before you hit anything."

Some poor Alfa driver crashed, and although the next car on the scene was Oklahoma Region's own Doc Foerster, who performed an emergency tracheotomy with a fountain pen housing, the guy didn't make it. No more *Ocho Millas*.

Kind of like the only race at Burns Park, just outside of Little Rock, but things were a bit more symmetrical at Burns Park. Instead of randomly-sized rocks here and there, at Burns Park all the light poles were the same size and the same four yards from track's edge. Drive around Lake Garnett in Kansas sometime. Wow! I guess narrow tires allowed narrow race circuits.

At Garnett, some cat lost the brakes in his Giulietta spyder and went down the turn 1 escape road, which happened eventually to be the main aisle of the spectator parking lot. If only the little old lady in the station wagon had waited until the end of the race to try to leave.

Now for the Human Side of the News

SCCA racing was more fun then, because you raced a stock sports car with a straight pipe and possibly with the windshield off. That way you had time to, for example, have a few drinks and launch a total stranger's outboard fishing boat into the pool of the Florence, Alabama, Holiday Inn, fire it up, and reenact Washington's crossing of the Delaware, using a bedspread on a broom as a substitute for the flag.

We couldn't stay there for the Courtland races the next year, so we stayed at a similar motel in Decatur, where Buck Buchanan, owner/driver of the Devin-TR3 *Pilsner Special*, rebuilt his engine Saturday night on his mattress. Of course, he reassembled the bed with the mattress upside down, but the maid spotted the oil dripping out of the box springs next morning and the jig was up. Luckily, the management had changed in Florence, so we went back there the year after that.

There was also the late night/early morning parking lot centered rite of bourbon baptism for several generally un-repentant Scotch drinkers. The SE Division of the SCCA in those days could put Stroker Ace on the trailer, and we weren't even doing it for money.

The Southern Race Car Experience in the late '50s/early '60s could've been written by Tennessee Williams and edited by Calder Willingham. There was a married couple with a business partner. The business partner and wife were doing things forbidden by the laws of God, and, at that time, man, but the husband didn't seem to know. Then one afternoon another racer met the husband having several beers, all alone, at a semi-popular watering hole. Hubby sat slumped over the bar like what is seen in any number of movies about such a situation. Names are changed to protect the innocent, the guilty, heck, everybody. "Hey, Sam! Whatcha doing? You look down in the dumps. Your bird dog die?"

"Naw. It's Jim and Susie." Omigawd, thinks friend. He's finally found out! After a pause during which the friend tries to think of something to say, Sam continues, "I don't mind 'em screwin', but now they thinks they's in love." Could you script it any more succinctly? Ask any acting class.

Another small racing family – dad the driver, mom and small child provided a more public entertainment. This was back in the days when the pits were simply located along the pit road, separated from the airport runway racing surface by the width of the pit road and a couple rows of hay bales. There was no paddock, safely tucked away from the action. People and their kids tinkered with the cars and strolled up and down pit lane watching the action on track and talking to friends.

This particular child – let's call him Billy – wandered around just like the grownups, but Billy was more interested in the mechanical aspect of things than were the other three-year-olds. Billy was curious and liked to inspect closely the float of a Weber carburetor, or the distributor cap lying there on a shop rag. Billy toddled down pit lane, picking up a part here, leaving another part there, until Mom would notice his absence. Then she'd step into pit lane and holler "Billy you son-of-a-bitch get back here!" In the club, for the longest time, Billy was referred to fondly as "Billy you son-of-a-bitch!"

I'd be happy to have some help getting all the details of this apocryphal tale, which might have taken place at an early Garnett, Kansas, race. The setting was one of those pleasant little motels, one storey, with rooms opening onto a central corridor. Someone was lobbing water-filled balloons through open transoms on that warm evening, and an annoyed victim, upon opening his door to apprehend the culprit, found that the fire hose was right there on the opposite wall. The obvious action took place, and then some poor unsuspecting soul opened his door and told the combatants to shut up so he could get some sleep. Did you know that one of those little fire hoses could blow out a motel room window from the inside?

That was a lot more fun than the no-beer riots at Garnett several years later. The young county attorney, a friend of mine, called every cop and deputy in the area and told them to bring all their dogs, trained or not! Then he climbed on the roof of a patrol car and told all within hearing that he was about their age, knew exactly what was going through their sozzled brains, and would release the dogs if they didn't disperse....

....and that anyone who harmed a dog would be shot. By the time all this took place the kids were tired, so things calmed down pretty soon. How many lawsuits would a speech like that get you today? Blessed days. Blessed days.

Years and technical developments proceeded apace, but Jim Hall still towed the Chaparrals behind pickups with camper shells - you can't take a semi into town if you need to get some welding done. Hardly anyone used big rigs. Leaving the Glen you'd see Surtees' formula car on an open trailer.

Gather close and try to imagine this scene happening in this modern age: It's the mid-sixties at the USGP at Watkins Glen, and there's a special auction at the Onyx Club, a pay-your-money-dress-nicely-and-drink-in-cozy-comfort little building near the old pits. A painting of Dan Gurney and the Eagle F1 car, done by a local artist, is being sold for charity, and the winner not only gets the painting, but also gets to be in Gurney's pit during the race itself. Dan is presented to the crowd, and the auctioneer warms up.

"Let's have an opening bid of $500.00!" (Call that two grand plus in today's currency). "Five hundred dollars," the auctioneer repeats. Silence; Dan smiles faintly and shifts from one foot to the other. The Yankees in the crowd freeze – any aristocratic tic might be interpreted as a bid. The auctioneer drops the opening bid, then lowers it yet again. Someone eventually takes the deal for around $300 and there are sighs of relief. Conversations roar back to their previous level. Graham Hill notices a camera pointed his way and instantly goes into full right profile mode; things are back to normal.

The day chivalry died in racing: March of '67. Sebring, Florida. It was the last-ever Le Mans start of the fabled 12-hour race.

I'm starting, in Joe Marina's Alfa Giulia Veloce spyder. With

1600cc and drum brakes we're, shall we say, well down the grid. Next to our car is the Matra Djet 6 of the all-girl team. Their starting driver: the Swedish model Liane Engemann, in her custom-tailored driving suit. I am getting a neck ache standing in my little circle across the track from my car; look towards the starter; look towards Liane. The starter is walking toward his position; Liane's getting tense. Oh yeah! She does a great tense!

Then I have an idea! When Jesse Coleman drops the flag, I'll sprint across the track, waving to Mom who's blessing all the drivers from the balcony of the ARCF Club, beat Liane to *her* car, and graciously open the door for her! But, what if that constitutes some sort of illegal assistance? How little I knew of the sporting attitude of the times. I chicken out and in my emotional combo of race-start excitement and self-loathing over my timidity, I avoid a huge clot of traffic in front of me by zooming off shifting first-second-fifth.

Actually, you'd have to say chivalry died the evening before the race. I was at a party given by a well-known U.S. driver. It was a good, healthy, solid and loud party. Around 11pm there was a knock on the door. Smiling host answers door. It was Janet Guthrie. "Look, (John Doe)," Janet said. "Liane and I have a 12-hour race to run tomorrow and we need our sleep. Can you keep it down?"

Still smiling, host replies "Blow it out your ass, Janet!" and slams the door in her face. That pretty well buried chivalry right there.

Meanwhile, back at the race, with just a few laps to go, Bill Pryor's lap times grew much longer. A quick check of the official hourly charts let us guess that whoever was behind us couldn't catch us (for whatever lowly overall position it was), and that maintaining his usual speed wouldn't have let him catch whoever was in front of us. Bill takes the checker and comes in – everything looking fine. I open the trunk and there's the battery, lying on its side and connected by the hot cable only. Bill has a look and says "Oh! That's why all the lights would go out in Big Bend. I'd pull way over to let cars by and if one passed, I'd have an idea where the hairpin was. I'd hit the brakes and everything would light up again until the next time I got to Big Bend." We could have just dnf'd with no electrics but, as the heathen would say, "fate smiled upon us."

That kind of made up for the time at the only Daytona 2000km race (designed to run just longer than Sebring's 12 hours); we'd had to take several laps to replace an oil filter gasket(!) that I, myself, had installed very carefully, and then had Ham Vose re-weld the Panhard rod, where it had broken right next to the gas tank. He gas welded it in place (it's still attached this very minute) while firemen crowded around with extinguishers at the ready, possibly hoping to be in a dramatic photograph in next year's program. With 2 laps to go, the generator, which had worked loose some number of laps before, let the battery run down, and the car died behind the pits enroute to the horseshoe. In those days you had to take the checker, and on the track at that, so we lost second in class and $750 – a decent sum in the mid-'60s.

Dreams Really Do Come True

When Bill Pryor and I decided to have a go at an SCCA championship in the mid-'60s, we dove into the Production Car Specifications (PCS) book to see what car might have an edge. There were two. First was the G-Production Matra Djet with its 1300cc engine, twin Weber 40DCOEs, three different wheel diameters and several sets of transmission ratios. We picked car number two, the H-Prod. Morgan 4/4 Series IV. Its 1340cc English Ford engine had about 18% more displacement per pound of vehicle weight than the Sprite opposition, 15" wheels, and it cost $1700. We could have finished 1-2 at the Daytona runoffs in '67, but there was a misprint in the specs that changed my life from that point on. I would have just gone on to other things, whatever they might have been, had I won that year.

The engine specs gave the carburetor type as a Solex do. We called Arnolt, the one-time Solex importers. We even called Germany, eventually. There was no such thing as a Solex do. So, the SCCA let us run the puny Zenith 25mm throat that was fitted as standard equipment. Not only was the carb so fundamental that it didn't even have an accelerator pump, the intake manifold was right out of the *don't design a manifold this way* illustration in any automotive handbook; every change of direction of the intake charge was a right angle. We, and eventually just I, raced through a few years, eating up the Bugeyes in the corners and lagging down the straights. Then one day I glanced into the latest specs.

The carb for my car was a Solex dd. I did what we should have done at the very beginning; I called SCCA headquarters. The earlier book was a misprint. What they meant to say, was that the car could use any Solex downdraft! Immediately I got a proper English Ford quasi-streamlined two-barrel manifold and mounted a monster Solex off a Borgward onto it. Seems like my comparative lap times everywhere dropped about three seconds.

Two main things contributed to my national championship win in 1981. First, in 1980, I decided to just go watch the race, instead of entering. Sitting outside turn 1 at Road Atlanta and watching the teensy Sprites buzz thru the turn completely eliminated the fears I'd had driving in my Mog, as the turn approached at the end of the front straight at a heart-pounding, oh, 80mph, with the theme from *Grand Prix* blaring in my head. I'd been scared of cars going that slow? Including my car? Ridiculous!

Then the following summer I went to the Road Atlanta driving school and was simply given a 300ZX to burn through a tank of fuel, after I emptied the tank of a 300Z. Let me tell you, four hours droning around a track on a lovely day with no pressure certainly got me familiar with the place. Most of the turns seemed like old friends when the '81 Runoffs took place, even in the rain. Of course, a small miracle – oxymoron, excuse me – a *Miracle* helped. We left the rain tires in Tulsa, so I had to buy a brand new set, just before the race.

Randy Canfield and all the other *good guys who usually win*, put on their rains that they'd hauled around maybe for years, just like I would have, if an angel hadn't fogged the team's collective memory of what was loaded in the motor home. Have you ever heard one of those racing philosophers say, "Why does the winner thank God? What about all those other drivers?" I say every winner should thank God, period. I won. Thanks, God!

Racing's a gamble. I've always wondered if I'd had the subtlest of premonitions that the HP championship would be mine. I'd ordered a thin sheet of pure silver, more conductive than copper but less malleable, to be made into a head gasket. Somehow it never got delivered on time. Wouldn't that have been a real hoot, when they tore down the engine at post race impound?

Then again all sorts of things came together in cosmic convergence for me to win that thing. The rain tires for one; having to buy a brand new set since we forgot to load them. The car wouldn't start for one very cold qualifying session – the hot plugs had been left behind too. If I'd been able to run that session, well.... At a kind of *triumphal procession* regional race back at Hallett, those little gearbox leaks at the Runoffs turned out not to be loose bolts but a spreading crack, and the box failed about 15 minutes into my run.

That means the car would have broken while I was in the lead in the Championship race – and maybe if I'd put in the silver gasket, it would've blown. There are a few things I don't like to think about and this is close to the top of the list. Again, thank you, God! Thank you very, very much!

John Apen built a Morgan like mine a few years later, except his looked like Roger Penske's crew put it together. He was running a strong third with a horribly slipping clutch and retired, saying he'd just save it until next year. Only next year the SCCA bumped the car from H all the way to F-Prod where the same car, but with a Weber-carbed 1500cc engine, was already ensconced. End of story.

Another lawyer-vetoed plan involved longtime friend, Steve *Yogi* Behr, fellow denizen of our *Land of the Motorsport Fringe*. Steve had a friend who came into a good hunk of money. What to do for grins? How about starting a skin magazine; it was called *Cheri* in those days.

Immediately, our new publisher received offers for liquor ads, beer ads and tobacco ads. Hell, the thing was about breakeven at the very start, with the cheerful side benefit of having girls walk unbidden into the office and get naked at all hours.

My plan: For $500 to cover labor, and a few large cartons of product, my race Morgan (already painted a color closely resembling that of the skin of your favorite blonde, otherwise known as

'81 Ford truck *Bright Caramel*), would carry the *Cheri* logo on both sides of the hood, and across the back panel. The sneaky part, not to be revealed until after the race, if we did very well, and otherwise a secret forever, was that the mottled background of the hood and rear panel would be made up of thousands of tiny pubic-hair triangles *decoupaged* onto the bodywork. Cutting and pasting the tiny things from the magazine photos, we reckoned, would take about 40 hours and result in cramped scissors fingers and considerable eyestrain.

If I won, *Cheri* would pay me $10,000. Again, liability concerns shot the idea down. And oh yeah, that year was 1981, when I won. Hey, maybe someone would have leaked what the *paint scheme* was and they wouldn't have given me the President's Cup too.

The Old Good Ol' Boys

Okay, here's another story, not about us. At Daytona back in the late '60s, a Carolina dealer has entered a NASCAR Plymouth in the 24-hour race. NASCAR was pretty close to stock back then. We were impressed with their setup, including crew uniforms. We didn't recognize the entering dealer, but I'm sure he wasn't one of the big names of the time. Their jacks and jack stands were painted to match the car, too. Wow!

They had the car up in the air and on all the drum brakes (there's a memory for you) technicians were painting radial stripes in several colors of heat-sensitive paint. White stripe, blue stripe, yellow stripe, orange stripe, purple stripe. Hi-tech as all get out!

Car goes out, runs a couple laps; next lap driver doesn't even try to make turn one, just continues around the oval and creeps into the pits. We're back in our garage stall now, three bays away from where the Plymouth crew eventually pushes the car back into their space.

We wander over to have a look. Out come the matching jacks and stands. Car goes up. Wheels come off. Paint stripes? Black, crackly and flaking off. Not a speck of color of any stripe all the way down to the hubs on any wheel. Crew quiet. Seems like the car started the race and drove around for awhile. It was quick enough down the backstretch but he was lifting off for turn one about the middle of NASCAR 4!

In 1968 I had my own personal NASCAR experience when I went to the Curtis Turner driving school at the Charlotte Motor Speedway. We saw some movies, got talked to a bit, and Curtis *his-own-self* dropped by, trailing an aroma of Jim Beam. The highlight of our instruction was to drive a real NASCAR car on the oval. First though, we thrashed Neil *Soapy* Castle's short-track Chrysler around the dirt oval. Then the bad news: the previous class had managed to wreck our car, and hopes for its repair in time for our session had come to naught.

Crestfallen, we were told that we could drive our own cars on the oval as fast as we wanted. There were a couple things to watch out for however, since work was being done on the infield. The gate in the outside wall on the backstretch would be open – and it opened to the inside. That took away about a lane and a half, so if we went high on the banking we had to keep bearing left when we got to the backstretch. Oh, and it would probably be a good idea to go high on the banking in turns one and two, so we could look over the edge and see if a road grader was preparing to come across the track – or a dump truck or cement mixer, for that matter. None of us hit anything.

I decided to cruise by Holman-Moody in my '68 Dart 383GTS convertible on my trip home. They were very nice to me and showed me the stacked racks of Le Mans GT40s, still covered with racing dirt. I particularly remember the pink and gold one. Are they for sale? Of course, and that useless Honker Can Am car is too. Whaddya want? Oh, $7,000 for any one; might knock off a bit, if I took two or three.

Well, let me see, I'd have to drive back to Oklahoma and then return with a trailer, and I was just kind of tired of driving. I'll think about it, I told them, but on the road I decided I didn't want some big old Ford-powered coupe – and who wanted a car called a *Honker* anyway?

At least I was consistent in my aggressive non-relationship with all things Ford. In 1962, at the Bossier City Pipeline 200 all-comers race (Roger Penske, Lotus 18; Lloyd Ruby, Lotus 18; some local in an Alfa Veloce – that type of field), Jesse Coleman introduced me to Carroll Shelby, who was looking for a bit of financial help to get his Cobra into production. Oh, I'd heard rumors about that friendly guy, kind of *con-man-ish*. I felt ambivalent about the idea, and anyway I'd always thought the AC roadster was ugly with its catfish face. I loved the concept though, because I remember when folks would put a Chevy in an Austin-Healey. The resulting car was actually lighter, never mind tons faster. But, on reflection, I took a pass. Real smart.

Then Versus Now Redux

How things have changed since those prim olden days of the sixties, back when hippiedom was just getting started, and darn near everybody else was uptight. *Playboy* magazine was still kinda naughty.

Remember romance in cars? Did *Playboy* ever put out (no pun intended) a collection of those wonderfully accurate sports car/cartoon drawings? I never had a subscription, but if I saw one of the drawings in an issue on the newsstand I'd glom onto it, buy the magazine, tear out the cartoon and glue it onto our basement bar (it was in the Car Room).

About the only one I can remember is a picture of a Craig Stevens type helping a lovely girl into his AC roadster and saying to an older lady in a fashionable doorway, "Don't worry – I promise I'll have your daughter in bed by midnight." Nudge-wink spicy in those days.

Of course, for a few years there was *The Bog* at Watkins Glen during the Fl weekend. Through the years a few cars, and finally a bus, were dragged into it (how the heck do you drag a bus? Somebody must have had a set of keys). That was rowdy, drunken and scary; although you would have probably been safe passing through the area if you took off your shirt, waved it over your head and screamed gibberish.

For a social evening, the thing to do was to wander over to the area behind the pits, where some fans (even at this late date, I'm not naming names) were showing porno movies on the side of their van. Sociologically fascinating, and I'm not referring just to the mixed crowd of mostly strangers who stopped to watch. Those were the good old black and white grainy copies of copies of real people doing it in sixteen millimeter reels of film. Not a shaved anything or a tattoo in the bunch. No phony passion. Often the participants would turn and address the camera, *à la* Paris Hilton but with more class. Someone always promised to bring a lip reader to the next cinema session.

Quick summary of how to go Major Racing in 1969:

- Find excellent Alfa Romeo Giulia SS, 18,000 miles, for $3,200.
- Put on straight pipe and install Conrero cams (Retrospect: Don't bother with the cams).
- Mount driving lights on stubs where front bumper was removed. (Oh yes, intermediate step: remove bumper).
- Borrow wheels from all friends' Alfas: 4, 2, 1, whatever.
- Can't find black contact paper in Daytona for numbers? Use dark green fuzzy shelf liner paper instead; tell tech it breaks up boundary layer airflow drag.
- Go to Daytona. Pay entry fee. Buy a dozen Goodyear Blue Streaks.
- Be possibly first pit to install wall-to-wall carpeting, deli table, 64-cup coffeemaker and little hanging baskets of artificial flowers.
- Prepare to race for 24 hours and have fun.
- Around midnight, clutch refuses to disengage. FIA rules state push starts are illegal. Exit pit stops by jacking up rear of car, start engine in second gear, rev to 2,500 rpm, pour water under rear tires, drop car off jack, thereby further impressing steward whom you'd already told about fuzzy numbers/boundary layer.
- Sell several unused tires to local Alfa racer.
- Replace second gear synchro, fix clutch linkage, sell car for $2,700. (Retrospect: Don't sell car.)

It was at the same Daytona 24-hr in '69, where Jim Garner's Lola was leading, when the car pitted and people fussed with it a long time and one of the crewmen said they had a couple radiator leaks, or at least water running out somewhere, and they'd have to retire. I gave the guy a couple cans of Stop Leak and said they might as well try it – don't recall how much more work they did on the car, but it finished, and won!

I have a beautiful full page color photo out of *Road & Driver Graphic* that shows only that car with our Alfa Giulia SS close behind. Fun racing. Fun memories. When/where else were there major races with a Ford GT40 (several, actually) and a Sebring Sprite with chrome wire wheels in the same event? It never went fast enough to use the banking except to make a wide turn from the road course onto the oval at NASCAR Turn 1.

George Waltman also raced his Morgan +4 Super Sports that year by himself. Since you could, by then, only drive 4 hours with 1 hour off, he'd come in and take a nap while his mechanic went over the car from one end to the other. He ran a steady Daytona 20-hour. I wanted to offer my services as another driver, but my pals talked me out of it. Boy was I easy to influence in those days.

I think that was the same race where Smokey Drolet pulled her Mustang in for re-fueling to discover that her crew had miscalculated the time for her stop and were all off to the john or having a late snack in the then-existing paddock cafeteria. She actually honked her horn for service and eventually somebody showed up.

The 1970s: What's it All About, Alfie?

In 1970 at the Questor Grand Prix, Ontario Motor Speedway's inaugural event, it was F1 vs. F5000. Think about that! Only $25 bought members of the Speedway Club a ticket to a coffee-and-doughnut early morning Q & A session with a slew of drivers (mostly from F1). It was hugely entertaining; there were almost no questions from the small audience.

Graham Hill, Denny Hulme and folks like that used their time slamming one another's driving abilities and commenting on the girlfriends of non-attending drivers, many of which were of the local-talent, semi-professional variety. I remember that someone had a little tape recorder sitting on the table. What a hot item that tape would be today. Now, F1 drivers wouldn't show up, even if it was $2500 a ticket.

But a change was definitely in the air. It wasn't just a glamorous and mysterious sport anymore – the drivers were presented, believe it or not, more like everyman. Oh yes, Peter Revson is the heir to the enormous Revlon fortune, but for awhile, as the press would have it, he had to attend to the family business from time to time between races. Piers Courage seemed to be heir to the Courage Brewing empire – he wasn't – but that was the focus applied to interpret the way he could be found grubbing about the Team Lotus F3 cars in Charles Lucas' official factory team. He worked at something, you see, even if his wedding to the Lady Sally Curzon, a gorgeous bit of nobility (who was also a Mary Quant model), was the London social event of the year.

Ah, brushes with the famous – how pleasant they can be, and occasionally how disappointing. Case in point – thanks to my friendship with Andy Sidaris (we met when he was producer and director of our two live Can-Am telecasts in the summer of '71), I was introduced to Jim Garner and we discussed the prospects of my managing the James Garner Racing Team, with his driver Bobby Ferro. It looked like a good setup; we would provide a new F5000 for Bobby to race, a motorbike and four-wheel/off-road machine for Mr. G to rove about upon. Also we'd assemble a crew, do vehicle maintenance – all the usual stuff. For the life of me I can't remember what (if anything) I was to earn for this service, but in any case, I knew we'd do an excellent job.

I hauled off and bought a brand-new Lola T332 and a nice new motor from somebody of good repute. I made semi inquiries, not partial questions, but truck leasing information. Bill Pryor worked up several logos and paint schemes for James' approval. We were putting together a fine big-time operation, although today its scope might compare with just one of the better efforts at the SCCA Runoffs.

One day I got a letter from a California legal firm. I was to proceed no further in our preparations and was not in any case to use James Garner's name in any negotiations or circumstance. That was that.

It never occurred to me to ask Jim what happened, even through Andy. Maybe Garner and Ferro had a falling out. Maybe the lawyers, as they are so wont to do, threw up all sorts of potential liabilities Jim might, well, be liable for. Maybe Jim just had better things to do with his time.

I kept the car for a year or two, not because I wanted to, but because nobody wanted to buy it. It never occurred to me to try it out for myself, because I never cared for open-wheel racing (a rational analysis of its dangers would get it banned next week). No hard feelings. I got back in my Morgan 4/4 and pootled off down life's highway.

Another quiet sociological revolution; suddenly it's all about money-money-money. If you want the exact dates for these things, ask Chuck Dressing. Motorwise, if he doesn't know a particular thing, remember that Henry Adamson does.

This phenomenon was started by Colin Chapman fielding his Gold Leaf Team Lotus cars in advertising colors rather than national colors livery. Have you got a million dollars? Well, some kind soul might sell you a tiny part of an Indy team. Lord Hesketh's F1 team (remember the teddy bear in a racing helmet?) had a Rolls Royce to get around Monaco, and had another Roller dedicated to just making runs to the wine shop to haul more champagne to his yacht.

For real culture shock, watch that 1975 racing documentary originally entitled *One by One* and re-released in 1978 as *The Quick and the Dead*, (much too insensitive for today's market). A huge multi-car pileup at an F1 race, completely wiping out several cars, was priced out by the narrator as costing, gasp, three or four hundred thousand dollars. Can you buy a half-dozen carbon fiber nosecones for that kind of money nowadays?

Are you old enough to remember those wonderful crossover days, when not only F1 drivers drove sedan and sports car races and ran European rallies (real road races back then), but NASCAR guys ran Indy? An Allison, LeRoy Yarbrough and/or Cale Yarborough on the oval. Going the other way: Foyt and Andretti doing *rather well* in the Daytona 500? Can you remember when someone would win a NASCAR superspeedway race by *several laps?*

Betcha completely forgot such a thing could happen. Richard Petty, once asked why he didn't try Indy, replied to the effect that too many Indy drivers walked with a limp, and some of their hands didn't work completely right.

My only racing scar, and boy do I intend to keep it that way, was from running John Bernardine's Alexis/Climax FC at Texas World. We had to take the seat out for me to fit, and in my eagerness to get on track, I was able to ignore the unpleasant sensation arising from sitting jammed up against the return pipe from radiator to engine. Centrifugal force jammed me onto it on the banking too. It really didn't hurt too bad, but it eventually roasted through my skin and a tiny bit into muscle, leaving me an interesting football-shaped scar on my right hip. Maybe I could integrate it into an original tattoo, but then folks might think I had a Harley. Anyway, talk about a fun car: 6-speed gearbox and 9000rpm redline. Can't remember how much driving I did, but I sure shifted a lot.

Think about the originality of Indy cars in those days. Narrow tires allowed all kinds of experiments, and the rulemakers' fears that someone might have a very successful innovation, if all cars weren't made nearly identical, didn't exist. Yunick's magnificent sidecar – it interested Chapman, so what might it have led to? There was the Golden Flap Special, a traditional Indy roadster with an airfoil vertically mounted on the right side; turn the wheel to the left and it swung out to provide centripetal force. The Fageol Twin Coach Special with a Porsche 911S engine at each end. My all time favorite was the Mac's Special: a car with a 2-stroke 2-cylinder snowmobile engine at each corner. I never heard it run, but 8 2-stroke cylinders equal 16 4-stroke cylinders, as far as exhaust pulses go, and that 2-stroke sound must've been indescribable. Anybody know where it is today? Let's go play with it!

Watching race movies from a few decades ago isn't too much of a time warp. The cars look similar to those of today, minus the modern snoot-in-the-air look. When I see the size of the sideburns on the drivers though, I feel that I've truly aged.

Remember when racing was to be the sport of the '70s? The real sport of the seventies turned out to be just trying to cruise at 70 in the middle of nowhere and not get nailed due to that dumb 55 crap.

At least it became a sport for *everyman!*

And hey, remember those Elvis movies? Remember his movies with all those lovely girls? How about his movies with neat cars? *Spinout, Viva Las Vegas.* They had girls too, of course. Well, there was an SCCA race at Texas World Speedway, that neat place in the middle of no place, in the late '70s. It was like being in an Elvis movie. It can easily be argued that Texas women are the most beautiful in the world, and for some reason, there were an incredible number of them at that race. I wonder why. Just one of those statistical things, I guess.

Not that races in Texas were ever short of sex appeal. In the '70s at the Victoria and New Braunfels airport races, a squad of *safety marshals/stewards* was assembled, of the va-va-voom kind. In general these fine gals wore low cut tops and short shorts; bras were apparently optional. On the false grid they'd check that drivers were belted in, and they paid special attention to seeing that the crotch strap was secure by bending way over and yanking on it. If you must be distracted on the false grid this is as good a way as any.

There's a photo somewhere of a topless sweetie waving the checker as some modified zips across the line at TWS, but I was told it was staged. Okay by me.

At the Austin street races, last held in '76, most corners featured a honey in the mandatory white, as in wet, t-shirt. You watched for those flags, boy.

The first Austin race was in 1964 and the winner of each race got a silver tea service, and their names were entered in a drawing for a new Mini. Yes, a free car! The British consul in Austin knew how to sponsor a race, and a non-SCCA race at that.

Of course I have another odd runoffs story, from 1975, when I also ran a Renault-powered Lotus Europa in DP. It was quite competitive, except against the Group 44 juggernaut's Triumph TR6. Anyway, it was a really fun and smooth car to drive, although I'm sure anything felt exceptionally smooth after stepping out of the Morgan in the previous practice session. We were hoping for a decent result, but – we were sabotaged! That was the report from my crew chief, just before the warm-up.

How was it done? Something in the gas? Something obviously and deliberately broken? No! Someone had stolen one of the pushrods! And had sealed the rocker cover very smoothly with anti-leak blue goop, just like my guys who built it.

The explanation was, well, not sabotage. All year we'd been running synthetic oil, at the time notorious for a lack of shear strength (and thus, even today, specifically not recommended for Mazda rotary engines). The oil carried so much more heat than *regular* oil that we took out the oil temp gauge – it was always pegged – and I just watched the water temperature, which was down 15 degrees due to the thermal help from the oil. We also had to put in a new cam every three hours of racing. Are you ahead of me?

The cam was wearing out not because of the oil, but because we had the tiniest amount of valve spring coil bind, and at the Runoffs the new springs bound up at maximum lift and bent one of the short pushrods just enough that it popped out of alignment and dropped into the oil pan.

That was reminiscent of one of our Daytona 24-hr. attempts in the Lancia Stratos when we had a persistent misfire, but only on the banking. Turns out centrifugal force was swinging out a too-long coil wire just in time for it to slide between the coils of the right rear suspension spring, where it got squeezed enough to short out through the suspension. All racers could probably put together an encyclopedia of stuff like this.

In '76 at Sebring the entire pit crew wondered how we'd missed Joe Marina going by with 3 laps to go in my black Lotus Europa; he came by just about on schedule next time and next lap took the checker. Months later, he told me we hadn't missed him – he had spun and killed the engine, and by the time the corner workers had pushed him to a place of safety long enough to bump-start the engine he used up almost exactly a single lap's time.

It was over 25 years ago that I got a huge head start on political incorrectness when I, with mock seriousness, told the Board, or the *Inquisition*, or whatever the ruling body of the SCCA was called at the time, that I was going to propose, from the floor, that all corner and safety workers must be within 15% of their recommended weight for their height in order to be able to renew their licenses.

You'd never have guessed that the late Dave Dooley could break out in a nervous sweat that quickly. Then I told them it was all a gag, and proposed a statement that it was the *Sense of the Meeting*, or something like that, that the 55mph national speed limit should be returned to states' control. They thought that was just fine. Sighs of relief.

No one can do anything but praise SCCA workers, though. If they're big, they're easier to see. They're the world standard, with continually augmented and reinforced training.

About a third of a century ago was an era when drivers received multiple samples of cologne at registration for the runoffs. The company was the race sponsor. It was also about the time that the arguments against letting rookie drivers race big production and sedans was fading away, helped along by two rookies winning A sedan and A production championships at the ARRC race at Riverside. An idea arose that there should be an actual book of instruction and reference for course workers, and my long-ago friend Ken Wagner was asked to compose it. Compose it he did - I heard it was over a hundred pages, and this heavy duty tome shocked the club into saying, "never mind!" I guess Ken left the club a few years later, probably from under-appreciation and burnout.

Opposite pole: I took the lovely Carol Annie to the airport race at Okmulgee, Oklahoma. It was her second race, so she was an old hand. Therefore, when there was a call for corner workers, I volunteered her. She was put on a station with a National Guard radioman for communications – it was his very first race. The station was near the end of the longest straight, right next to the pavement like God intended.

On the second lap the entire nose broke off a Lister Corvette, so she waved the yellow flag vigorously until the field had passed, and then, waving it over her head, ran out to the middle of the track and dragged it out of the way while the Guardsman reported her progress on the radio. She was applauded for her actions after people heard the story during the Saturday night party. "I couldn't just leave that big thing out there for somebody to hit." she said modestly.

Compare that to an English rally, the real-race-on-closed-dirt-roads kind, in the early '90s. As an invited observer, I was out early as the stage was being signposted. It was a scene right out of the Peter Sellers movie, *I'm All Right, Jack*. Worker comes up and says to Marshall: "I put a right turn arrow up at the end of the straight, but it's a left turn."

Marshall asks, "Why on earth did you do that?"

Worker replies, "Rules say all turns have to be signed and I'm out of left turn signs. Anyway, the navigators will have pace notes."

"Let's see," I thought to myself. "I'm up to about 80 on this dirt road and my navigator calls out 'left turn coming up' at the same time I see a right turn arrow. Trust the anonymous pace note writer or the anonymous sign hanger?" It didn't catch out a single driver! Miraculous!

You should get right on line and buy Brock Yates' *Cannonball* book. From the standpoint of our two runs, Bristol 410 saloon and Volvo 242GT, dead last and mid-pack finishes respectively, they were a day and a half of paranoia, bracketed by great parties at each end.

Tex Arnold and I ran the first *One Lap of America* in a Honda CRX. To show that everything was on the up-and-up, Brock informed the highway patrols of all the states involved, and thereby presented the absolute hands-down best argument against that truly idiotic 55mph national speed limit. Around late afternoon we were in a standard medium density traffic flow east out of New Orleans, across that little Alabama hemorrhoid by Mobile, and into Florida. Traffic was running a bit over seventy.

A few miles into Florida, we came up into the sixth or seventh row of cars running nose to tail behind a trooper doing, of course, 55. There was a lot of CB use in those days, and we could hear folks, especially truckers, asking what the hell was going on up there – the compression wave effect was slowing them down to a near stop in the jam extending most of a mile behind us.

I got on the CB and asked Smokey what was happening. I was told that some crazy car group (he got that right) thought they'd be racing through Florida and the authorities were going to show they enforced 55. We got into a pleasant conversation for the next few minutes, as I played innocent. In the gaps in our talk, the truckers could still be heard wondering why traffic was at a near standstill. The cop and I were still talking in that rolling parking lot, and he eventually pulled off. Before he left the *superslab* though, we were going a hair over 65! I was kind enough not to ask that if he was so intent on enforcing 55, why was he now doing 65? If he'd slowed suddenly, there would have been a humongous accident behind us. I couldn't have that on my conscience. Traffic soon moved back up to 70ish and thinned way out.

Later we found out that the police had run three 55mph pace cars that evening; ours was the last, as the word got back to headquarters that huge traffic jams were resulting from the cops trundling along in front. Wadda bunch of politically motivated maroons Congress was in passing that speed limit bill, and that rat Nixon in signing it. The Prez also closed the *gold window* that controlled government spending and therefore inflation – the foreign governments could no longer threaten to buy gold with devaluating dollars. Look at us today.

Some California University physics research department computed that the same fuel saving could have been attained by telling everyone to put 4 pounds more pressure in their tires. Time is the only un-renewable resource. That first prototype *One Lap* was a bit of a bore. I'll only tell you about my experiences on the second one in person, but I wouldn't have missed it for the world.

I lost a heck of a photo once too. It was right there in the viewfinder, which I'd been squinting through for half a minute. It was at Watkins Glen in the late '70s during a Formula One weekend. We were up there with the Cooper-MG for the vintage race, and a nice guard let us go up to the box seats above the pits. It was a beautiful day, and the final practice session was ending.

We were right above the Ferrari pit, it turns out, and coasting in comes Gilles Villeneuve. Joe Marina hands me his new camera - Miranda? Yashica? I zoom in and out as Villeneuve talks to his crew. Traditional sort of shot; I don't take it. He takes off his helmet and shakes his curly locks from side to side. Would have been pretty good, but my reflexes weren't fast enough. He stands up in the cockpit. Seen that before. He puts one leg over the edge onto the pavement – traditional glamour photo, never mind.

Then, just as I'm thinking that all I'd do with a photo here would be to eventually throw it away, Gilles puts a finger to his right nostril and blows his nose. For a few milliseconds the setting sun catches the two-foot-long stream of snot rocketing to the tarmac with a golden gleam. I froze on the shutter, but it's forever in my mind. You can take the boy out of Canada, but....

Later yet, we had towed the Cooper up to the Glen with Joe's 280SE sedan. (They say proper aficionados refer to the place as *Watkins*, but I've never ever heard it used in conversation. Then again, I don't get to Sardi's restaurant in N.Y.C. all that much). Heading into the sunset on the return trip it was impossible to see the feeble glow of the alternator warning light until night fell. Dead battery; what to do? After a few minutes fretting over hooking up a positive ground battery in one car to a negative ground in another we bought a roll of huge wire. We ran the wires from the Cooper battery to the Mercedes battery, holding them in place on the cars' bodywork with lots of duct tape.

We fired up the MG engine and set it at rapid idle, fast enough to indicate charging on the ammeter. We went through tollgates. We stopped and re-fuelled, the un-muffled XPEG motor blatting away. Nobody ever said a thing to us. We made darn sure we checked the Cooper's fuel level every time we gassed up the Merc, and pulled over occasionally to check the temp gauge in the Cooper. We actually got back to my dealership without further incident, and had fun explaining to everybody next morning what that bizarre-looking setup had accomplished. Isn't it fun to fix stuff?

Mine All Mine: Hallett Motor Racing Circuit

It's not surprising that from time to time people ask me why I built Hallett; or more accurately, Hallett Motor Racing Circuit. Yes, I got carried away with a touch of Euro-British enthusiasm when I was 39. It just seemed like the thing to do. I had enjoyed road racing for over 20 years by then, and I also figured it shouldn't be bad as an investment. In hindsight, I should also have added a ⅛ mile drag strip and raked in money on Friday nights, but staffing the place was always a problem, like with any enterprise.

We thought we'd get lots of spectators from Oklahoma State University's many thousands of students, less than two dozen miles away, but that turned out emphatically not to be the case. When Paul Newman showed up for a pro race, with about a week's notice, we still only had a few thousand spectators.

Regardless, having a true gentleman racer compete at Hallett was a delight. He is at least as nice as everyone says. When Karen gets in her *worrying mode*, I tell her I'll quit racing when Paul does; at the same age that is.

When it was built in 1976, the batch plant that made the paving material didn't really care about a couple miles' worth of material, so the stuff they delivered was like I ordered an oatmeal cookie and got a brownie. It was oh so soft; you could dig the heel of your sneaker into it! I paid to repave it and that was almost as bad. The third time, the paving contractor did the job free, but I still had to buy the materials. We eventually limed it to help it stick together. Marty Marina, my track manager, was asked to consult before the '84 Dallas Grand Prix. She told them that their pavement would come up. She was right.

Folks would say to me, "It must be fun to go drive around your track." It was so darn much work, though, I never drove around it all that much – no long, relaxing straights! I'm proud to say that Skip Barber told me that if you could drive well at Hallett, you could drive well anywhere. There was hardly an ordinary turn in the entire layout, no swoopy-doopy motorcycle turn in it and no (ugh) chicane.

Investment-wise, well, my current financial guy says that if it had been properly amortized and depreciated and things like that throughout my ownership, I might well have broken even and maybe, just maybe, come out a little bit ahead. I then asked him if I should therefore find some suitable land and do it all again and he said, "No!!!"

The year we opened Hallett we had a vintage race with a dozen or so entries. I'd run the first few Monterey Historics at Laguna Seca, and Steve Earle and I had lunch one day to discuss this vintage phenomenon. Recognizing that the VSCCA had been running at Lime Rock and Watkins Glen for years, we came up with the idea that we might offer a *participation trophy* in the form of a tetrahedron (three-sided pyramid with triangular base) with the tracks' names engraved, one per side. These would be given to folks who finished Monterey, Hallett, the Glen and Lime Rock in the same year. This was probably the last time that the Monterey Historic Races and Hallett were ever mentioned in the same breath.

We had SCCA drivers' schools, of course, and the Skip Barber school came by Hallett for a few years, too. I also had fun inviting various lovely young things to be trophy girls, which the drivers very much enjoyed.

After one event, my good Nashville friend Tommy Dews was asked by the younger friend of our trophy girl if he could give her a ride around the track after the ceremonies were over. She was a living doll of, oh, about fifteen – maybe sixteen – maybe fourteen. Tommy had her buckle up in my '74 Saab Sonnet (why did I ever sell that delightful car?) and around the track they went, at a sensible speed.

Tommy, who'd been through the drivers' school, was explaining how the various turns should be taken, and ran a few consecutive laps. As they prepared to take another lap, the delightful passenger remarked, "Gee, I'd do just about anything to be a trophy girl."

As Tommy began to reply, he glanced over, and her decorous white blouse had somehow come unbuttoned, not completely, but *unbuttoned,* if you catch my drift. Tommy said he couldn't remember if he said anything or not, but he put on speed and whipped into pit lane at the end of that lap. Somehow, her blouse was properly buttoned when she got out of the car. I know because I helped her out of the car and nothing seemed to be a whit unusual. I checked closely.

Let's see, she'd be in her mid-forties now. If she reads this, we might consider her application to be a vintage race queen.

It is nice to know that there are now low key clubs scattered throughout the country that hold road races, so everybody is not under the bureaucratic weight of the SCCA. Also *lapping days* and *high-speed touring* and such lets us nutzoids take our street cars onto the track (why does every single blessed TV announcer call them *racetracks* over and over and over?) and scrub off 25,000 miles worth of tire tread and brake pads in an afternoon. There are even the fringe-of-the-fringe events, like the 24 hours of LeMons at Tracy Speedway in California with $500 as the maximum you can spend for your, well, racing car.

We did our part once, long ago – a two-year race at Hallett, never mind that 24-hour stuff. The race started Le Mans style and went from 11:45pm, December 31, 1978, to 12:15am January 1, 1979. It was a very special event, as earlier that day six inches of ice coated everything. This made the quick way through some of the turns a dive into the drainage ditch, Nurburgring Karussell-style, using the banked berm to keep the speed up. Tulsa local John Farnum won in a Honda Civic with studded tires (we hadn't foreseen the weather when we wrote the rules); but as legends often develop, people who heard about the event years later believe the race was won by the second-place car, driven by Danny Sullivan.

Danny drove my Saab Sonnett III with William (don't call me Bill) Jeanes as passenger. William said he wished he'd thought to bring a tape recorder along, as they kept each other in hysterics for the full half hour.

Qualifying wasn't held at the track, but at the Hilton ballroom the night before, with the drivers timed removing their helmets and driving suits and then putting them on bikini-clad models. The models had offered to do the job *starkers*, as they say on that odd island near Europe, but we thought the staff and management of the hotel might take undue notice.

As it was, the intense media coverage we were promised (how often does something really different happen on New Year's Eve?) never materialized. We were told later that folks didn't like the name I'd given to the event: *The First Annual Showroom Stock Champagne Suck*. We could have easily changed the offending word to *Slurp*, if someone had only told us.

We put an ad in *AutoWeek* the following year for a similar race, but got only a few entries and cancelled our plans. The qualifying plan for that event was to have models wearing only several dozen Post-It Notes stuck to their bodies, with the lap times written on the hidden side. A driver was to remove a single note with his teeth. A one-second reduction in the lap time selected would be granted if the driver wore a blindfold and was spun around a few times before going for the timing slip, *piñata*-style, but with teeth.

Maybe I should copyright this idea, along with my plan to have vintage race queens for vintage races. A major venue, such as Road Atlanta, might have quite a good turnout of candidates. They would have to be at least 36 years old and wear one-piece swimsuits. Oh, and industrial-grade pantyhose would be permitted. I suppose a rule stating, "a candidate can be under 36, if for every year under that number her bust measurement is an inch over that number." would be a wee bit too much. Yes, and with all the plastic surgery being done these days, we might have someone show up with a body as grotesque as if her surgeon was moonlighting from Orange County Choppers.

So many fun events: from little regional SCCA races to Brock Yates' *Cannonball Baker Sea to Shining Sea Memorial Trophy Dashes* and *One Lap of Americas*. Long ago, I looked forward to racing on real roads (Ponca City, Garnett, Daytona), but today I do kind of miss those airport courses, where you could take yourself to the limit, and past it, executing lurid spins and have absolutely nothing to hit.

In summary, I'd do it all once more; but these low-key mistakes, given the relaxed racing environment of that time, aren't like breaking a bone or several in a scary crash, thank God, but like having little kids whacking you with little hammers from their Junior Carpenter Sets on the elbow, on the knee, on the toe, on the back of the neck. A lot of little psycho-financial bruises that just make it kinda hurt to move.

But one pass down that Sebring backstretch, in those days a mile long and fifty yards wide, getting lapped by Andretti's Ferrari prototype and Yenko's 427 Camaro – five-dimensional stereo – will make it all worthwhile.

The Media: Less is More

Could somebody please squirt some superglue in all the telephoto lens mechanisms at race telecasts? Putting some kind of brake on the lateral pivot would help too. Watch an old race movie sometime. If two or three cars are approaching a curve the camera doesn't move. You are there, looking through a window, watching the action.

What happens these days? Here they come. Camera zooms in as the lead car approaches. Car quite near, camera zooms back; car into turn camera zooms in tight, so the viewer has no idea of the configuration of the turn. Hey, what happened between those two cars about a second behind? Then if a single car heads toward a camera through some of those silly esses or chicanes the camera wobbles back and forth to keep the car in the exact center of the screen. Just stop it!

There's so much more attention mediawise (especially on TV) to racing these days that it must be inevitable that with this great amount of material being presented there's much more opportunity to offend, well, me.

Seriously, doesn't every major road race, F1 or sports/GT cars, feature an intro with the announcer saying, "This course offers few opportunities to pass"? Look at all the ugly kinks and *bus stops* on long straights. Ringworm on the lovely classic bodies of historic circuits.

It's for safety? Then continuously widen the runoff areas as the straightaway progresses. Also, pave those areas to do away with that stupid sand. Oh, does this widening cut down on the spectator areas? Heck, the big guys get most of their income from TV anyway. After the straights are restored, and the runoffs are widened and paved, make sure that all around the track the barriers are as far back as possible, so the vehicle can be slowed down as much as possible, and won't have all or part of it ricocheting back onto the racing surface.

Also, now that we all know how wonderful carbon fiber is, – ban it; fewer flats. What about the expense? Okay, grandfather the ban in. For what a largish piece of carbon fiber bodywork costs, you could pay the salaries of a group of aluminum panel-beaters for a month.

Of course, in even the lesser series, if a favorite is running around back in the pack, someone is sure to mention, "He needs a full-course yellow!" I recall a recent race at Laguna Seca, when someone lost a complete nose panel. In any rational universe, a corner worker would evaluate a suitable gap in traffic and scramble out to retrieve the piece – even the pudgy ones could handle a big aluminum panel, let alone carbon fiber. But no, the cars circulated under a full-course yellow for *four laps* and the race finished behind the pace car. Hell, red-flagging the race while someone got one silly piece off the track would've been an infinitely better procedure. What do the "officials" think? The pace car adds to the spectacle?

We had a double fatality at a drag strip here, during testing. A rail job flipped and came straight back up the strip, driver unconscious. Killed her and her son, who was sitting in the family car by the start line. Way back when, there would have been photos of the smoking wreckage in the paper, but not any more. Sensitivity.

The acme, or nadir, of crash coverage came back in the late '60s when a network broke into regular Saturday programming to say a driver had been killed in a support race for the biggie at Daytona on the following day; and maybe we should send the kids out of the room, because they were going to show the crash in the next minute.

Ooooh! We can't – well, we don't – do stuff like that nowadays. It's like somebody said about the argument against Native American mascot names. What we could use these days is a good dose of *insensitivity training*.

At one time Oscar Koveleski had a column in the SCCA magazine analyzing the biggest crashes in the latest club races. It went away in about a year. Was it Oscar's boredom or nervous lawyers? Today, there's barely a whisper in any club publication, SCCA or even vintage, when something awful happens. Not necessarily the best way to handle things.

Motorsports television coverage is somewhat different in Europe. For example, we'd been in Italy for the 50th anniversary celebration of Ferrari and a German film crew was shooting various color scenes for a documentary. We got to see the result on TV. It was a comparison of the Ferrari event with a simultaneous German Opel Club meeting back in der homeland. Scene: well-dressed lady delicately wielding knife and fork during dinner in a Ferrari tent. Cut to: German crawling out of a tent at dawn in his underwear and eating half a candy bar, while finishing off a can of beer he found at tent's corner. Stuff like that.

The grand finale was magnificent. Ferraris driving off into the sunset was followed by a wet underwear contest for the Opel men. Girls did the judging – I couldn't understand the narrator's description of the criteria, but you probably have a good idea of what they were. Then the winner whipped off his briefs and put them over the head and face of the female MC holding his trophy. Yes, I mean trophy. She pulled the crotch to one side and made an "Ooh, stinky!" face. Fade to credits. Yes, they do things differently over there.

Is there a point to all this? To quote my friend, Peter Egan, "I think you see my point. Which is good because I can't remember what it was." There will always be differences between then and now. Why does it seem *then* is always better than *now*? Someday *now* will be someone else's *then* and it will be better too, maybe.

Ferrari 3Z at Sebring in 1980, when you could still vintage race your street car

1st Annual VINTAGE GRAND PRIX
December 1st, 1985

Winning the first Palm Springs Vintage Race 1985, Morgan 4/4

HP Opel GT at ...ett SCCA National ...8

Me, Bill Pryor and Tom Davis before the 1963 Targa Florio. Photo by Bernard Cahier

ANATOLY ARUTUNOFF
President

AUTOMOBILE RACING CLUB OF OKLAHOMA, INC.

1844 Northwest 23rd Street, Suite 10
Oklahoma City 6, Oklahoma   JAckson 5-9607

My company when we went racing in Europe, summer of 1963

Driving the Flamiminia Zagato from Sicily towards Spa – the bumpers are in the Fiat wagon in front

Polishing our first European trophy. After the Targa Florio, 1963

...had fun anyway. Lancia Flaminia Zagato, Nurburgring 1963

Driving the race car to the Targa Florio 1967

Targa Florio 1967, a face in the crowd

Targa pit lane 1967. Notice the tag on the Chaparral

Parc Ferme 1967 Targa. Do mice eat fiberglass in Sicily?

1967 Targa Florio -- 1st GT over 2 liters, unclassified – only 5 laps completed (7 of 10 required). The car I gave away – albeit on legal advice. Spectator bored already? Nothing like turning your back while sitting in an impact zone!

Toly, Brian Goellnicht and Peter Law, Lotus Europa Twin-Cam

he last real Targa Florio, May 1973. I Drove the car from Tulsa to the boat and back

I'll race most anything, most anywhere. The Italian Line, the ship, "The Michelangelo" 1966

Alan Bolte and me at the 2000 Historic Targa Florio in Sicily in my '63 Lancia Zagato

Monaco-Sestriere Rally 1988. Cooper Mark IV Sports

1989 Coppa D'Italia. Award for "Most Sympatico" Karen & Toly

-Mille Miglia scruitineering, the Cooper Mark IV

Mille Miglia 1994, Karen & Toly, only American Bodied Cunningham

Crossing the finish line, Pet *Egan and I wir* *the first La Carrera, 1985*

Da Lauro Restaurant, Modena, Italy with Sig. Lauro. Everything is all about cars in Modena

Cannonball London to Monte Carlo. Toly and Trace Sheehan, my brilliant, handsome actor stepson in the "rental Peugeot"

Trace, Karen, Toly, Spark Pug and Mille Miglia in the Morgan. Christmas 1996

Me and Bill Pryor holding a picture of me and Bill Pryor at the Lane Motor Museum. Photo of the Lancia Flaminia Zagato in the 1963 Targa Florio

French road sign

Galleria Ferrari, Maranello 96. Old fat guy having fun

And on the 8th day He said, "Let there be fast cars, fast food and fast women."

Racing in Europe
Thank You God!

I've said it in public and I'll say it again here: all the car stuff I've done is a sort of cross-section of what you would have done, if you'd been young in the sixties and had the money. I had the money and inclination to do more, but I didn't. Puritanical streak maybe or, perhaps, puritanical racing stripe.

"We're Here to Race"

When we went to the '63 Targa Florio and were told they never received our entry. They then signed us up on the spot, saying, "We're here to race, not to keep people from racing!" One might think that this would have been a good enough omen for our four-race European adventure, but our hotel wakeup call really confirmed it.

You see, the hotel at least, had received our reservation request and honored it, but since we were coming from the States, we sorta got shuffled to the bottom of the list. Thus, one of our rooms was a converted office in the basement, with cute little double doors. Double glass doors, that is. They had sweet little lace curtains cinched together in the middle, which we were able to spread out to cover most of the glass, although the lace was thin enough that you could read a large newspaper headline through the door. The occasional hall passerby would stop and peer in at us. We were a large Okie terrarium.

Also, the shower was like a closet that opened directly into the hall, and Stirling Moss, in his briefs, opened the door on my co-driver's first wife and stood there admiringly, while she giggled and went through all those useless *hiding* gestures you've seen in innumerable movies. I'm not sure which one of them enjoyed it more. Later, Stirling told everyone in the bar about it and she had a bigger grin than he did.

We had actually just met Stirling Moss, not *Sir* in those days. He was traveling round Europe with a BBC TV crew, who were recording his thoughts upon seeing all the famous race circuits after his retirement following his horrific Easter Monday crash in '62. One evening after dinner, and, of course, a little wine, Stirling asked if he could take the Flaminia for a spin; he'd never driven one.

Off we went, Stirling driving, me as passenger and Bill Pryor sideways in the back. With the car's slightly mis-aimed American headlights and Stirling's ever so slightly mis-aimed eyes – nothing to worry about. He's still Stirling Moss. We pulled around a donkey being led down the unlit street and it was redline city.

The seat was low for me and Stirling noticed it too. "How do you see out of the bloody thing?" he asked, as we passed 65mph and he shifted into third. "Do I look over the wheel or through it?" he mused, as we slalomed through clots of black-clad pedestrians out for their evening stroll on blacktop roads.

We were in fourth, not going really too fast, when it hit me; very shortly there was a humpback little bridge, followed by a hard right which would arrive about the ETA of our touchdown from leaping off the bridge. I was curiously calm. "Toly Arutunoff?" people would ask in a far-off future, of, say, 1972. "Wasn't he that guy who was killed with Stirling Moss? You know, like Nelson with de Portago."

We hit the bridge with Moss chatting about something or other, Goodwood or Silverstone or perhaps Pryor's wife in the shower. It seems like he somehow turned the car while we were in midair and we landed pointing in approximately the proper direction, which Moss put right with a twitch or two of the wheel, without a pause in his conversation. I was so happy. I am unable to remember anything of the drive back to the hotel, but I think that was where the 25¢ full glasses of Scotch came in.

Anyway, the hotel garage was occupied by the Ferrari team, while the personnel stayed at a different hotel. Our deluxe basement room had small windows opening out into those below-ground *light boxes* or whatever they're called.

Now it's just past daybreak. We're sleeping off a marvelous Sicilian dinner followed by 12oz glasses of Scotch for twenty-five cents each, a result of the proprietors visiting friends up in the hills for the evening and leaving two pre-teen sons in charge of the bar. A glass of scotch was about a quarter, wasn't it? And when you have a glass of something you fill it up to the top, don't you? Well then, kid, keep pouring.

So we awake to the crunching sound of tires on gravel. The room darkens as something is backed over the space where light comes in. Then Guido fires up the Ferrari Dino sports racer with the exhaust pipes practically sticking in our window! Wotta noise! Wotta smell! Wotta dose of carbon monoxide! Can you think of a better way to wake up on the first day of your Italian racing adventure? Me neither. *Mag-freaking-nificent.*

How stock was sports car racing in the good old days? Well, in the '63 Targa officials made us remove the little hoop rollbar behind the driver's seat, which we had to put in to run the Lancia in an SCCA race to get the feel of the car at speed. The Italians said it was stiffening the chassis. There was a neat rule in those days: if your car was a production car, you could lighten it up by 10% and modify the body contours very slightly, and tidy up the inside of the engine. Our redline was 6,000 in top, and 5,600 through the gears. The lightweight Flaminias that showed up, I was told, could turn 7,000. Of course, they might have been fibbing.

At that wonderful '63 Targa Florio there were girls around, of course, but there really weren't any pit popsies (as they were called then), roving singles or small groups of young ladies. It was Sicily, remember, but in the pits and connected to some car or another was a mature woman we referred to as "Miss Animal Sex." It looks silly in print, but as I so often say, you shoulda been there.

She was definitely a *type*; not your generic sexy good looking female. If your imagination is really good I offer this description: an earthy, glamorous, heterosexual Martina Navratilova. Hard to get your mind around, but that's the best I can do. Okay, I'll make it easier. She looked a lot like an unrestored, club-raced version of Francois Hardy, the French girl singer, who played the Sicilian driver's lover in *Grand Prix*.

On to the race! Bill Pryor drove the first 3-lap stint. He gashed his head open on a cinderblock overhanging the pits as he got out and took off his helmet. Then, trouble, but not from poor Bill's accident. You weren't allowed to refuel your own car if you were a privateer. In fact, four crews had to share the same pit, giving each group, behind the pit counter, about 1½ square yards.

We'd figured we could safely make three 44-mile laps per tankful, but without much leeway. The *Supercortemaggiore* dude filled the tank and it burped the way it did at a regular gas station – the filler nozzles were the same type. On the road I'd learned that the burp meant the last gallon or two could go in, but more slowly. I told our helper *"e'non pieno!"* – it wasn't full – but he disagreed with me and put the cap on.

See what my timidity got me? The car ran beautifully, but on the last 44-mile lap the fuel warning light started blinking way sooner than we'd figured it would; in fact Bill told me it had come on only 10 miles before he pitted, downhill past Campofelice toward the seaside straight of 3+ miles. Now, here it was blinking, as I left Collesano, a bit past midpoint of the lap. I cut the engine on the downhill parts, and had to honk to get locals off the road; they couldn't hear me coming. Catcalls and whistles as I passed. Then as I entered the straight, with about 6 miles to go until the pits, the engine quit. Running outta gas in our first major European race.... why didn't I insist that Rocco put in some more gas? Just 2 liters would have been more than enough.

I coast to a stop and just across the road is a solitary individual, an angel, standing by a Renault R8. *"Benzina?"* I holler.

"Si! Si!" he replies, and by the time I've crossed the road he's gotten out a bottle and a siphon hose. I put a bottle (1 liter? 2 liters?) in the car and we both grin and wave as I take off gently. I get to the hairpin left, 150 yards, uphill, to pit entrance, and the car staggers. I back off the throttle to a crawl in 3rd gear. Pit entrance is steep! A hundred feet to go and I make it in first gear, driving on

the choke lever.

Since Bill's sewn-up head wouldn't be comfortable in a helmet, I drove the third and last stint, tank filled to the damn brim this time. Two or three cars in our class dnf'd, so we were second among stock Flaminias, with the two lightweights one and two. They'd all had problems in their pit stops; Bill showed me a lap chart. If I hadn't run out of gas we would've won – it wasn't the time lost putting fuel in at roadside so much as it was the slow progress coasting down hills and the gentler runs uphill, where I'd been short-shifting. Well darn it anyway. We got a standing ovation at the trophy party, with everyone clapping and chanting, "O-Kla-O-Ma!" They didn't do Hs very well.

By the time we'd cleared out of the Jolly Hotel Monday afternoon, driven to the Messina ferry (no foresight in booking the Genoa ferry, the way we'd come down, meant no available space going back), we only had a couple days to drive to Belgium for the Spa 500km race.

That's right, we drove the "race" car. No autostrada in southern Italy in those days. Have you ever driven while *very* sleepy? Of course you have. Awful, isn't it? And it's especially awful when you have your crewman, Tom Davis, snoring away in the passenger seat.

Bill and Donna were ahead in the Fiat 1400 station wagon we'd obtained for a service vehicle. Bill drove it as fast as possible and we just stayed behind, an easy drive for me. Belgium went kinda okay – too many weird little details to recount.

We could have dusted the Lawrence-Tune Morgan +4s the following weekend at the Nurburgring, but a kindly garage attendant in Belgium had topped off our brake fluid reservoir from a can of brake fluid, open, which had been sitting near an open doorway in the rain! A few laps into the race and it was *no* brakes.

Bill and Tom were driving this time and Bill got to find out the brakes had taken the afternoon off. There's a bend at a hillcrest under a bridge that he'd been taking with a "confidence lift" and occasional touch of the brake pedal, when the rain or snow there was evident (the weather can be sun, rain, fog, snow/sleet in the one 14-mile lap). Bill thought, since it was now very wet and a Filipinetti 2-liter Porsche Carrera was closing quickly from behind, he'd just pop the brake a good one and let him by before the bridge bend. He hit the pedal and it fell to the floor, at which point Bill decided to really concentrate on driving. He got through the corner beautifully and when he looked in the mirror the Carrera was way back. Made Bill feel rather special.

So the Lancia crept around until the end of the race, while more and more parts fell off the Mogs. Two of them beat us home, so we were third out of four in class. Our timing showed they'd slowed down considerably with much of the race left to go, and then one of those curly-headed blonde Brits looked over my shoulder and said, "Oh, you're on the same lap!" and gave the Mogs the *faster* sign next time by. If I'd been more secretive, we might have caught them. Were we forever to be novices? Of course!

Hey, the '67 Targa was worse. My co-driver not only left the (his) Ferrari SWB at a garage up the course to be checked out (which meant desperate measures and dramatic Italian hysterics by my niece, Kiki, before we were allowed to retrieve it before the start), but when the police dropped me off at the garage, there he went with the car! He'd gotten another ride before me! So I had to walk over a mile down course to the start, and the first cars were sent off before I made it back. I was leaping into ditches when the racecars came by.

Our car had developed a blown head gasket, but all others in the over two liter class had blown up or crashed on the first lap! This was the first year in which you didn't have to just finish, but had to complete 7 of the 10 laps. I pulled into the gas station on the 3 mile straight to add water (the station was open for business, of course – it's Italy!) and the car made a loud noise when I shut it off. I should have just let it cool, dribbled water in, gotten a push start from the friendly Sicilians respectfully watching me from a distance and kept going. But I let it cool until the leader went by on his last lap, and then I drove around briskly to the checker. It ran pretty good. Should have gone an hour earlier – hadn't done 7 laps and though we were the only finisher in class, we didn't get that gorgeous trophy and a letter from Ing. Ferrari and Lord knows how much publicity and bragging rights.

Another quick story from '67 Targa: Tommy Wiking (a Swede in case you hadn't guessed), racing one of those fiberglass bodied Minis, walks up to us in the pits just as someone mentions that the news of the day is that Twiggy got married.

"Married?" asks Tommy. "I didn't think she had any room for her own sex organs, let alone anybody else's." He zoomed off and crashed at the second turn several seconds later – cold Dunlops!

And that was the Targa when the officials insisted Phil Hill present his racing license to prove who he was. Did the Chaparral team have to borrow our jack to make it through tech that year or was it in '71? I know the crew was complaining that the Italian food in Italy wasn't near as good as the Italian food in Midland, Texas.

Ah yes, 1971, as we prepared to take the 454 c.i. alloy-head Corvette to the Targa Florio, my co-driver-to-be, Charles Lucas, asked me if I could find a Plymouth Superbird for him, geared for European cruising speeds. Could we? Heck, there was one collecting dust at our local Plymouth dealer: 440 wedge, 4-speed, AM radio. Would we please take it away for $3,200? I guess so. We ordered bigger wheels, taller, for longer legs, but someone made a mistake and we got nice wheels but the same stock diameter. We did put in a 2.73 or 2.93 or thereabouts axle ratio, with appropriate change in the speedometer drive gears.

Driving it around Sicily elicited wonderful phrases shouted our way – I wish I understood the dialect. One imprecation I did understand (must have been a visitor from the mainland) was, "Why don't you just buy a bus?"

The car had such wonderful aerodynamics that it was whisper-quiet at 110mph. As we swooshed northward after not running in the Targa – that story to follow – we were passed by a 280SL, on PROVA (test car) plates, easily doing 125 or so. Bill nudged me. "If you don't pass him, he'll tell everyone he outran a NASCAR racer." I put us on his tail at 140. Passed him at just over 145, and then remembered we had *stock tires* on the 'Bird. Lifted off and let him by; smiles and waves and enthusiastic body motions. It must have been a prototype 350 or 450SL under the 280 bodyshell. Fun. Fun, fun, fun.

Oh yes, the Targa itself. 1971 was the first year the FIA insisted on rollbars. We'd brought along a cutaway of the Vette's super-structure from the dealership's book, but they insisted – and we'd known about it – on having an engineer's testimony that whatever structure could withstand 7.5 vertical G and 1½ lateral G. I asked a local engineer SCCA member for a piece of paper, but he must've feared the long arm of the mafia and wouldn't comply. Years later I realized that one of my father's two-dozen engineers, preferably one with WWII experience in Italy, would have been glad to testify in my behalf.

Anyway, we kept putting the car on the grid, reassured by Count Pucci, a heavy-duty local, and then those "new bastards from Milano" (not our words, believe me) would tell us to take it away. Upshot; we didn't race.

But you should hear the stories my niece tells about when we ran out of gas in the Vette one evening before the race, and I sent her off in a Fiat 1200 with three grinning locals. She's 5'9", had long blonde hair – just the way they like them on the island.

She said the continuing swatting of their hands off any available part of her anatomy would've made a great drum solo in a Duke Ellington composition. You mean that bit in "Black, Brown and Beige?" I asked.

"No," she said. "something more like oily, garlicky and sweaty."

Bill Pryor took some Brit's girlfriend around the circuit. The week leading up to the race itself is practice week. No, not official practice – that's a few hours on the day before the race, but believe me, it's practice week. The locals generally stay off the roads comprising the circuit, or if they have to go out, they drive in the race direction if at all possible. Since there aren't all that many completely blind corners on the route – 50 or 60 maybe, in 44 miles – a driver can certainly express a little enthusiasm in getting the feel of things.

Bill and the young lady belted themselves in and off they went. He took that monster Vette up to the yellowline whenever he could (first was good to over 60mph), and went leaping from crest to crest of the road heaves in the ancient tarmac. Worked up a regular sweat, he did – opposite lock around the hairpins, all that fun stuff. Got a nice odor from the competition brakes. He even caught himself holding his breath several times. He kept the car under 150mph on the 3-mile straight, just to be conservative of the machinery.

The girl was quiet; he figured when she screamed or whimpered, he'd back off a bit. They turned off the circuit and headed back for the hotel. "That was fun," she said. "I'll bet in the race you go really fast!" Bill told me he had no answer.

Anyway, Luke bought both the Superbird and the Vette, and in part payment he found me a Scott Flying Squirrel. If you don't know what that is, consider it a homework assignment.

I have a love-hate relationship with the Targa Florio – love the event and hate the boneheaded things I've done there. I'm not even going to begin to tell you about 1973 when I took the Lotus Europa twincam to the last Targa Florio. This time we put in a rollbar to FIA specs, thus avoiding the tech hassle we had in '71 when our aluminum-head, full comp option, 454 Corvette was excluded… ah well. Actually, some official or other came by and said our Lotus rollbar wasn't legal. We showed him the rulebook and he smiled and walked away. If you want more stories, ask Allan Girdler sometime.

I've thought it over for awhile, and have decided to use this really neat guy's real name. We met after that final Targa on the beautiful Italian liner Raffaello, the lovely and brilliant Kathy Sawyer and I. She'd been planning a European trip and I showed her how to slightly rearrange her schedule, so I'd have someone to dance with on the ship, being timid and all. We chose a table for eight – it's fun to meet folks under such formalized and pleasant circumstances and seated at our table was the marvelous Mr. Santangelo (my spelling might be in error).

On the week-plus trip we had deep and continuous conversations with Mr. Santangelo, whom I don't recall ever seeing anywhere on the ship besides our dining table. Anyway, what with our philosophical discussions only interrupted by the time between meals, the other guests at our table for eight faded until they were like extras in a movie, which featured only the Santangelos, Kathy and me. I remember getting into a mild argument with a man who was connected to the Hammer films from England, those entertaining

Christopher Lee vampire, werewolf and castle things. Today, I wonder who the other three people were.

Mr. Santangelo had been an Alpine soldier in the Italian army in WW1 (when the Italians were on our side). He had a son who raced a Corvette until father and mother found out about it – after a crash. He told me about all the spas and springs in Italy for any specific disease you care to mention, all put there by a loving God for our healing. He said that he came to America as a poor youth and had worked his way up until now he owned paper mills and the forests to supply them, and many other things besides. "Only in America!" he said.

The missus sat quietly by for the most part. The staff was especially deferent to him; I figured it was an Italian-to-Italian thing. Then we got to Genoa, where the car and I were to board the ferry to Palermo.

These days, rapid turnaround is the procedure for ocean liners. No longer does the crew spend the night in New York City, Cherbourg or Southampton. Passengers are rushed off in late morning and the next bunch boards in late afternoon. But this was in the good old days and we were on an Italian ship. Disembarking was in the mid-afternoon after a nice lunch – then customs, baggage, etc. etc. We were sipping our espressos and sambucas con mosche when we were approached by a bright young man in a blue uniform with those double-row buttons down the front, brass, of course, like Red Ryder wore. "You can disembark now, signore." he announced.

"Let's go," said Mr. S. I replied that Kathy and I had to go through customs and supervise the Lotus rollout from the hold. "None of that," said our host. "Your car and luggage are together on the pier!"

The young man in blue smiled at us and said, "When we are in Genova, Mr. Santangelo owns the port!"

Well now! Golly! We all stood; Mr. S shook our hands. "Have a good race," he said, and the couple strode away with the boy in blue. We never saw them again. We left the ship. Nobody looked at our passports. The dockside platform was deserted – except for a Lotus Europa, just washed and shining, with our bags next to it.

Months later, I sent them a Christmas card but never heard back and I eventually lost their address. It makes one wonder…

Flashback: 1963

Racing internationally used to be like buying a glove and taking the field with the Yankees. Mail your $5 in for your FIA license, take your car to the race and have a go. However, just like it's difficult to get into the Historic Mille Miglia these days, it was hard to get into Le Mans back then. In 1963 we'd sent in our entry along with other applications for the Spa 500km, Nurburgring 1000km, and the Targa Florio, but got back a pleasant letter saying we were rejected by Le Mans. We were the only Americans racing in Europe in '63, except at Le Mans, and before we got to Le Mans as guests, later that spring, they simply didn't know who we were.

After our back-to-back-to-back decent showings in the three other races, we found ourselves hanging with the organizers of not only those three, but Le Mans. From the Targa there was Santa Claus' Sicilian brother, Pietro Pottino, Marquis di Rosa. The name of the Spa organizer escapes me, though I remember walking through the Belgian drizzle with him as he said, "You know, Spa ees called ze pisspot of Belgium."

Next, there were we, at Le Mans as spectators, staying at a nice downtown hotel (it helps to have friends in high places), sitting in the bar with Jacques Finance of the Le Mans organizers, who told us, "We now have four non-starters in the race, but it is impossible for us to admit you at this late date." I'll bet if wife Karen had been there, she could've talked us in – even though she would've been 16 at the time! It would've been fun; we had the spare wheel and tire and were still running the car's original brake pads. Talk about showroom stock!

We're still in the bar in the hotel in Le Mans, with all those FIA organizers. Augie Pabst and Walt Hansgen stuck their heads in the door and said, "Hi!" Then Count Johnny Lurani says to me, "But wait! I like the way you drive. Why don't you come and stay at my villa on Lake Como with your lovely girlfriend and I'll see to it that you have a drive in the Monza Formula Junior Grand Prix."

Possibly Count Lurani thought, as the creator of Formula Junior, that an American couldn't hurt in the promotion of the race, but then it doesn't seem that Italians ever *need* to have a race promoted to *them*.

During the moment of my slack-jawed silence, Bill Gavin (who later oversaw the Ferrari Can-Am effort in the U.S.), pulled up a chair and added, "I took the liberty of talking to Lancia on your behalf, and they'll go through the car after every event for a token $50 or so; and if you'll stay over here and run a bunch of GT races, I can get you appearance money of about $200 a week, plus expenses." That's what, $1,000 today?

I don't need to suggest to the gentle reader what any sensible person would say. Unfortunately, I had too much ego to just relax and accept the role of *international playboy* that God had assigned me. "Geez, thanks," I said modestly, "but I promised dad I'd be home in July to learn more about the family business."

What a lie! I'd promised dad no such thing, and if I'd phoned him with the news I was staying in Europe to race, he'd have given me his full blessing. Talk about the sin of pride masquerading as modesty! Talk about being a drooling idiot. Maybe I was scared at the thought of being up on that Monza banking in the middle of a pack of Chianti-dosed Nuvolari wannabes in open-wheeled cars. Who knows?

I wake up kicking myself and screaming every few months when I remember this scene, but the attacks do come less frequently with age. From a spiritual point of view, as my niece Kyra told me, "God gave you the test of success and you tried your best not to get an A. There's a great fantasy story by some Englishman called *The Green Door*, if you'd like to read something in a similar vein. No cars in it, though.

Ah, that wonderful European racing trip. Why didn't I stay? Why didn't I go back next year, with the off-season spent thinking over what went right and what went wrong. Could it actually be better that I didn't go back? It is now a shining temporal jewel in my life and the lives of my friends. Glowing there in memories, a *special thing* that one picks up and examines fondly. Possibly, but I bet it would be a bigger jewel or maybe a trunkful of treasure if we'd stayed. Either way, I'm glad we went!

The more I think about it, the harder I think it must be for modern young car enthusiasts, especially potential racing drivers, to understand the beautiful simplicity of what it was like to go racing in the '60s and early '70s. One wonders, was it the continuing layering of bureaucracy that leached or burned the simplicity out of it, or was it the growing commercialism that required more and more restrictions to separate racing people from the common herd of spectators? Probably it was some sort of synergy between the two.

It is interesting that after the Le Mans disaster of 1955 some places banned car racing for a time; and yet safety regulations for cars themselves were unchanged. Spectator safety was improved, and that was about it. The way vintage racing and rallying safety regulations stiffened after an accident in Italy must have been due to a greater sensitivity to danger in this increasingly paranoid world. I can't help feeling that having to wear a fireproof suit and trick your car out with rollbars and extinguishers and such, appealed to the egos of the vintage racing drivers. "Look at all this equipment. Ain't I special?"

Today's 25-year-old with some disposable income does not have these options. Imagine buying a Miata or Chrysler Crossfire and deciding to run a big European road race. You write for an entry form, return it with a few hundred bucks and take yourself and your car across the Big Water. Oh yes, you need to buy your international racing license first.

There's one story out of a long-ago *Christophorus* (Porsche's house magazine) that relates the essence of what that wonderful and fading term *motorsport* is all about. A couple South American guys (I think Argentinian) decided to tour Europe in 1964 or '65. They want something sporting, so they buy a Porsche 904.

When Porsche built the 904, I figured they were finally on the right track, and then they built the ugly, unbalanced and perpetually popular 911. What does that tell you about the state of the great unwashed – moneyed, but unwashed?

So anyway, these guys drop by the works to pick up their 904, and Porsche says, "Why don't you race it in the Reims 12-hour coming up soon?" So the guys buy their el cheapo FIA licenses and show up at Reims. Their spares consisted of the spare tire and a fanbelt. Well, they said, we were told Porsches were quite reliable.

Reims is the way to run a 12-hour race. First you have a big party and then start the race at midnight. That way people watch for a little while, go catch some zeds (do they say that in England?) and come back for breakfast and the finish. The factory-breathed-upon 904s all break their throttle cables (I vaguely recall) and Our Guys win the U2L GT class. They take their two-foot-tall trophy and go on their way, never to be heard from again. Rank amateurs save factory bacon. What did Ustedes do this summer? "We drove our car in *una carrera* and won a *muy bueno trofeo de plata*." That is *motorsport*.

Zourab Tchokotua and Tommy Hitchcock showed up at the 1963 Targa Florio with their GTO – first race for Zourab, I think. Tommy had some experience. When we saw them at the 1964 Daytona Continental the following year, they had a new Cobra with a basic rollbar. They asked Bill and me whether they would need any additional lighting for the nighttime portion, besides the stock sealed beams. We told them that would be a very good idea since the track, unlike today, was completely unlit, except for some light by the starter's stand. Buy a car and race it – not any more.

The Way Things Should be Forever

Let me give you an overview of – not a typical trip, because all my trips had their delicious differences – but a particular trip. The plan was to run a GT race in Sweden and then swan around the continent. We'd planned to tow the new '66 427 Vette with a Stage 1 Yenko Stinger, but the brand new trailer broke on the New York Thruway. We towed the trailer empty; Bill drove the Stinger and I drove the Vette.

We got on the Thruway with three axles and got off with five. What confusion! Bill asked if a light went on atop Governor Rockefeller's desk or something.

Okay, got that behind us. Met my folks at the Plaza in New York. They came to watch us sail away to Sweden on the Gripsholm. This was the *Return to Sweden* year, and the Swedish-American line asked us if there was any particular Swede we'd like to meet! Car-focused at the moment, we said Eric Carlsson, completely forgetting Anita Ekberg, Britt Eklund, etc. Onboard, males were outnumbered 4 to 1 by females – college students returning home. That's a novelette in itself.

So, we get to the track at Karlskoga, and are told that Mr. Carlsson is being run up to meet us from recce-ing the Tulip Rally in Holland. We protested vigorously, but the next day, there he was, and though we'd interrupted his plans, he could not have been nicer. The GT race was cancelled – it was formula cars only, but we'd been informed earlier, so we let our newfound friends Charles Lucas, Roy Pike, Piers Courage, Chris Irwin and various race officials hare around the course in the Vette after official activities were over.

An interesting event took place in the F2 race the next day. This fairly quick new guy by the name of Jochen Rindt just couldn't quite catch the leader, a guy with a long name. It might have been Freddy Kotulinsky – or not. So, with a few laps to go, at a tight 180 at the end of the back straight, Rindt just didn't brake, from a good 20 yards behind the leader, and smartly punted him off the track. That Jochen would be going places, everyone agreed.

Piers and I swapped cars – for keeps, or so we intended. He gave me his factory special Lotus Elan (Lucas, Courage and Pike were the factory F3 team) and a swell car it was! Then a day later Piers told me we'd have to swap back, since the customs duty on the Yenko Stinger was about equal to its purchase price in America. I have no real reason to doubt his explanation (cf. Perfidious Albion), but I think he really just wanted his keen car back. Later that same day, we gave Frisbees away to various drivers.

So we were at the Karlskoga track for the Kannonskloppet races, spectating, but with the Vette and Stinger we would from time to time attract a few of the *Flickas* who didn't want to exert sufficient effort to get to the F2, or even the F3 drivers. Somehow we had become encumbered with a young lady, who might be described as a young Swedish Goldie Hawn on really bad drugs, or maybe it was just seething Scandinavian enthusiasm (pardon the oxymoron).

She was one of the 1% of Swedes who didn't speak English. We couldn't understand a word she said and we couldn't shut her up. Buying her drinks so she'd at least be quiet when she swallowed, didn't help. I'm sure we could have taken her off somewhere and selfishly abused her for our entertainment, but we weren't British and besides, we were tired. What could we do?

I looked around the room in a cinematic heaven-help-us gesture and there he was – Jimmy Clark, eating alone at a small table against the wall. Bill and I stood. She leaped to her feet, still jabbering. Bill took her hand. I led our trio over to Jimmy's table.

"Excuse me, Jimmy," I said, "but we have something for you." I stepped aside and Bill seated the girl opposite *Our Hero*. As they stared at each other in silence – she had actually fallen mute and he was pleasantly nonplussed – Bill and I split. I'm sure everything turned out all right.

I'd first seen Jimmy Clark in the dining room of the Glen Motel a few years earlier, chowing down with someone – not Chapman. Another guy came to fetch Jimmy just as Dick Irish and I were leaving. Jimmy was ahead of us as we came to the stairs. He stopped, looked up and – you're all familiar with the phrase – his face lit up. I've never seen that phenomenon before or since. We walked over and looked up too. There she was, and the man who led Jimmy to the stairs said, "Jimmy, this is...." I'd give you her name, if I could. It dissolved out of my memory around 1980.

Long honey-blonde hair, cashmere sweater, whipcord slacks and not a lot of fussy details. She was just all flowed together in her clothes. She smiled and said, "Hi, Jimmy." He sorta oozed up the stairs and she sorta oozed down the stairs and somehow Dick and I managed to slip by. We knew we'd seen something beautiful happen, just like in the movies.

But think about Sweden! An F1 World Champion dining by himself on a race weekend? Things were realer then. We were fans because we loved the sport, not because it was sold to us. If you knew someone attached to the Circus, and were sufficiently foreign where you were, you'd get invited to a party where all the drivers were present, not because of sponsor pressure, but because it was a party.

Sure, the Shell man was there, and the Mintex man, the Esso

man, the Bosch man and the Goodyear man. But they too were there because it was a party, not a commercial obligation. Not to mention the presence of, mixing eras and metaphors, a Wal-Mart warehouse stock of metric *woogy*: short, medium, tall – slim, nice, stacked, Rubenesque – blonde, brunette, redhead. Pick a characteristic from each category, move your head no more than fifteen degrees in either direction, and there she is. I think the formula for the permutations and combinations of the above characteristics is 3!x4!x3! I've forgotten lots of math, but the factorial exclamation points in that formula are certainly appropriate. The scene was simply *The Way Things Should Be*. And believe me, they were.

Oh, and trackside at that Swedish race, there were a couple other moments that help to define the era. Piers Courage and Charles Lucas were fiddling about the rear suspension of the Lotus F3 team cars, when Jack Brabham (whose F2 Honda-powered cars won every race but one that year) quietly walked up. In a moment or two, Piers noticed the nearby feet, looked up and said, "Copy anything you want, Jack."

Brabham replied, "I can see why it doesn't work." and walked away. Then, later that weekend, the report came that Ken Miles had been killed at Riverside testing the Ford J-car. A driver who shall remain nameless paused for a few seconds. "Hmmm. We all move up one," he said. Bob Varsha would have wet his pants.

A few days later we wound up at a race in Holland at Zandvoort. A couple officials came up and offered me $100 to start the Stinger in the GT race, so I said fine! Now this was the Stage 1 Stinger, with maybe a dozen or two more hp than a standard Corvair, and, thinking we'd be towing with it, I'd specified the shortest possible diff ratio, meaning that in practice, before the start-finish line, I was at the redline in fourth gear.

Then it began to rain before the standing start. I'm on the back row, and with my rear weight bias and short gearing I figure to really get a great jump off the line. Flag drops. I pop the clutch, and immediately drop a slug of rainwater, which had puddled up on the rear deck, right down through those scoops the Stinger had back there, and into the carbs and onto the ignition. Well, the engine barely kept running, and by the time it cleared out I found a delightfully empty track in front of me. It was a great place to watch the race from, as I had just enough time to learn the track in the wet before I began to be lapped. Fun!

Then I sold the Vette to a European friend of mine, but before we left Holland, Bill, friend and I are sitting around our cozy suite at the hotel. Bill and I are going to go scope out the town. "Don't go yet!" exclaims friend. "A few of the young chambermaids are coming by for a party!" Yeah, right, we thought, and split. We returned from our leisurely stroll (is there really any other kind?) to find a couple little Dutch girls (not little really) adjusting their uniforms and giggling. Friend, fresh out of the shower said, "I've tried to get them to stay, but they have to get back to work. You really should've stayed." Yeah, but if we'd stayed I'm not sure I would have told you the story.

The Stinger got Bill and me all around the continent and with its short gearing and tail-mounted engine was at its best on Alpine passes. Thinking about how clever we were, Bill and I checked into a nice little suite at the Crystal Hotel in St. Moritz.

The bellboy had told us that each lamp in the sitting room had to be turned on individually, and as I fumbled around in the dark, in the open-curtain, brightly lit room at an angle across from our window, no more than fifteen feet away, a bare female leg flashed into view. It was not hallucination. A lovely teenage blonde, enraptured with youth and, perhaps, all things Swiss, was dancing naked around her room. Of course we never turned on a light, and the next evening at the same time we pulled a couple chairs not too close to our window and got the same show again. Blonde. After shower, rubs hair with towel. Drops robe. Dances.

Next morning at checkout we met her and her folks. American, from Ohio, I think. Bill and I stumbled through things like "Nice meeting you, but I guess the odds are against seeing any more of you. I mean unless we get to Ohio." David Niven would have done it much better. Double entendre – single entendre – triple entendre, David was the master. We shouldn't even have tried. Even after all these years I bet I'd recognize her navel – three dozen years can't make that much difference, can they?

Another evening, tired out from driving back roads to Vienna, we spot the Hotel Imperial and pull up in front. It was midnight. "Do you have a room?"

"Sorry, we are completely full." We slouch toward the door. "Just a minute, gentlemen; how about the Imperial Suite? It is available." How much? "Two hundred dollars (!!!)." Remember, this was 1966. Thank you; we'll keep looking. "Just a moment! How about sixty dollars?" We took it.

We had to sleep in one bed. It was, however, about nine feet square. Besides the bedroom, bath and dressing room, there was a nice sitting room, of course. Was the suite really 3,500 square feet? The figures of 22 chairs and 17 love seats/sofas stick in my head. That sounds ridiculous, but the place was full of furniture. I'm about 6'2" and I could sit in the tub with the water just above my chin; I could stretch out on the bottom of the tub without touching either end.

As we dressed leisurely the next morning, our cigarillo butts kept disappearing from the ashtrays. We spoke loudly to each other and went into the bedroom, peeking around the door (the doors were twelve feet tall). We saw a chambermaid instantly look in to see if anything needed to be cleaned up. Best $60 ever spent on lodging, as far as Bill and I are concerned. I hear that the rate has gone up and it's Jagger's favorite suite in the world.

The funniest part of the Stinger trip was when Bill and I, *back-roading* it as usual, crossed into Italy late at night on some deserted route. Ten kilometers into Italy, we were ambushed by Italian customs agents. They noted our passports and the car's registration, and walked to the back of the car and bade us open – the trunk. I fought back a grin, flipped up the lid, and there in the feeble glow of the under-hood light the little flat six sat, cheerfully idling away. Both agents stared at the engine, neither wanting to reveal his confusion to the other. Bill and I, by now, were biting our lips. They waved the cover shut and us on our way. Maybe you had to have been there. The Yenko Stinger, what a terrific car.

The beginning of the Stinger's downfall had come, though. I began worrying about an oil change with several thousand miles on the car, and so we stopped at a roadside oil change facility in the Netherlands. I was looking around for a lift or a pit or some way for the Dutchman to get under the car and was surprised to see him simply stick a tube down the dipstick hole and suck out the oil. Now, even the base model Stinger has a finned and baffled sump, and while you would think that gravity would eventually get all the oil to any spot of the sump, whether it was at the drain hole or under the dipstick hole, especially as the attendant was poking the tube this way and that, we found the car wouldn't take the specified number of quarts of oil Yenko's book said it would hold.

Guess what happened! We didn't know that the oil change also included a kerosene flush and it hadn't all been removed; probably all the oil hadn't been sucked out even before the flush went in. So, scratching our heads, we motored off with perhaps two quarts of kerosene and four of fresh oil in the sump.

Was this before or after our "invitational" race at Zandvoort? I can't remember, but trouble never arose on the short and gentle trip to the Queen Mary and across America to Nashville, where I sold the car. I don't know whether the new owner changed the oil, but eventually (fairly quickly) the engine started making *those noises* and was rebuilt. I was told there was a strange smell of kerosene when it was taken apart.

The car was soon thereafter rolled off an earthen dam somewhere in Tennessee with no injury to the driver or passenger. Years later it was restored in Dallas and now lives in Springfield, MO. I'd love to drive it again. I was told a decade ago that that would happen.

Charles Lucas, who we met in Sweden in 1966, founded Titan Cars and was this close to fielding a very competitive F1 car, motor and all, pure Titan. He became a good friend, as did his close friend, the late Piers Courage. I am deeply honored that Charles was best man at my wedding and that I am the Godfather of Charles' number one son, Sprog. I mean Piers. Charles called the tyke Sprog so often that even as an adult he still sort of looks like Sprog to me.

Years later Charles introduced me to both Lord Hesketh of F1/James Hunt fame and Bubbles Horsley; believe me, his name does not begin to do him justice. I met the Heskeths and Horsley at the younger Hesketh's 21st birthday party at a house about the size of one wing of the Pentagon. There were midnight fireworks shot

up into impenetrable English fog and all that sort of thing; to give
you an idea of the shindig, just let me say that the Dom Perignon
champagne was served continually in the indoor tennis court. The
unbroken rhythm of the corks popping behind the partition was at
the pace of the hammers pounding in the Anvil Chorus.

I was provided with a lovely date for this occasion and with confidence released by a glass or two of the only liquid around (they
were even handing groups of bottles of D.P. to the rock band), I decided to make a friendly move on the beauty (think of a kind of
AMG–modified Audrey Hepburn), but got nowhere. Heck, it
wasn't my fault that she was someone's mistress. I just wish someone had told me beforehand.

The band eventually got very sick onstage, but no one seemed to
notice. As the evening (well, morning) drew to a close, the depart-
ing crowd was energized by the valet parking attendant roaring up
the drive in our means of transport, Charles' orange Plymouth Superbird, slewing to a stop in a sharp-intake-of-breath's distance
from a bunch of Rolls Royces and a few of those old green English
cars that used to win Le Mans in the twenties. I've spent worse
evenings.

But how silly of me; you wanted to know more about Hesketh's
house. Okay, here's how I was told to reach a large oriel window
on the top floor to watch the midnight birthday fireworks, fired off
by the champion of the fireworks competition held every year at
Monaco. Yes, fireworks competition. It's Europe.

Here goes: "Walk down this hall, Toly, and take the second set of
stairs you come to. Take them all the way up (the champers fuzzed
up my memory of the number of floors). You'll come out in an
apartment; go directly across the room, through the door, and take
the door to your right out of that next room. Turn left in the hall.
Walk to the end, turn right, and in several strides there's your window!"

There were several shadowy shapes near the window – since
there was only about a 15-watt bulb every thirty feet in the hall. I
couldn't have recognized my own mother. There was a muffled
boom outside and then the fog briefly turned red. Following
booms: blue fog, green fog, etc. No one had spoken yet. There was

some sort of finale: mixed-color fog and several explosions. Then silence. I dared to speak, "We Americans are raised knowing about British understatement," I murmured, "but this is ridiculous."
There was a faint chuckle, bemused, superior. Then the shapes faded away. Going back, I never saw anybody in the halls or on the stairs. What the Heck? I'm an American. They'd probably sent me up the servants' stairway.

If some of what is contained in these pages is the worst of what life has tossed at me, I can only conclude I have been blessed from both birth and heaven above. I'll take my 49 remaining years (the Bible promises every man 120) and get on down the road, steering with my knees.

Driving

The first car I ever steered was a '38 Caddy limousine, on Mulholland Drive, at age 4. Since I couldn't reach the accelerator I had to sit on Kenny the chauffeur's lap. All these years later I still remember the feel of the steering as I turned the wheel, probably at a throbbing 15mph or so, and I still can smell the broadcloth interior, gently releasing the trapped aroma of many packs of Chesterfields. That Caddy had 3-filament headlights, with little red, white, and green indicator lights across the bottom of the speedometer: city (both beams straight ahead and down), passing (the traditional dipped pattern, down and to the right), and country (high beams, natch). Are bulbs available for them today? Probably on eBay.

Then one day in Bartlesville, OK, when I was about eleven, Dean Radefeld brought (I think he drove it – he only lived a mile away) a motorized go-kart to my house. His father had built it, and it was powered by a ¾hp Maytag washing machine motor. Yes, Virginia, when you lived out in the country, you might have a gasoline-powered washer.

The feeling of just pushing on a pedal and moving down the street was one of newly discovered and limitless power – I felt like I had to actually keep pushing the accelerator, as if it were a pedal car. After a couple fast-slows, though, I got the hang of it. It had a lever-operated clutch, which took up the slack in the belt drive. That was the first time I ever felt intoxicated.

Skip ahead to getting a Doodlebug motor scooter at age twelve: 1 ½ hp, fluid automatic clutch and what one would call a live-man's throttle. What would our insurance company or NHTSA think of this arrangement? It had one lever operated by the right hand. Squeeze it to close the throttle and apply the rearwheel-only brake. Turn loose of it and you might find yourself at 31mph!

There was no kill switch except a grounding strap you pushed against the sparkplug after lifting the foam-slab seat off, so if you were out of control (as out of control as you could be with 1½ hp), you were on your own. It was simpler to kill the motor by pulling the choke knob below my left cheek.

Then, fast forward through the 98cc James 2-stroke (50mph), the 8hp Powell (65mph) and the 26.5 c.i. Indian Scout (85mph).

One day mom asked me to move her 1949 fastback Caddy out of the drive for some reason. As a joke, I yelled upstairs and said Don Hinkle and I were going to take it out to the country club. We about dropped our teeth when Mom yelled, "Just have it back by four o'clock!" What a feeling of command! I was 14. We didn't stop at the country club; we drove around until 4.

Later that summer I visited mom's friend in the Pacific Palisades, who had a son my age. Upon arrival by cab to spend a few days as a guest, I discovered he'd gone up to his father's ranch; but Mrs. Stout, always obliging, said I could take Claud's Peugeot, if I wanted to go anywhere.

Imagine loaning a stick shift convertible to a 14½ year old in the L.A. suburbs! The car looked like a 4-door VW with a fabric roof that slid all the way to the back window. It was a 1949 or '50, I think – a 206? It had a separate key for the door, spare tire, gas cap, glovebox, trunk and, as I recall, the gearshift. Oh, and the ignition, of course. It had those cute orange-lit trafficators for turn signals – the kind that spring out from the B-pillar and bob up and down to get the other drivers' attention. It also had huge yellow headlights that I never did find the switch for. Bugs me to this very day!

So as you see by the ripe old age of fifteen I had a bunch of driving experience, all illegal. But heck, there sure wasn't much traffic back then in those necks of the woods.

Seems like often when you're young you are ready for it to be tomorrow, next week, next month, well, as long as that doesn't bring school closer during summer vacation. As I age, I often seem to be a season behind. I might have inherited this from my mother, at least. Around Independence Day she'd exclaim "Fourth of July! Summer is nearly over!" You'll have to do the Russian accent in your head. Think Zsa Zsa Gabor, but with more class. Anyway, a few times the seasons changed with a jolt when I was young.

The Caney river runs along the north edge of downtown Bartlesville, then wanders around out in the country someplace and you cross it again about halfway between B'ville and Tulsa. In late August or early September I drove alone down to an evening movie in Tulsa, with a snack afterwards to give me the blood sugar to get home awake. The late summer smells were everywhere with the top down; in the evening the buildings of downtown Tulsa radiated heat into the night. I took the old road home, and just north of the tiny burg of Ramona, I crossed the single-span steel bridge over the Caney. The water was forty feet across at most. As I passed the north end of the bridge, it smelled like autumn. Wham! And it smelled that way the rest of the way home. I forgot about this for a year or two and then one night, Billy Kaufman and I were returning from a similar trip on that road and it happened again. Billy noticed it, too.

It happened maybe once more after that, but we'd both mentioned it to friends and once, so many years later, somebody said, "We came back from Tulsa last night on the old road and it suddenly smelled like fall when we crossed that little bridge, just like you said." I wonder how many days leeway there is in that situation. I wish I'd gone the next night just to check it out. I haven't been on that road at that time of the year for ages, but for some years before and after, it would snow down to that north bank and there would be no snow in Ramona. Snow lasts longer than a nighttime. Zephyr, scent, meteorological event?

Lost Places

Past times are lost, though we have the memories. But, there are – or were – lost places that no one remembers. Driving that Porsche to Vanderbilt from Oklahoma on US 60 across southern Missouri between 1959 and 1961 brings one to mind. There was a section of the road so twisty that a sign advised you "No Passing Zones Not Marked Next 60 Miles" and the daytime speed limit was 70. I asked a patrolman about the arrangement at a coffee shop. "With the limit at 70, we don't have to worry about stoppin' anybody for speedin'." he advised me. That's my kind of highway philosophy. That was in a little town, soon bypassed, named Cabool. The question of what is an Afghan name doing in southern Missouri beats me.

On that 650-mile drive I used to count sports cars. I met 8 to 12, usually. Mostly MGAs, then TR3s, a couple Healeys, the odd Jag and Alfa, and once, crossing my headlights at a remote T intersection something flashed through my vision. Was it a Zagato-bodied Maserati 2-liter? Whatever it was, it was going the other direction – with verve.

One day I was in the twisties and there was a red-on-white sign on a post ahead, "Odd Acres." A few more miles: "You're Almost There." Then, "Slow Down for Odd Acres." In front of the small frame building, "Here It Is." A couple miles farther, "You Passed Odd Acres." Then, when it was almost out of short-term memory, a sign fifteen feet up a tree, "If I Were You, I'd Go Back." I never did and, of course, I wish I had.

Then there was "Judy's Museum," marked with a little red square on the map, south of 60 on one of those Missouri county roads called OO or ZZ or PU, about five miles out of the way. From time to time, if I stopped in Poplar Bluff for a meal or a night, I'd ask about it. No one knew anything about it and I was too imperceptive to notice if furtive sidelong glances were exchanged by the natives when I asked. It eventually disappeared from road maps. Paging Stephen King.

Odd Acres was most likely a gift shop. Maybe my single purchase would have kept it in business. Maybe it was run by gorgeous, witty twin sisters. And the museum! I bet Judy was there in her establishment having brandy and coffee once, when I thrummed past in the distance in the Porsche. After all, running the only Krafft-Ebing exhibit in southeast Missouri can be a lonely job.

Do you remember something that no one else does? Something

in the public arena, that it seems like nobody noticed? In the late '50s the *new highway 75* wasn't so new anymore, and straight and wide as it was, almost no one used narrow *old 75*, except folks who lived along it.

So it was odd that a mile down old 75, for a few weeks during a few summers, there was a trailer-mounted fruit stand. The shoulder was so narrow that the edge of the contraption almost overhung the road surface. Even though every time I saw it I thought it quite un-usual, I can't tell you if it was a freestanding trailer or the rear of a utility truck. Also, though I sort of crept by it, because the road was narrow and a few strange people were always standing about, I could never tell what the stuff in the racks for sale was!

I'd go by, and think, "What were those things?" and if I remem-bered to go down that road again, it was dark and they were gone; or I'd remember a day or two later and they were gone then, too. None of my friends, who also drove around aimlessly in those days, can remember that whatever-stand. The inventory was proba-bly divided up between Odd Acres and Judy's Museum.

It was about this time that I thought about carrying a camera with me to document the always different condom machines in gas sta-tion johns across the country. It is a shame I didn't; a book of these photos would probably be a good seller.

Then there was the Red Top Café, somewhere in the Florida pan-handle, over four decades back. It was the end of spring break in '61, and two frat brothers and I were heading back to Tulsa U. from doing a telephone remote bit of reportage from Ft. Lauderdale for the school FM station KWGS 89.5. As of this writing, it's still broadcasting, more powerful than ever, with way too little jazz and way too much BBC.

Anyway, it was getting late, it was a bit foggy and ahead of us a red neon top – the boy's first toy requiring coordination – glowed through the mist as the Corvair thrummed along some nameless 2-lane road. A real local roadhouse! No burger joint for us tonight; it's to be a greasy spoon instead.

There it sat, an Edward Hopper painting commissioned by Ten-nessee Williams. My friends, their imaginations numbed by the acres of females we had seen on the beach (a very few even wore those bikini things!), ordered hamburgers, but I opted for the steak. The burgers came without ceremony and then Tugboat Annie's little sister presented my entrée. They must've been saddened to part with it. It was a culinary heirloom. I was hungry. I tried cutting it – oops! – across the grain. Cutting with the grain was little better, but I eventually hacked off a corner and took a bite. Meat-flavored balsa wood fibers instantly wedged themselves between every pair of teeth in my head.

I thought perhaps a cup of the Red Top's coffee-flavored battery acid might dissolve some of the fibers, and indeed, several slipped free, but I suspect it was the erosion of a layer of enamel from my teeth that provided the extra clearance. The guys said the hamburgers were just fine. I can assure you of one thing: I wasn't hungry for another twenty-four hours. How can food be that bad and not make you throw up? There's a Master's Thesis right there.

How many ways can you find to get from Nashville to Courtland, Florence or Decatur, Alabama? We were probably coming from the airport race at Courtland, since it was a Sunday night in 1960. We were on a narrow road and hungry, and there on the right was a little café that was obviously the front parlor of a middle-size house. The only chain restaurants we knew of those days were Holiday Inns, and there sure wasn't going to be one of those for quite a few miles. So café it was.

It had a screen door and the main door was open because it was a pleasant evening. The food was okay, I guess, but it's difficult to taste your meatloaf or fried chicken or country ham or whatever it might have been, when you keep sticking your fork in your ear. That was because the waitress/owner kept walking by.

With her accent she was likely a German war bride. No, too young. Probably the daughter of some scientist at Huntsville Arsenal, where they were working on building those rockets. Equal parts (you're gonna have to be old to get all of this): Sophia Loren, Elaine Stewart and Tina Louise (Ginger on Gilligan's Island) with Cyd Charisse's walk. All this was poured into a cocoa-colored knit dress.

Unexperienced as I was, I don't know if they had ladies' unmentionables then with edges and seams thin enough to be invisible under a knit dress. I can only testify for sure that she was wearing a dress and a ring. Oh, and shoes. I'm pretty sure she was wearing shoes.

You bet we planned to eat there, every future trip to or from Courtland, or Selma or Huntsville. We all make plans. Never found it again.

A number of years later I'd taken a trailer down to the port of Houston to bring back one of the two Piper Le Mans cars I'd bought (unwritten law: it's *bought* under $1 million; over that figure you're allowed to use the word *acquired*.) For feminine company (and to help push the thing onto the tilt-bed trailer) I'd asked a charming Indian lady to go along. I'd used her as a model once and if you would like to see a fine abstract partial figure study of a Native American framed in the cockpit of an Alexis FC, drop by sometime. They're surely the only photographs of their kind in existence.

With our easy load-up and early departure northbound, we had developed a breakfast appetite before a Waffle House appeared, conveniently at a highway exit. Parking the rig was no problem since they weren't very busy. Okay, *now* it gets strange. As we entered and took seats opposite the counter, the slim and not unattractive waitress behind the counter drawled to someone, "You really wan (no *t* was enunciated) three aigs?" I saw none of the five customers respond, but while she was speaking, the cook, a perfect Li'l Abner type, black hair hanging over brow, broad shoulders etc., stopped putting bacon on the grill and turned to watch her as she spoke. Velma and I did a quick check of the menu and looked toward her expectantly. "Yep, he really wans three aigs," she said again, and again the cook froze in pose and rotated like a robot to watch her speak.

A few minutes passed as we smiled, twiddled our menus back and forth, and tried to make eye contact. "Doan fergit them three aigs," she repeated, as I computed the cook was laying down maybe, just maybe, 3 strips of bacon a minute. Of course, he rotated 90 degrees to absorb her comment.

Two more minutes went by and possibly two of the customers took a sip of their coffee. I leaned over to Velma and whispered, my lips hardly moving, "This could be some kinda Candid Camera setup. Casually look around and see if you can spot a hole that could have a lens behind it." I did the same; we spotted nothing. With my hunger and lack of sleep I'm not sure if the *aigs* thing repeated again or not, but shortly thereafter, we got up slowly – to see if that might generate some service – and left. We were there over ten minutes. I didn't see anyone served. I didn't notice most people even drinking their coffee. Had we stumbled into a totally stoned little group at 8:30am? What on earth could have been going on?

After the inaugural La Carrera in 1985, I decided to drive back to Oklahoma by heading east in Mexico, crossing the border at Calexico, which was smaller than a border crossing on a movie set, and go east by north to eventually hit I-40. Look, gang, there aren't that many nice paved roads down there. Hey, when you've run a Copperstate 1000 in Arizona, taken back roads to California two dozen times, and laid out and put on a few one-thousand mile touring rallies in New Mexico, you just have to figure you could again find that un-trafficked desert road I took toward home with long straights, beautiful sweeping turns, and occasional blind 40mph-max dives into arroyos. You may just have to figure that, but you'd be wrong. Where is that road? I've never seen it again.

Denise McCluggage tells of a time on a rally in the Eastern Bloc where they stumbled on an open but unpopulated Grand Hotel all marble and gilt in the *Back of Beyond*, just waiting for High Party Officials to drop in. Well, if I ever find my lost hotel I'll go inside, like Denise did, and not just whiz by.

Of course, if you're driving a new Morgan + 8, almost to Italy and skimming through the Alps in France? Switzerland? in mid-afternoon, you'd not really want to stop. I'd just had a fun dice with a Mercedes 6.3 sedan, all *burghered* up with a businessman in every seat. They saw me coming up behind and decided behind is where I should stay. *Gott Straffen England* and all that sort of thing. It was all in fun; they were smiling and waving, and I was finally able to discern a no-opposing-traffic bit out of a steep climbing right-hand switchback with the mountain on the left. I didn't want to violate the break-in rpm limit, but full throttle just once wouldn't hurt. So, as the 6.3 actually took the line (he could see that no traffic was coming, too), I took an apex so late that I think it was actually on the straight part and rumbled by on their right up the hill. We all waved, as they lit fresh cigars and dropped back.

It was mere moments of smugness later, that I swooped left over a hillcrest and saw, below the road on my right, a fairytale hotel. Not the castle kind of fairy tale, but the pale blue and cream kind, with thick round roof overhangs, and a sign with the same typeface as in old Mother Goose books. "I'm gonna stay there next time," I promised myself. And I will too, if I can ever find the blessed place!

Karen and I have taken a couple of backish-type roads to the Italian border, but no luck. I'm going to have to devote several days of taking one road after another, up and down, left to right on the map, until I've found the place. Lousy job, but somebody's got to do it.

Then there's the road I sort of deliberately lost, from the Sopraelevata 4-lane to my hotel in Genoa, to put my new Morgan +8 and myself on the boat for New York. How I miss the Italian Line!

It's a warm autumn evening and there's the sign: "Hotels Alberghi." An arrow pointed to the upcoming exit. Really? Here? Heck, I know where the hotels are! I start by taking the next exit. Hmm, trickier, than I thought. I eventually find the Piazza Corvetto and take a street that looks promising, then zigs and zags. Hmm, Here's the Corvetto again. Okay, next street to the left. That's not it. Maybe I can find – yes! Piazza Corvetto. That big road across the piazza must be it. Three lanes in my direction; it must go somewhere important, like the train station near the port and the hotel. Interesting – the street narrows to two lanes in my direction. Well, there's, of course, less room for streets down toward the port, which, of course, is the oldest part of town. Just as I finished the rationalization the street became one lane my way, three lanes in the opposite direction. Worrisome. Then! My lane is blocked and I'm directed to the right down a wide alley. People have to step back into the little bars and cafes as I rumble by. Another right turn and ahead I see the busy traffic of a real street! Except the exit is blocked by a pair of those fancy metal pylons!

Now I have to back up over a quarter mile. Bar patrons are applauding and laughing; all right – snickering. One hour has passed, story not over! Fifteen minutes later somehow I find myself next to my hotel, but one lane over from the driveway access. No problem, I'll cross this small square, run a bit up the road opposite, turn around and I'm home. Only when I get to the road opposite it's one way! And it takes me over a hill and, well, I got to the hotel. Don't remember how. Not in the best of moods, mind you, but nothing that a few minutes in a swell Italian bar can't cure. From then on, I've followed highway signs. Religiously.

Signs I follow, but long ago I got leery of taking route advice from strangers. Actually, on the very same trip where I learned that lesson, I also got conditioned against letting other people drive. I don't mean that I attempt to wrestle the wheel out of the grasp of someone when I get into their car, just that, well, after that trip, I feel better when I'm driving.

It was enroute back to Nashville after my first-ever victory, at the Hammond, Louisiana airport course, towing the Lotus 7A with my '61 Corvair Monza. Bill and I had decided to play it safe and gas up before we got on the Natchez Trace Parkway and headed NNE from near Jackson, Mississippi.

A friendly fellow customer asked where we were going (Nashville) and then asked the details of our route. "Up here a ways," we said. "we pick up the Natchez Trace, off onto US45 at Corinth, north to Tenn 100, east to Nashville."

"Hey, you don't need to do that," he informed us. "I towed a trailer to Nashville last month and the Trace is complete all the way." Hmmm. My map was two years old, but it didn't even show the Natchez Trace as *under construction* for the last hundred miles. But what the heck, Pryor, you take it from here and I'll sleep until the next gas stop somewhere close to home. So off we went, found the Trace, and headed northeast.

You should take the Trace, if you ever have the opportunity. Although the speed limit is 50, and lower in some places, it's free of commercial traffic and not all that many cars use it either. Sometimes there are no cops, sometimes lots. It now goes off I-40 from southwest of Nashville, across the northwest corner of Alabama to

Jackson and continues down to Natchez. There are frequent points of interest with interesting dioramas, plaques, views and suchlike. There's even a gas station.

Bill woke me to congratulate ourselves for deciding to stop back there at the Shell, because although we originally planned to stretch our fuel load to get to the one and only station on the Trace, not only would we have run out of gas a few miles short, the station would've been closed by the time we walked there and the Lotus had very little fuel left, assuming we'd had a means of getting the gas from it to the Corvair. Smug with the drowsy memories of my triumph, I dozed off to the thrum of those $20 J. C. Whitney duals. I awoke to a drum solo while being shoved against the seatbelt, and focused my eyes on a throng of saplings being mowed down by the front bumper.

"I didn't go to sleep! The road just ended!" Pryor beat me to the punch. Yeah, sure! But that's exactly what happened. Bill was cruising along about 60 on the velvet asphalt, when he was pleased to notice the roadway flaring into four lanes. He saw a thicket dead ahead, and, fearing a microsleep moment and erring on the side of caution, he hit the brakes at the same time he noticed an object, still on the pavement, out of the corner of his eye. Microsleep no, thicket, yes. The thing to one side was an ancient yellow stop sign with those glass beads in the letters – remember those? – propped against a cinder block.

He got most of our deceleration done before the wheels hit dirt; and thankfully be, the stuff we ran into was a little new growth from what had once been a heavy equipment parking area. We escaped with a few tiny dents in the bumper, and were both remarkably alert for the rest of the trip.

My last flicker of trust in strangers' travel advice was extinguished after a family promised me that I-40 was complete to Nashville from Memphis a few years later. It was daylight and I didn't hit any small trees, but I had to make a 14-mile backtrack on the *Interstate to Nowhere*. Since it wasn't patrolled and I was in my Vette, it didn't take long. So now I thank folks for their advice, smile, and drive off on my planned route. If there's a mistake, it is my very own personal error, thank you very much.

I used to have a tepid sort of superstition that if we had trouble with the towcar/trailer going to a race, we'd have no trouble during the race – inductive *reasoning* at its worst. Thing is, it was true in hindsight! Not that we would have problems in the race if we had zero problems on the trip. I think we drove too late a lot and thus developed weird ideas like that.

I lost a bridge once too, after I'd seen it several times. You Floridians should be familiar with it. Before the Interstate and the Florida Turnpike, going to Miami for the boat to the Nassau Speed-weeks meant driving down US 27, I guess. Somewhere down there, on a lovely 4-lane divided highway, a concrete arch bridge looms up in the distance. When you get close to it the roads split to go around it, and then resume their former proximity a little ways farther along. What is/was it a bridge over? Anybody go to jail for fraud? Did anybody ever drive across it – maybe the big wet place was filled in? If the bridge was already there, why go to the trouble of filling anything in? Boondoggle bridge.

Roads Worth Remembering

I might have lost some roads, but there are several I remember. I don't keep them in mind for their driving pleasure, although of course that's involved, but for the way they look from the driver's seat. My all time favorite is a bit of Wilshire Boulevard eastbound, just out of Westwood. The road curves left and right, dips and rises, all simultaneously in view, with lovely medium-tall buildings on both sides. At night it's magical; in daylight it's only lovely. There are also a few miles east out of Raton, New Mexico, also curvy and dippy. These roads fit into some arrangement of my brain. There are many places I really like to drive, but these roads resonate somehow, like yellow and orange marigolds clustered together. Northeast out of Amarillo the road is so brilliantly white that I like to drive it just for that.

I had a yellow Alfa Junior Zagato which I'd driven to California, and niece Kiki had both an Alfa Duetto and an Alfa Quattroruote Spider. She decided to move from LA to Tulsa, so Bill Pryor, Brian Goellnicht and I drove the three cars back. Big deal, you say, but here's the way we did it.

The slow car of the trio was obviously the Quattroruote. So it always led, with its windshield folded down and the driver wearing goggles. We took back roads as much as possible across California, Arizona and New Mexico. To give you an idea of how long ago that was (1971), a bit of our route that was dirt then, is 4-lane now. The Quattroruote driver drove on those deserted roads as fast as he dared, and the other two cars followed maybe a quarter mile apart, watching for a brake light flash that would mean cops. Maybe a fifth of the route was on interstate and I think we saw one patrol car on the whole trip.

If there was a mountain road that tended eastward, we took it. The trip took four days and they were solidly exhilarating (except for the Jr. Z. driver, who never got as much wind in his face as the drivers of the two convertibles. We'd planned on making a great entrance into Tulsa with our Alfa flotilla, but got separated in western Oklahoma somehow, and so straggled in hours apart. It was as thoroughly satisfying a hundred-hour period as I've ever spent, car-wise (not counting the Cento Ore di Modena).

The only problem we had on the entire Alfa trip was that Bill, driving the tail-end Duetto on that little section of dirt road, and therefore staying well back to avoid the clouds of dust kicked up by the first two Alfas, had the fuel pump quit working. We waited when we got to the paved part for a little while. Eventually no dust, but no Bill either. I drove back to find Bill leaning on the Duetto, smoking his pipe and admiring the scenery. After we diagnosed the problem, I took off my shoe and gave the pump a healthy whack and it started working immediately. Like I said, no more problems. Just good old-time sporty car fun.

My niece Kyra and I were in France in her 1750GTV Alfa, and while cruising about 90 were often passed by families in Citroens, Mercedes and such, who looked over at us in curiosity as to why we were going so slowly. Well, the redline on the Alfa was kind of low, at least for an Alfa, and I never liked to push things mechanically.

Later I found out why the low redline: Italy had passed a law stating that cars sold to those under 26 and over 65 (I think), couldn't go over 175kph, 109mph or thereabouts. So, Italian carmakers lowered their tach redlines to equal the specified speed in top gear. Nothing else changed.

That's the proper way for an industry to think. Compare that to the USA and the imbecilic 55 limit, to be enforced on all roads that had any construction or maintenance funds from the federal government. Well, there was a section of about half the Kansas Turnpike that had been built completely with private funds. Kansas said they'd leave that at 75mph, per the law.

"Oh no!" said the feds. "You're not in compliance with the spirit of the law." Kansas backed down.

What a bunch of chickenpoops! They should have said, "If you mean all roads in America, then put that in the law."

I drive a few tens of thousands of miles per year and whenever I see a Corvette on the Interstate, it, oh so rarely, is passing anybody. In traffic they are the least aggressively driven. Other cars pass them. Is it an awareness of their cop magnet status? Seems to me in general that there's a lot less of that *c.m.* stuff these days. I'll have to get a Z06 and find out for myself.

Somewhere I still have my little Corvette lapel pin that GM sent me when I got my first Vette. Buyers also got a subscription to Corvette magazine and even way before that national 55mph silliness it was amusing to read the articles about touring all sorts of places with straight roads leading to the horizon or twisty roads through the mountains, with never a reference to using the performance of your new 396 c.i./425hp Corvette. Apparently it was just a kind of a special car way to see the countryside. It wasn't too terribly long after those days when one could find a full-page Ferrari ad which showed nothing but the logo across the bottom of a close-up of the speedometer with the needle somewhere close to 300km/h.

Inspired by *The Slow Corner*, an article in *Road & Track* analyzing traffic safety in the northeast United States, I wound up with a half-cubic-yard of car safety books and articles from several different research institutions. And get this - the last year when Montana and Nevada had no highway speed limits, guess where those two states ranked in fatalities per passenger mile? 24th and 25th!

Smack dab in the middle of the 50 states! They were only that high because when you crash in one of those states it took a lot more time to get an ambulance to you and you to a hospital than it took in Wisconsin or Kentucky. Of course, Nader, Claybrook and even Elizabeth Dole (what kind of Republican is she anyway?) took no notice of any rational analysis. *Speed kills*. What rubbish....

Everybody should drive fast, really fast, once in a while. Yeah, I know: conditions permitting. And I agree: *All* conditions permitting. For Pete's sake, folks, don't do anything dangerous. By the way, my attorney did not tell me to state the above. Remember common sense?

Driving fast transforms you. You'll get your alertness back. You're a good driver right now, of course. And of course you're alert at 30mph or 50, whatever. You're driving a car, and looking out for stuff; but a nice 110-120 lope down an empty Interstate or western 2-lane gets the look way down the road part of your synapses working.

On a twisty road you can have a great workout by just staying in your lane – where you certainly damn well belong – but quick driving under twisty circumstances sharpens up mental gear changing from one physics problem (this turn) to another (the next turn). Long straights are great for learning how your vehicle feels in a high-speed panic stop, especially if you don't have ABS. Pick a definite point way ahead, blast toward it and try to judge the spot to nail the brakes to stop right at that point. The intensity of a few of these experiences will embed them far enough into your brain to make them together a valuable resource in an emergency, but check your tire pressures first!

Interstate – late afternoon or early evening. Somehow suddenly there're no cars ahead and nothing in your mirrors. No trucks. It's *your* road. Where did everyone go? How pleasant! If a single car goes by it simply punctuates your isolation and restarts it. For the icing on the cake, somebody catches you at a high rate of speed, so let them get a half mile or so ahead, to roust out Smokey, and settle in for a comfy 100mph gallop. You can cover a decent amount of ground at 100. Then somehow there's traffic, and you're back to normal velocity, but definitely awake.

Some traffic engineer somewhere must know what year it was when traffic density was lowest on paved highways (WWII and the gas rationing years don't count), and it has to be admitted that major arteries between and around cities were always busy. You can still find empty roads out west and even in a state as populous as Arkansas or Mississippi, so while more and more cars are sold, maybe in the "greater scheme of things" traffic concentrations just eddy and swirl and rise and recede across geography in a *fractal meets chaos theory* hydrocarbon dimension.

Oh well, it must be age, or a more relaxed driving attitude, but I don't press on as fast as I used to. The speed limits are more reasonable; traffic really moves along from Oklahoma on out west; and cars themselves are so darn quick that to feel like you're making one really work you have to put yourself at a lot more risk, both legally and momentum-wise. I'd like to know the insurance setups certain magazine journalists have: Usually Fast and Occasionally Arrested must make for considerable financial drain.

A fun part of youthful highway exuberance was that I'd had a radar detector since the late '50s. This particular model went off sale sometime in the '70s but I still have one or two around here someplace. It looks like a tan crackle finish box the size of a stack of three decks of playing cards. It hangs on the sunvisor and has a 3" wedge of plastic protruding from the front – the antenna. It had no adjustment besides the volume of the warning buzz, which I think was just the radar frequency heterodyned down into an audible frequency. Oh my, what a feeling of freedom for many years! Hear that buzz, stomp the brake. Ease along for a half-mile or more and there was Smokey with that big apparatus hanging on his side window. Give him a cheerful sports car wave, wait another half-mile, then nail it. There wasn't much radar development until that imbecilic 55 nonsense, but then CB radio more than made up for having to belong to the detector-of-the-season club.

CB was quite a polite medium early on in its history. Bill Pryor got chewed out in Los Angeles for saying either damn or hell in '75. Then it degenerated until in the mid-'80s, people who were wired on some chemical or another would keep up a filthy stream of talk for hundreds of miles. There was some base station near

Jacksonville, Florida, where a guy who sounded like Bluto in those Popeye cartoons kept up a steady stream of crud for as long as it took me to get into and out of range, driving past en route to the Daytona 24-hours. I heard him two years running. Then something must have put him out of his misery.

Late-night CB grin makers: the honey-voiced women jumping into and out of conversations with one trucker after another, not promising, not even hinting, barely, about accessibility of their charms. There was the quite rare, "I'm just a lonely blonde lyin' here by the fire with nothing on but this radio." At the far end of the social spectrum were the hookers broadcasting from the top of Monteagle Mountain between Nashville and Chattanooga. You can still pick up some stuff like this near the Amarillo truck stops. Thank God radio doesn't transmit actual physical contagion.

Yes, CB sure isn't what it used to be, but late at night it's still useful. "Breaker one-nine" is a time-warpism that no one uses, so "Westbound Yellow, you're clear for sixty miles" can get you "Ain't seen nothin' since Flagstaff," but if a convoy has a multi-sided conversation going, you'll more than likely just be ignored.

Towing back from the Monterey Historics awhile back I slowly gained on a 240Z painted that *spoiled hollandaise* brownish or-ange. The license plate read *Bunsie*. I picked up my CB mike to get more info on the pretty driver's claim to fame. She had "Love a Nurse PRN" on a bumper sticker so I knew she was familiar with evaluation of things anatomical. But she didn't have a CB. So I'll always wonder exactly how good a backside has to look before a lovely creature advertises it on her license plate.

Nice long open straight roads on a sunny day are fun when you feel like just flooring it, but I'm uncomfortable playing the '50s game of "wottle she do?" Well, these days, she'll do somewhere around 150. Okay, so I went 160-plus in the Miura and my three Corvettes, and near that in my lightly modified RX-7 twin turbo. Those were all *once* and a longish time ago.

You drive away from home in a *raw* car – something with the top down and at the very least no power steering – your rump reading the road through simple upholstery; powerful engine, but not too much, so you can use all of it from time to time. When you feel all this at the beginning of a trip, your mind expects an adventure.

A coupe? A modern GT or *sports* car? You might have just left home but you're taking some *home* with you in the comfort of the modern car. For the greatest reach and span of adventure, you must start from home, so you can go home and tell people about it

Why do I have an affinity for fundamental cars: MG, Triumph, ever so just barely a 190SL? When you get into a car like this, the spirits of its designers say, "We think that this is enough to get you to your adventure. Try it."

Going around the block can be as big a thrill as going around the world. Call that block, that little piece of earth, that smudge on the map of life, yours! I've done it in a simple kart, driven it in sports cars even fast and fancy ones around blocks all over the world that I wish I could remember. Mathematicians know of at least 11 dimensions that can be measured by quantum physics but maybe, just maybe, the existence of a 12th dimension is dependent on re-membering where you were on the block in that place you can't quite bring to mind in a year that escapes you at the moment.

Crashes and Near Misses

I don't think I'd be here if it weren't for Guardian Angels and I'm not referring to those guys in red berets. I mean the invisible ones. In the downstream pages I recount my few accidents, only one of which was a real dilly. Now think about it, how many incidents such as these have you had? Some crusty philosopher said that losing something was God's way of telling you that you don't really need it, so I'm very thankful to God for getting me through situations where I could've lost my life.

May, 1960, heading up to the Indy 500 in my Alfa 2000 spyder. I'd gone through Nashville from Tulsa, not exactly the shortest way round, to see if Bill Pryor wanted to go along, as I had tickets for a pair of good seats. Of course, I never bothered to call and tell him I was coming, so by the time I got to Nashville, he was out on a long date. I over-nighted in one of those $7 motel rooms then abundant, and headed up the road.

Somewhere in southern Indiana there probably remains that long, narrow 2-lane bridge over a sizable rail yard: a big, tall, skinny thing, almost Disney-like (Hey, I used to go out with her!). As I approached the narrowing-down transition section, over the bridge crest came a new Pontiac convertible: maroon, top down, four howling male passengers, smack dab in the middle of the road, at about 80. If I'd been five seconds ahead or he'd been five seconds behind, squish.

On a rainy night in Nashville in the Porsche Speedster, I pulled up in the inside lane behind, gosh, another Pontiac, at a red light. After a few seconds I decide to move over to the empty outside lane, not that the Porsche was all that likely to out drag the Pontiac, but, well, *just because*. I see headlights off slightly to my left in my mirror, hear a hissing wet-road skid sound for an instant, and – Wham! – a Ford knocks the Pontiac a car length into the intersection, just as the light turns green. Why did I move? You already know what I think.

In January of 1958 in the same Porsche, Don Neptune and I were returning from a *let's just do it* drive to L.A. Route 66 had occasional stretches of four-lane, and it was on such that we were creeping by a semi, which was throwing up an opaque wall of slush from the thaw of the one-foot snowfall the day before. The big snow berm on the road edges indicated that a snowplow had been through recently. The truck began slowing and I thought to myself what a nice guy the driver was to help us get by. Actually, it was his instinct of self-preservation, for as we emerged into clear air past his front wheels, there was a three-foot wall of snow where the plow driver had apparently decided it was quittin' time for the fast lane. I got my foot off the accelerator about the time we punched through, driving blind for a couple seconds, while the drift slid up and over the tiny windshield. We were now sledding through the foot of snow about 50mph, but the smooth belly-pan and the front wheels acting as rudders gave us a graceful arc back to the slow-lane cleared pavement. The semi had slowed to a crawl and no doubt was making plans to pick up survivors, so we opened the doors (side curtains, remember) and waved thanks.

It's a blessing that I've had so few crashes. It could simultaneously be said by some observers that this blessing came via the avenue of my being a timid driver. Yep, bunches of us guys (and don't forget the lovely Saralou Goldtrap) used to drive fast. Of course, cars in those days were much slower; 100mph indicated got you brief, but definite notice, when you told the gang at The Mug rootbeer drive-in.

Acceleration counted back then too – it took a lot less road for a friendly competition – but there was a definite priority given to top speed. If you could hit the peg or bury the needle on your (folks') car's speedometer, you rated. Since solo runs were scoffed at by one's peers, you needed one or two witnesses in the car with you for it to count. A girl or two, although unneeded ballast, helped in the driver's ego department, when they described the just-completed run with flushed cheeks and that now obsolete characteristic: *girlish excitement.*

Somebody had carefully marked off a quarter mile stretch on the mile-long straight from town towards the country club, starting at the convenient highway sign adjoining the entrance to the Mug parking lot. My Golden Hawk with its 275hp (SAE; optimistic) held the record, even before I put the McCulloch 5psi centrifugal supercharger under the hood. At the highway drags, no one was even in the same league when I'd slipped the 4.11 diff under the car, replacing the stock 3.31. I didn't leave it in for long after I twisted both axles, with skinny tires and no limited slip!

Stock, that lovely 352 c.i. Packard V8 managed to edge the second-fastest car, a car which surprised everybody. It was Don Neptune's pretty '56 DeSoto hardtop. It was pale yellow with a gray spear down the side, which had a slight lavender tinge. The Hawk was a stick (3-on-the-tree plus overdrive), while the DeSoto was a 3-speed Torqueflite with pushbutton control. The Hawk had a 3.31 axle ratio; we never even thought of looking in the DeSoto owner's manual to see what its ratio was. Heaven knows how fast it would've been with its medium-sized Hemi if it had twin four-barrel carbs like the limited production Adventurer, which came a year or two later.

My worst crash happened at the end of a drag race in an undeveloped industrial park in southeast Tulsa, running the Golden Hawk against an ex-John Zink NASCAR Pontiac (back when NASCAR meant showroom stock). I'd had an occasional brake problem at highway speeds – e.g. a coyote or a squirrel would run out in the road and I'd hit the pedal and it wouldn't go down more than half an inch and *nothing would happen!* A few whomps on the pedal and suddenly the brakes responded normally. This couldn't have happened more than three times over a few months.

I eventually took the car back to the dealer and told them to replace the distributor shaft bearing, and, drumming my fingers on the roof, said that there was something else important and when I remembered it, I'd call them. I didn't remember until it was too late – *way* too late.

That drag took place on a street ending in a T intersection. After the recent tune up, and with the timing where it should be instead of wandering about due to the sloppiness in the distributor, I ripped past the little stake indicating the end of the quarter-mile with 112mph on the speedometer. I must say that this was after the addition of the McCulloch supercharger, but without that 4.11 rear axle, which I'd bought complete – brakes and all – for about $120 brand new from Studebaker.

And now, back to our accident! I hit the brakes, and nothing happened. It was about 3:45pm, February 19, 1958. I'd had nothing to eat that day. My apartment, in an old house, reeked of dog poop from the landlady's two Great Danes who didn't get outside much. I'd had a disagreement with my girlfriend. I was enrolled in at TU and I planned to drop a course, but chose the much more entertaining idea of a drag race. It was a gloomy day.

If I'd had any sense, I would have slapped the shifter back up into second. I do remember hitting the brake pedal more than once, but I think eventually I froze on it, instead of pumping it again and again, while watching that big dirt bank approaching. With brakes, a month before at this same venue, I was able to stop more or less gently with a hundred feet or so to spare, but I'd used that hundred feet up in way less than a second, so I braced myself against the wheel and said "Sorry, Jim," to my passenger Jim Yates.

You may notice that when you fall asleep slowly on an airplane it seems as if the engines quit, because your hearing shuts off just a hair before sleep actually arrives. Yes, well, I heard the accident! That was probably because I had to run over a curb before I got to the dirt bank twenty feet beyond.

Jim had put his seatbelt on really tight; mine wasn't exactly loose, but not snug. Jim got a one-inch cut on his forehead from just skimming the dash, along with some hip bruises from the belt. I would've suffered about the same, but I had to deal with the wheel. I took a thumb-sized hunk out of the hub with my upper front teeth. It took four upper incisors out roots and all, broke off my canines, and did all this without even cutting my lip, let alone breaking my jaw. My loose belt resulted in compression fractures of three lumbar vertebrae.

The outer belts on the Hawk were connected to the trailing edge of the doors, (no one could rescue you, if you were unconscious), whose latches operated normally after the crash. Jim got out stiffly, and I rolled out onto the ground. With my back hurting (and I'd had lower back problems as an adolescent) I made sure I could wiggle my toes and move my legs.

Jim helped me stand up, and I could walk and sit down, but couldn't get up without help due to the pain. Upshot, I was in traction a few weeks, wore a brace for a few months, and got some nice false teeth. I was also 4-F, but I don't recommend this particular sequence of events as a means of avoiding military service.

There was another crash, again involving faulty brakes, at a National SCCA race at Lake Afton, Kansas, in 1972. To give you an idea of just how long ago that was, Dorsey Schroeder was racing an 850 Fiat spider in H Production! My race mechanic at that time was in the long tradition of people who worked on my racecars. They all mostly ignored what I told them to do, and since I was too lazy to face the minor task of getting someone who would follow my instructions while in my employ, I thereby brought lots of crap upon myself. It's annoying to continually make other people's mistakes instead of your own.

This particular young man was just itching to update the Mog's front suspension. Its sliding-pillar mechanism, lubricated by an occasional ballet-inspired toe push on a floor-mounted plunger which let engine oil squirt into the pillars' cylinders, along with the Mog's live rear axle, made the car handle like a large, floppy go-kart. Believe it or not, it was predictable in its sloppiness, and analysis of the tire wear showed that all four corners were doing their jobs.

Well, against instructions the kid converted the front suspension to teflon-lined cylinders with no provision for lubrication, a system which remains on the car to this day. I think. See what I mean? This stiffened the front suspension a bit, turning the car, with its limited slip diff, at anything less than full throttle, from an understeering pig to an *Understeering Pig*. That wasn't all he did, and that mod has no bearing on the accident. He also laid hands on the rear suspension. Now, there wasn't much he could mess up back there: the lever-action shocks had thicker oil in them, and there were small lowering blocks on the rear axle, but he got, in a phrase from *Close Encounters of the Third Kind*, "creative, not constructive." He decided to invert the backing plates on the rear drum brakes. To make them easier to adjust? To bleed? He unknowingly swapped right for left and vice versa? Who knows?

Anyway, the racing season, like most of them, had its ups and downs, and boy did I want to do well at the late-season Lake Afton Grand Prix west of Wichita, Kansas. My friendly nemesis was Dr. Charles Rogers in his Bugeye. There were several other H Production cars at every event in those sweet days, but Doc and I were usually the two up front pecking at one another in the way small cars seem to do.

Lake Afton had a 4,000+ foot front straight, slightly uphill and then slightly downhill. The Mog's aerodynamics weren't well-suited for that sort of thing, but I figured if I could get a good jump at the beginning of the race, I could pick up some useful tows from a faster class car, who for one reason or another might be starting behind me. Hmmm, how could I get that early edge? Although at the green flag the Mog, with its almost 20% advantage in displacement per pound of car weight would out torque most Sprites, I'd be in traffic, so the slipstreaming advantages of all those cars in front of me (and by the way if you ever turn right, as well as left, it's slipstreaming, not drafting) would be more than offset by the big clog in traffic for the first lap or so.

I took my MV Agusta for a ride over to the club house series of very closely linked turns on the backside of the course: a medium-speed left and then a right-left-right wiggle through intimidating water-filled barrels. This led into the wide open gentle zigzagging backstretch, flat out for all but the fastest classes, into a tightening right followed immediately by the near-hairpin right, back onto the front straight.

I figured that by going a bit too fast to make the last right by the clubhouse, I could shoot across a mildly bumpy lawn and re-enter the course without letting up. Not only was this path about ten yards shorter, but the dust kicked up when I went off into the little area, where cars occasionally dropped wheels off the pavement, would make any following car think I was going to spin back across the track, as happened occasionally, when a driver really wanted to stay on the track itself.

Gang, it worked like a charm! A few laps into the race, with Doc on my tail, I took a deep breath and shot off the road, full throttle, driver's left, at about a 20 degree angle to the blacktop. Great dust cloud! And Doc must've hit his brakes, because when I rejoined the actual track, leaping and bouncing, he was at least thirty yards farther back! What a tactician I was! And that TR3 or MGB right behind him, a victim of an early spin, was going to pass him before the hairpin and then give me a wonderful tow down the front straight! *Except....*

Thanks to the reversed rear backing plates and the full compression of the rear suspension as I raced across the grass, the frame or leaf springs had sheared off the bleed screws of the Mog's single-circuit system! I arrived at the hairpin with a dent in the firewall where the brake pedal had hit it, managed a downshift, which slowed me down a bit, and opted for the escape road to the left. Well, it was an escape road in my imagination. Although paved, I found it led directly to the lake's spillway, a nice section I could've easily taken at, say 5mph. My reflexes though, honed by (A) racing experience, and (B) no brakes, just twisted the wheel hard right and I went into a ditch.

Analyzing the situation later, I probably could have made it around the corner on the track, mostly sideways, and motored on gently to the finish sans brakes, as I did years later in a showroom stock RX/7.

This crash was like falling into bed. The five-point harness distributed the impact and the Mog's frame splayed outward ahead of the firewall, gaining additional resistance from the lateral tension shearing of both motor mounts. I climbed out of the car and walked back to the corner, just in time to see Dorsey Schroeder's Fiat 850 instantly splay out both front wheels when he hit the brakes and his tie rod broke. It's amazing how fast a car will stop when that happens!

Did I fire the guy who redid all these details? Me? Heck, no. He quit at the end of the season, a race or so later. I hope it was due to embarrassment.

But now for a crash that was all my fault. The car was my beautiful Abarth 2000SP sports prototype, a 1970 model, back when prototypes had two real seats and those cute license plate lights, as delivered from the factory. This was a vintage race in the late '70s at Sebring, where we'd run the car in three twelve-hour races when it was new.

This was the real Sebring, not that big kart track that's there now. A pair of mile-long straights connected by a corner of *pick your own* radius. The esses, Big Bend, the hairpin, and turns 1 and 2: nothing to hit on the outside of 1 and 2, but fast enough to be one of those real tests of *manhood* people talk about.

Gorgeous track and a gorgeous car, sitting there on the grid, among those common, good-peasant-stock Porsche 906s and such. My car had fouled the plugs enough while idling for ten minutes on the grid so that it had an almost total misfire over 5000rpm. I cleared it by turning the fuel pumps off intermittently until the hot lean burn cooked off the plug deposits without harming the pistons; and then I was ready to make my move. Unfortunately, on lap 4 the car ran way wide as I entered the high-speed left first turn.

Did I have a flat? Is that why the car went lumpity bumpity for fifteen seconds down the backstretch at 60mph on the pace lap? Did I have sense enough to pit? No! Why heck, I must have just run over some sand on the track or something. I whipped the car around in a tight right u-turn and set off after those pesky Porsches.

What had happened, boys and girls, is that the right front wheel wasn't steering anymore, so while I could make a normal-feeling hard right, and the car tracked nicely straight as I approached the esses, when I turned the wheel left the car turned just a bit, but not quite enough to avoid going off course and hooking the tirewall and bending the frame.

Ed Swart in California has the car now; a similar model to one of the cars he drove to the two-liter European Sports Car Championship. If I'd only zigzagged to see if the car felt the same in both directions I'd still own that beauty today. Sigh.

Finally, there was a memorable incident when I wasn't behind
the wheel. Don Hinkle, Ed Turner and I had just left Johnson's
Drive-In at the intersection of U.S. 75 and 60 and headed south. It
was one of those slightly crisp fall nights in the early '50s, still and
moonless. Don was driving his family's '50 Olds 4-door, two-tone
green with that exterior sunvisor of the period. The car had a recent
tuneup, and so, as teenagers were wont at the time, we agreed that
we really should find out if it would bury the needle on the
110mph speedo.

There were no cars on the road, high beams on at what passed for
ablaze in those days, and we passed the second one-mile-apart section line road where cross traffic might've been coming east from
Bartlesville. Then Don floored it. The three of us were in the front
seat – cars might've been wider in those days, but we were definitely narrower – and the new white concrete was an exciting blur
as the Rocket 88 kept winding. "There's a hundred and it's still
climbing," said Don after a quick glance downward.

"I'll watch the speedometer and you keep your eyes on the road,"
offered Eddie. From the outboard seat, I saw, far in the distance at
about 45° to the right, headlights approaching on the next section
road.

"See the lights ahead on the right?" I asked. I thought Don nod-
ded slightly, eyes dead ahead, both hands firmly at ten-to-two on
the wheel.

For a few seconds I stopped thinking. A primitive fear response?
I wasn't afraid, just curious! "It's on the peg!" exclaimed Eddie.
The approaching car was not going fast, even allowing for our
moving parallax. He'll see us in plenty of time and there's a stop
sign there too, I thought. We're still wide open and here comes the
intersection and – *He Didn't Stop* – and is turning left in front of
us!

Don locked up the brakes, as the citizen slowly ran the stop sign
and veered across our path. We passed him at about 30° of rotation
into our counterclockwise spin and our lights picked out a '36 Lincoln Zephyr coupe that might have been painted black when it left

the factory a decade and a half earlier. We did a remarkably smooth 210° to the left, with the tires offering a condensed operetta from soprano to basso, went off the road on the other side in a slight arc, and backed up a gentle bank.

Our momentum had carried us a couple hundred yards beyond the fated carrefour and we stopped across the street from a country beer bar, with several customers already outside and others caroming off the *Rainbo is Good Bread* screen door in their eagerness to catch some of the excitement.

We were instantly surrounded by applause, salted with "gollees!" (people didn't cuss in public in those days) and "Hey Merle did you see that?"'s. Our hearts weren't racing any faster than the time Billie Sue almost lost her top at the Sanipool. Youth rebounds so quickly, or, perhaps, just doesn't recognize when it is nearly squished like a bug.

Numerous beers (all longnecks back then) were proffered, but we figured it'd be for the best if we all went to my house for roast beef sandwiches and cokes. We helped Don clean out some dirt and grass from the rear bumper valance and called it a night. Half a century plus years later I hope it's not too late to say, "Thank you, Lord for now and then!"

Historic Rallies: Better Cars,
Better Food, Better Wine

I can't be the only one remembering the thrills I got as a youth when reading evocative place names or phrases: Santa Fe, Eagle Pass, somewhere beyond the west, tickets on the Super Chief, the Targa Florio, Julie Newmar. I could go on and on (and often do) and so could you.

I'm an odd sort of snob. I don't want everybody hip to Jaguar and Ferrari, but by now that's a hopeless case. They're just big businesses. My gang knew about them and craved them because of what they did, not because of slick up-market advertising campaigns. I most certainly don't mind all the play the historic *Mille Miglia*, the Monterey Historic Races and Goodwood get, though. There's more than enough of anything at those events for all and sundry to appreciate. Anyway, the ad guys will never hype Mugello, the Targa Florio or Bristol cars. Or, in fact, lots of the vintage races in America. Never mind *see and be seen*. Just go see them.

Some have come and gone, like the truly wonderful *Coppa d'Italia*: three hillclimbs and a five-lap race every day for four days. No repetition of venues, and you were in your nice hotel early enough to clean up for dinner.

Karen navigated the '89 Coppa for me and quickly learned who likes whom best from among the participating nations. At each checkpoint the navigator gets out of the car and watched the official clock on the checkpoint desk with the objective of slapping the car's timesheet down on the desk at the exact second the clock indicates the car's perfect arrival time. Our overall position put us in front of a German team and behind an Italian team – we were lined up nose to tail waiting for our chance at the clock and could pull up and to one side to check out the car close to the timer's table if we so desired. Karen noted an emerging pattern: Italian team zeros every checkpoint. We're off a second, sometimes early, sometimes late. The Germans are always two or three seconds off. This went on for four days! Karen figured we would win the non-Italian Congeniality award.... which we did. *Most Simpatico Team.*

Now she refuses to do anything but hold the route book so I can read it, like a page-turner for a pianist at Carnegie Hall. And just because I threw a fit at her missing a turn to a checkpoint on Mt. Etna in Sicily on another rally and practically threw her out of the Cooper so I could storm back down the mountain at full speed before the checkpoint closed. Missed it by about 15 seconds. To this day she claims hardship even though I left her at the mountaintop bar (believe me, it's not there any more!) with a bunch of English-speaking German rallyists for company.

I recommend the *Cento Ore di Modena*, four days of driving near Modena with a few laps of the Fiorano track thrown in, and, when I was there, dinner amongst Sig. Righini's incredible car collection. Is there no limit as to how many supercharged prewar Alfas one man can own? How he got them is a great story, but not for here.

The *Coupe des Alpes* is a fun, three-day run from Evian in France over a couple dozen of the highest Alpine passes, winding up in a luxury hotel on the Riviera.

You really shouldn't miss the *Liège-Rome-Liège*. Although it doesn't necessarily start at Liège or go to Rome, the route takes you through several countries with TSD checkpoints and tulip rally instructions. It is really, really fun, scenic, and all that good stuff.

If you like the sensation of beating yourself over the head with a steel mesh bag full of old stopwatches, the *Rally des Alpes* is for you. It's several days and a few countries' worth of rally dilemmas. Whenever you see the registration line full of old open Alvises and Bentleys full of grizzled Brits with briefcases full of local maps and wearing enough stopwatches to fill up that bag I mentioned, you know you're in for a real job. For a non-speed event their scrutineering once was tough enough that a couple people had to go have panels welded into the rusty spots in their floors. That's the Swiss part, I guess. They claim it is the toughest historic rally in Europe, though, so give points for full disclosure.

The *Giro di Sicilia/Targa Florio* – piggybacked long and short rallies – is very nice too. Everybody should run the Piccolo Madonie circuit once in their lives; just remember in the good old days it was about ⅔ as wide and cambered.

The *Kitzbuehler Alpenrally* in Austria does a clever thing. Tech inspection is also where they select the cars for the concours at the end of the event, and it's the only rally where I've been given a pair of socks (amongst other souvenirs) with the rally logo on them. There was also a nice shirt, but only for the driver. In the years I've been away maybe they've added underwear. Who knows? This rally is where you'll get stuck behind a nice Teutonic sort in his 300SL or BMW507 pootling along at the average speed designated, totally oblivious to the narrow mountain track just ahead, where Fangio himself couldn't maintain 50kph.

I was behind the previous year's winner in a Jag, who honked and pulled out to right and left trying to get by the German, who then sped up as the Jag found a wide space to pass; they both over-shot the next turn, but by golly, I didn't. The Jag out-dragged the Merc in reverse and when he caught me, I waved him by, with a *thumbs up*. He was laughing and so was I.

You could also check out the *San Remo Historic*, the *Coppa Milano-San Remo*, etc. etc.

There is a bit of overlap, but it's safe to say that, if TSD and/or track competition is involved (you run TSD laps on tracks too in many rallies, as fast or slow as you want, but trying for identical lap times), the more serious the competition, and the more likely you'll need an FIA certificate for your car, saying it is what you claim it is.

Lots of the *fun* rallies simply grade you on not missing check-points. In other words, you car's reliability is the only factor (besides a total ineptitude with the route book) in getting an award. So look in the international vintage car magazines and email or fax the organizers. They love to have Americans in their events!

Down Mexico Way, 1985

The inaugural *La Carrera* recreation took place in October of 1985. That first race started at the arch at the very edge of the little town of San Felipe, Baja California, on the gulf of the same name. It wasn't so much a leap of faith to go down there, so soon after the Mexico City earthquake had cut off all communication with the event organizers, it was just thoughtless optimism on my part. So Peter Egan and I drove down in my IMSA street-stock RX-7, leaving his wife Barb in Ensenada to do social studies at Husong's. We noted only a few dangerous spots, and retraced the course a couple times to see if some dips in the road could be taken at top speed. They could.

We also realized that fuel was going to be critical. Not because of the local Pemex concoction at the single station in San Felipe, but because we might just run out. The 120 plus mile course length was about the max range of the car at full throttle.

The staff and onlookers at the Pemex station were in a frenzy on race morning when I announced our intentions to fill up with the standard semi-kerosene grade swill instead of Super. They did everything short of importuning the Blessed Virgin (although someone kneeling by the Coke machine may have been doing exactly that) to convince us that our engine would be a useless lump by the time we got to the first turn. They did give themselves some leeway there. The first turn was a fast 90° left some twelve miles up the road.

As a Mazda dealer, though, I'd been assured by our service rep that octane be damned; with the extreme quench areas in the '84 non-turbo rotary engine, any petroleum product with viscosity low enough to get through the fuel pump would provide more power than American regular gas. So, with blessings showering upon us, and only the most halfhearted attempt to shortchange us gringos, we headed for the start line.

Because of the conditions of geography and recent calamity, there weren't any communications between the start and finish officials. GMT or WWV or suchlike radio time signals were to be used to send us off and clock us in. However, several vehicles ahead of us either hadn't showed or were non-starters, so we were flagged off seven minutes before our official start time.

We were assured that the army would make sure that no other vehicles would use the road while we cars and our motorcycle-racing brethren were having our few hours of fun, but Peter, I, some luggage, and a brimful tank had just reached the serenity of about 5,000rpm and climbing in fifth gear, when down the middle of the road toward us came an ancient camper shell mounted on a late '40s-vintage red (once) Ford pickup. It lurched and teetered toward the shoulder to give us racing room just as we hit a small depression that, at speed and with our full load, ripped off the bottom of our front spoiler. "These people really know how to close a road." commented Egan, as a glance in the mirror showed the driver scrambling from the truck to pick up his souvenir of our passage.

The race went well. It usually does when you wind up winning, doesn't it? On that long, uphill straight from San Felipe, with the RX-7 loaded to the gunnels, we actually got a beep from the up-shift buzzer. We were at redline in fifth, thanks to gas with octane low enough to suit the rotary's peculiarities. When we got up in the hills, I resorted to the old touring-day-at-the-Nurburgring trick of watching for clumps of spectators. *They* knew where we were most likely to go sailing off a cliff – and they were right! A couple times, when I wasn't quite sure if the corner was as tight as it looked, I relied on input from Peter and his Formula Ford experience. When he'd really plant his foot on that imaginary brake pedal in the passenger footwell, I knew for sure it was time to drop anchor.

We made it to the finish with the low fuel light on and the needle bouncing off the bottom peg, and after checking in we crept into town to fill up and compute that we had the better part of a gallon left. Peter looked at our time sheet, where they had not corrected for the seven-minute early departure from San Felipe. "You know," Egan mused, "next year Dan Gurney's gonna be killed in a Ferrari, trying to better our time!" But, darn it; they got it right in the final published results – nothing against Dan!

Our biggest competition came from some guys from TRD in a nicely hotted-up Mister Two. They ran out of gas, we heard, after they'd knocked off the mounts for their special front antiroll bar in the same dip that ate our spoiler.

We finally sold the RX-7 at the dealership, and I wrote up its history for the purchaser: Ran the first IMSA street-stock race at Sebring, qualifying fourteenth out of a whole lot, with absolutely stock suspension. It also won a pair of Escort radar detectors for me and co-driver, Chris Ally, as the car with the greatest improvement in position from the first to the second half of the second One Lap of America (easy to do when you're stranded in a snowstorm for nine hours). And, of course, it was the winner of the inaugural La Carrera. For some reason it always was a slug off the line, but top end was great.

Anyway, after the big win Peter and I serendipitously retrieved the rest of our luggage from a helpful crewman in another car, who was about to head for Montana with all our stuff. Went to the prize giving, had dinner, signed autographs for the men's room attendant (he probably wanted a tip instead) and split up.

Firsts: The Historic Targa

If you have the chance to go to the first iteration of an event, take it – somehow the pre-event fretting by the staff is released into *laidbackness* when the thing actually gets started and people are too tired to think up any more regulations. It wasn't for that reason that I looked forward to running in the first Historic Targa Florio back in 1986. The original event was simply so wonderful (the people, the food, the roads) that I just couldn't miss its revival.

These days it seems like every semi-major car club in Italy is putting on an event over the Piccolo Madonie circuit. It was an event with the best safety record of all the famous circuits, but it was halted after 1973 for "safety reasons!" The problem, of course, was that cars, even way back then, were warping themselves into machines that could race only on smoother and smoother tracks. This resulted in the ultimate sports illogic: You have to change your racecourse (which was obviously there first) or we won't come race on it. Since the Targa was pretty unchangeable, it thus could no longer be a part of the world sportscar championship. Ridiculous!

So Bill Pryor, his wife Ellen, Sally Clayton-Jones and I set off for Sicily. You should have been there. You could have entered with a teensy old Fiat (Abarth, that is) and you would have been more than welcome. To keep vintage enthusiasts from squashing bambini in the three towns the course traverses, the event was run in three laps, broken into flat-out competitive sections which stopped short of the towns which were more or less "transit zones" to be traversed slowly.

This allowed plenty of time for refueling (there was a station smack-dab on the course itself), potty stops (but if you wore a Pirelli cotton driver's suit you had to go local and pee at the side of the road), espresso and a wiener – *a wiener?* – at a refreshment wagon. Of course, whenever you stop, people give you all manner of things to eat and drink. They barbecue some mighty strange vertebrates and invertebrates in Sicily.

Before the event Bill had taken the car, the Cunningham C3, out for a lap, and he never returned (faint background music *MTA* here). The Panhard rod had broken, and a few locals in a Fiat had pulled up and insisted that Bill get in the car. He put on a big smile to mask his suspicion that a kidnapping might be taking place, but they took him to the family home and plied him with wine and local cheese. The cheese was hacked off a large slab on a side table; for a moment Bill thought it was a piece of sandstone to repair their front walk.

As a parting gift they gave him a brand new Italian mail sack, which I have to this day. Now, how would a family of goatherds in the Sicilian hills come by a new mail sack? Better not ask.

The same MO was appropriate a few hours later, when a charming local young man named Marcello led us to a place to have the Panhard rod repaired. With my feeble Italian, Marcello managed to communicate to me that he was in the legal drug delivery business, with a route through all the small Sicilian hill towns. I see. He wanted to drive the Cunningham to show me how well he knew the roads, but I humbled myself and told him I was terrified just driving myself and would undoubtedly faint or throw up as a passenger, while he demonstrated his mastery of the terrain. That pleased him, and he took us to a local bar run by the Latin twin of Harry

Dean Stanton. Marcello said his uncle was the sheriff and his father the *Capo*? "*Syndaco?*" (Mayor) I asked.

"No." Marcello replied firmly. "*Capo.*" Better not ask.

The barkeep, upon understanding that I was Russian, inquired if I was a communist. Upon my vigorous denials, he looked furtively about, and then whipped out a life-size pewter bas-relief of Mussolini from under the bar. One drink later (the *aperitivo della casa* seemed to be *grappa* and Tang) he showed me his brass fasces mounted on red velvet. A helluva souvenir to take to Oklahoma, I thought, but I realized that offering to buy it would have offended him deeply and thus wouldn't have done me any good either.

The event was great fun, although in a bureaucratic mix-up complementing the one at the start (the cars were started at 1-minute intervals, just like the sainted Targas of old), when only the first 15 or so cars departed in assigned order, the vehicles were kept in impound for hours. I managed to find a drivers-only tent with champagne, brandy (and twelve bottles of pop delivered by mistake) and lots of little salami sandwiches on gum-tearing hard rolls, so all in all, it was plain swell. Of course, there was a big poolside party at the hotel with lots of roasted Kliban sea creatures, plus lots of fireworks. They have a neat non-OSHA tradition in Sicily – the rockets explode about fifteen feet above ground.

Yes, they do things differently in Sicily. They are very kind – at their events they provide an English translation of the rules in the entry form. The catch is – those aren't *all* the rules. Case in point: At the start of this very Historic Targa Florio, people were zooming off in their cars, at one-minute intervals, almost like the real race. Some cars had just the driver; some cars carried a passenger, helmeted and belted, of course.

A proper English gentleman pulls up to the line in his Cobra, with his wife beside him in matching driver's suit and helmet; a well-turned-out *equipe*. The starter gestures for her to get out. Confusion. Astonishment. Start time is not many seconds away. An official opens her door and takes her arm. She jerks away. Voices rise, unfortunately in two different languages. Shouting now. The Cobra burps and the carb catches fire; meanwhile two guys are trying to undo her seat belt and get her out. Fire extinguisher goes off and a fistfight is narrowly averted.

Why did this happen? Well, because in the *Italian* regulations, you could only carry a passenger if you had a rollbar completely spanning the cockpit. The Cobra had just a driver's hoop. Later that afternoon most of the acrimony was dissolved by a couple liters of *Vino Corvo Rosso*, but not all of the acrimony. There'll always be an England, you know.

In one respect the Sicilians' attitude toward the British can be excused. If I'd had General Montgomery sneering his way across my artichoke patch a few dozen years ago, I'd probably do the same.

Our actual performance in the event can be summed up pretty easily: no trouble, fuel consumption a bit higher than expected, lousy brakes due to my driving away from rest twice with the handbrake engaged and thus temporarily warping the rear drums. Can you believe my co-driver (not Bill) did the same thing at the beginning of the last real event in '73 and thus put us out with a blown rear brake seal in our Lotus Europa – I have been a Lotus dealer twice, for Pete's sake. Anyway, I had the indignity of being passed at the same place on one particular stage on each lap by two locals in a Lancia Aurelia coupe being driven by a proper '60s-era-type Dago maniac.

The Velvetouch linings in the Cunningam's drums never faded, and at about ¾ normal braking retardation the back brakes would stop rumbling and the axle would start hopping. This crude antilock system not only looked dramatic, but several times it also introduced enough randomness in my direction of progress to blow out a half-century of accumulated plaque from my arteries.

A couple people in our class blew up or broke down and so we would up second in class and were given a couple of silver plates by lovely young things.

The formal prize-giving dinner was great. We missed the cocktail hour because our bus was late, but we fortunately arrived just as the dining room doors were opened. I told the Americans I was with to grab the first large table and we flopped into chairs at the big round table next to the door. Place filled up in less than a minute.

Then the fun started. You see, a bunch of wives thought they could stake out adjoining seats for their spouses who were finishing off their *Camparis* in the bar. Not in Sicily, buddy! Strangers smiled and brushed the ladies' hands aside and sat down or occasionally deliberately sat down on the hands. Then the husbands arrived. There were no more chairs, so the little Sicilian waiter threw his wiry body against the barely open door. Arms waved through the crack, grasping at his uniform. It looked like an outtake from that surrealist old French movie *Beauty and the Beast*. Imprecations and cursing!

The situation looked hopeless, but I knew it would work out before the doors were ripped off the hinges. Sure enough, *maitre d'* materializes, speaks through the crack in the door, another dining room is opened just across the hall, couples are reunited and just as calm descends so do the antipasti. The Italians have social timing down pat.

Las Millas Enchantadas, The Rally of New Mexico

It must have been the first touring rally we put on in New Mexico in the early '90s when we invited Brian and Marian Redman to be the Grand Marshals and storytellers. Brian was as good as he ever was and ever will be – superb. But according to wife Karen, off the record they were hysterical.

The late and wonderful Bob Sutherland (his Colorado Grand was, of course, our inspiration) had loaned us one of his new Maxton sports cars, that sparkling little device with the general shape of a Bugeye, but with the heart of a Mazda rotary. Brian and Marian drove it one full day with its lack of air-conditioning and its wind-tunnel-in-the-cockpit aerodynamics. They asked to drive the luggage van the next day, so I got the Maxton.

Karen felt as an organizer, she should ride with them (and she does enjoy her air-conditioning). If I could remember all the stories she told me that evening I still wouldn't repeat them, seeing as how they involved many details of their courtship and marriage. One included Brian's clothes being hurled into the swimming pool (by Marian) at, was it Monaco? Stuff like that, but much more intimate. While tale after tale spun out, to Karen's continuous breathless laughter, Brian was drifting the Econoline around and through the turns on the mountain roads that were that day's route – none of that shortcut to the next hotel, when the Redmans were in charge. We should have named the rally the *hysterical miles* instead of the *enchanted miles!*

Next morning I checked out the van. Plenty of oil, filled with gas. The interesting part was the tires: scrubbed about two inches up the sidewalls. You should have been there. I should have been there.

Plunk your Magic Twanger, Froggie

We also often meet people with lifestyles different from ours. One day on a rally in France, our cultural diversion/education was a tour of a cognac distillery. The huge vats and barrels of aging cognac exude vapors worth, could they be trapped and condensed by the entire industry, dozens of millions of dollars – a month! Those heavenly vapors are called, appropriately enough, the *angels' share*.

As we walked into an airplane hangar-sized warehouse and all took a deep breath, "How wonderful!" said a British lady of a certain age. "It smells just like Christmas!" How can we manage to spend the holidays at her house?

Did you know that in France, when you go into McDonald's to have a beer, there's classical music in the background? Karen and I came rumbling into Orleans, in France, in the Cunningham, enroute to the Channel and then England and then home. In a shop window was a little poster advertising a racecar spectacle the next day.

I drove over to the headquarters trailer in the morning. I wanted to run my car? Yes, but you mean I can? Of course! And since you are American, there will be no entry fee! Here are your numbers, *mon ami;* your practice session starts in a half hour. We put the Cunningham in the paddock and while I adjusted the brakes and checked the fluids, a local, apparently on an outing from the nearby laughing academy, seated himself in the car and made engine noises. Interrupted, of course, by laughing wildly.

During the whole weekend, first person to the grid was on the pole. Few people wore helmets. There were Alpines, old MGs and a spindly-wheeled cycle-car, including granny seated crosswise behind the driver, with her ancient unbuckled leather flying helmet rippling in the wind.

"You have a fast car, *m'sieur*. Please do not go out of control." No sir, I certainly won't, especially at the u-turn around a fountain, where water was blowing on the marble sections, which were part of the course. Spectators, including a lady with babe in arms, stood on the outside of the course, behind two-foot-high plastic wedges partially filled with water to keep the wind from moving them. After my session was over, I asked an official how this event could be sanctioned with such delightful disregard for modern safety precautions. "But this is not a race, you see; it is a demonstration, and the rules are quite different!"

Could we do something like this in, well, Akron maybe? String some yellow tape between the lampposts and prop up the odd hay bale against the bases of the statues and everybody get in his old car – an XKE is old enough – and thrash around an .8 mile circuit through the streets of downtown? Maybe in *New* Orleans....

Having become bored with having this kind of car fun, I just spectated a week later at a similar event in some smallish town, where there was two-way race traffic up and down a six-lane street. Part of the course was a left turn through a deep and door-less garage with perhaps a fifty foot opening. Prewar cars, hopped up Renault R8s and the usual Alpines partook in what apparently was just a Sunday afternoon's sport. Concession stands, of course, with cotton candy, scary-looking sausages and crepes. You can't have an event in France without crepes.

Driving around Europe, especially France, the thought of food as merely sustenance does not apply. Thinking of comparisons of Mc-Donald's, Burger King, Steak n Shake, Waffle House – not on The Continent, pal. You are going to find some restaurant, some *trattoria*, where the food will do more than comfort. It generally takes a longish time, but it will satisfy you like a good massage – or at least a foot rub. Eating in Europe is somehow beyond *food*, and yet to the proprietors, dedicated though they may be, it's just another day at the office. Yes, and high standards are a matter of course.

We were visiting friends, Jean and Sandy Ortlewell in southwest France who were having some renovations done on their 400-year-old farmhouse, when lunchtime crept around. We had: excellent local sausage, excellent local bread (baked that morning) and *tapenade*, accompanied by a nice local wine. All this was chewed and swallowed leaning on a counter in the kitchen or sitting on a wide windowsill. It was much more than pleasant. In the States it would have been a heckuva picnic.

But outdoors, ah! The *common laborers* had spread a clean cloth taken from one of their several hampers over planks spanning a pair of sawhorses. On this naperied table they set out red and white wine, a few small cheeses, a thermos of soup, a platter of cold meats and silverware! Okay, it wasn't really silver, but it was metal cutlery. The scene was a demonstration of one of many automatically performed French customs that unites their society: food is not to be slighted.

With age, though, French cuisine has lost a step. In the early '70s, the major *autoroute* (toll-road) stops had, besides gas and an espresso bar/cafeteria/lunchroom, a Jacques Borel restaurant. My niece Kiki and I decided on a very late breakfast and saw that well before noon the doors were opening to ol' J.B.'s, so in we went. The *maitre d'* was wearing striped pants and formal jacket. The food was, of course, exquisite. We had to order dessert at the same time as the meal, because they were built to order, and we decided on the volcano. This is the French name for baked Alaska, which, for you unfortunates who've never had it, is ice cream inside a cake, with meringue toasted on top, and flaming brandy running through the valleys of said meringue. Instead of the all-vanilla of the standard version, they offered the ice cream and brandy in your choice of many fruit flavors. When I asked how they could store that many kinds of ice cream, I was told that each order of ice cream was made and frozen while the customer proceeded through the meal. *Autoroutes* don't have this sort of thing any more. We did hit an American-like stop recently in the backwaters of central France (yes, Virginia, France does have backwaters), where there was a "fast food" menu! Hamburger steak, tripe or brain omelets were included on the menu, and if you didn't get your food in a half hour, it was free! I guess *fast* really depends on the native culture, doesn't it?

You should watch your speed on the *autoroutes* (81mph limit with some leeway) too, because some legislators are suggesting the adoption of the Finnish style of fines, based on your taxable income per year per your legal paperwork. The dotcom king of Finland, doing over 100mph in a 60ish zone, got fined over $30,000. Does this practice mean that, if you're on welfare and are stopped for speeding, the government gives you money?

The Italian Job: Somebody's Gotta Do It

A few years later we were asked to take the Ferrari 3Z to Italy for Ferrari's 50th anniversary party in '97. We got past all the little problems like lost car keys, missing rally passes, missing rally routebook, etc. etc. and were having dinner in Modena after the close of festivities. The waiter walks up to us. "Gonzales!" he says.

"Arutunoff!" I reply.

"Argentina!" he blurts.

"Oklahoma!" I riposte.

Finally, he decides to form a complete sentence, "Those people tell me you are Froilan Gonzales, the *Wild Bull of the Pampas*." I told him I was a decade younger, several inches taller, and several kilograms lighter, and, sadly, had never driven a Ferrari F1 car. If I'd played my cards right, Karen and I probably would have had a free dinner. I knew enough Spanish to write a nice personalized autograph, too. You can miss fun things when you are instinctively honest.

Late at night from time to time, Karen will affectionately refer to me as *her Wild Bull of the Pampas*. I give her a grateful snort!

But once again, I digress. Karen had fun back at our villa-hotel elevator. We were the only guests who were not members of the German Ferrari Club. The hotel had obviously converted a coat closet into the elevator. It was the biggest elevator I've seen in a little hotel, and brand new. So, Karen comes up behind three *Frauen*, as the elevator door opens. Karen has a couple big heavy bags of souvenirs. Gerda and Ilse and Brunhilde step into the elevator, stop, and turn around; leaving 25 square feet of empty space behind them. Karen says, "excuse me" and pushes her way in.

On the slow trip upward Karen said the scene was like something out of an Ingmar Bergman movie; she was facing forward and the women on either side of her had turned their heads 90° to stare silently at her profile. Karen smiled and said, "I'm sure your mothers taught you that it's impolite to stare," figuring they knew English. She said their heads whipped forward so quickly they adjusted their spines down to the third thoracic vertebra – and they moved aside to let her disembark. I've said it before and I'll say it again, "Don't mess with an Indiana University Basketball Queen."

On to the '99 *Liège-Rome-Liège*, where the competition actually only went from Liège to Rome (I guess you could have driven back to Belgium, if you wanted), there were a couple guys in an XK140. One was a Chicago businessman named Murray, bearing a resemblance to a meatier Richie Ginther, but reserved – almost shy. The other was a Fittipaldi-look-alike gynecologist with offices in Chicago and Rio. There's a story there somewhere that could put Richard Gere's *Dr. T. & the Women* on the trailer.

The 1,300-km event through Belgium, Luxembourg, Germany and down into Italy is kicking off from the stately courtyard of the *Halles des Princes*. With typical Belgian hospitality, although it's just past sunrise, the big marble bathrooms in the Halles are not only open, they're heated!

The Jag has been overheating on the chilly drive from the hotel, so a bunch of us dive under the bonnet to see what we can find. They're not particularly worried, since they've never finished a rally and, in fact, consider themselves quite accomplished if they can get to the first night's hotel. Okay! The electric cooling fan is shorting out, and when it runs, it runs backwards, diverting cooling air from the radiator since it's mounted in front.

They have not a single tool on board. Their spare tire is worn to the point of uselessness, but that's okay because it's also flat, and – what the heck – they don't have a jack or a knockoff hammer anyway. These various situations are addressed with the contributions of a dozen other teams, and the L-R-L becomes blessed for the clueless team.

They get lost, of course, but only at the end of the day's run, when they can't find the big hotel in Strasbourg. It's not like you can't find anybody to ask directions from downtown late at night in a major European city. No, it's nothing like Chevy Chase's experience in *National Lampoon's European Vacation.* In these surroundings there're hookers on every other corner – and you don't even have to know the language.

Murray and his buddy decide that if they have to ask one, they'll at least ask a pretty one. *"Oui, M'sieur, je conn...."* – but let me translate for you, "I'll show you to the Hilton, but you must take me there in your pretty car."

"Gosh, honey, it's a two-seater and full of luggage."

"That's OK, I'll just sit on the cowl and lean back on the, so handsome navigator." The Jag had racing screens only, no windshield. And, she could've added, "I'll do a little advertising by letting my skirt, such as it is, blow back in the slipstream, since I'm wearing no underwear."

So, they pull up in front of the Hilton. She's whistling and blowing kisses to the porters, doorman and occasional guest. Not to be outdone, Murray blows the air horns a few times too, just in case somebody somehow missed their arrival.

Then $50 changes hands – hotel directions are expensive in Strasbourg after midnight – and after convincing the young thing that no, they absolutely were not buying her a champagne cocktail in the bar, they put her into a taxi to return to her battle station.

As a rally, it doesn't sound much like the Susquehanna Trail or Hundred Acre Wood, does it? You know, they actually finished the entire 5-day rally, and at the awards dinner, after the cocktails and champagne and after-dinner brandy, Murray seized the microphone and gave a marvelously coherent speech, in which he enthusiastically described the high-speed police-escorted run in heavy traffic through the hills of Rome to the Cavalieri Hilton high on the hill as, "The best fucking moment of my entire fucking life!"

His co-driver attempted to hush him up, but Murray kept broadcasting at 110db, "This is Italy! They don't speak English here!" which sent the waiters into tray-dropping fits of laughter.

While we drove through Belgium and Germany, we were just road users like other traffic. The first town we came to in Italy, though, had cops blocking off cross traffic, so we could blast through.

Here's a perfect example of Italian police attitude. In my Alfa Giulietta spider I came up behind a column of three Danish car/house trailer combinations. It was at the beginning of a long but gentle downhill, and as I checked things out two Jags and an Aston, also in the rally, pulled up behind me. I swung out and had a look. Way down at the bottom of the hill was a yellow storage building, a good reference point.

So, I dropped into third and went for it. As I began to pass the second car/trailer, I realized that what I thought was a building was a yellow tarp-covered load of hay being pulled slowly uphill by a tractor. I knew I could make it with a few seconds to spare, and I (obviously) did.

In the mirror I see the blue light on the escorting police motorcycle come on, and he passed the Brit cars and the trailers and – and – and zoomed by me, waving me along. Then we came up to a couple trucks and he waved me by, but as the much faster English cars pulled out, he held them back.

Lesson: If you're in a rally in Italy, drive a red Italian car.

The only blemish on the event was the final-day accident involving the oldest car in the rally, a thirty-something Morgan three-wheeler, crewed by two sporting gentlemen in tweed caps, briar pipes, the whole bit. They lost a brake cable on a steep downhill switchback, resulting in broken arm, sternum, ribs, and a punctured lung. All agreed their fate would have been worse if they'd had seatbelts in the car.

A further touch of good fortune was that the Medivac helicopter had broken down. The local doctor was indignant that they wanted to fly all the way to Rome, "I am the expert, because I always treat the many accident injuries on that road." He proclaimed, "For the mountain accidents I am the best!" Wives and mothers of the crashers sent word from the hospital that next year they'd be back on the rally, just as soon as they'd gotten out of hospital and un-wadded the Morgan.

A Five Rally Tour

I guess giving away that alloy Ferrari 250 SWB conditioned me to be a bit more careful, thank you Lord. This particular incident would not have exactly been a giveaway, but it would have been a very unpleasant but necessary transaction. Oh, it was close.

It was at the end of a stage on the 2000 running of the *Giro di Sicilia*, an event where you drive around Sicily, logically enough, trundling through very warm city traffic, while people trot alongside to look at and fondle your car. At night you get to stay in hotels where the air conditioning is turned off by the light switch! Obviously, the management doesn't want you to try to cool the room down while you're having a nightcap in the bar with the policemen, who travel with the event (they get to have champagne at the finale just like the competitors). But that also means that on a hot night, if you want to be cool – more accurately, less warm – you have to sleep with the light on. A dampened hand towel, folded over, makes a refreshing sleep mask.

Anyway, at stage end we were stopped in the usual long line, waiting for something. The Italians always know what's coming next, but it's surprise after surprise for me. The spitting image of the actor who played the young Italian GP driver in *Grand Prix* climbs out of his 911S and walks up to me. "I very much like your car," he says to me. "How much does a car like that cost?"

As this was several years ago, I tell him that a Lancia Flaminia Zagato in rough, but running condition (gee, I just described my car) back in the USA would be about $27,000. Then I say, "Oh, excuse me. Let me introduce myself."

He says, "I know you run thees car in the Targa Florio in 1963."

"I'm Anatoly Arutunoff," I continue, and as I extend my hand I laugh and say, "This doesn't mean I'm selling you this car!"

I snatch my hand back before we touch as he says, "Oh yes, it means I buy your car. I have the money at the hotel!"

Wheeee-yeew! A handshake would have made me several grand richer, and earless. He was from Sicily. *No sale* would have meant something similar for little old me. I bet that after they found my body parts, he would have wound up with the car in any case. Like the guy used to say in *Hill Street Blues*, "Let's be careful out there!"

Yep, rough but running. After three consecutive vintage events in Italy, a set of Hot Wires (thank you Alan Bolté), a fuel tank cleaning, a few dozen *pull off road when engine dies, yank fuel lines apart in several places, blow out crud, reassemble and never mind about the clamps*, the car ran nicely. At the start of my first event that summer, the first *Cento Ore di Modena* (100 hours rallying around Modena), the car died and refused to restart for awhile. A combination of perpetually clogging fuel lines and a set of points that looked like they were made of used wooden match heads had me under the hood and in the trunk about every half hour. At prize-giving, where I nonetheless won my class (there was no one else in it, which helped immeasurably), the rally chairman, Sig. Bompani, said in Italian, "A man whose car was always breaking down, yet he remained calm" and gave me a nice silver cup. There's a cultural note for you; Oklahoma hysterics are interpreted as calm by Italians.

By the time I finished those five consecutive historic rallies, I was actually the teeniest bit tired of the whole thing! Incredible! I'd even gotten the taste of gas out of my mouth. I must be honest, though, I didn't finish all of them. At lunch on the first day of the five-day *Rallye des Alpes*, I officially retired. Talk about work! I had no navigator and the instructions were in kilometers. Yes, I had a miles odometer with the tenths numbers broken and a 2.2% error. I momentarily planned to go ahead each day to the hotel and just enjoy the parties, but you had to run the thing to find the hotel. The hotels were not named in the routebook.

At the pre-rally party, I ran into a nice couple from the southeast coast of America I'd met ages ago, the Huwylers. Mrs. H. told me, "Last year on the first day, I told Hans just let me off somewhere and I'd take a bus to the finish and wait four days for him. I was in tears. He told me, 'Don't cry darling. We won't do this next year.' And dammit here we are again."

That should have been enough warning for me, especially since I got lost on the little warmup/practice rally that very day. The beautiful city of Geneva is on a big lake. I was in downtown Geneva. I couldn't find the lake. 'Nuff said?

Karen had warned me that the brochure said the rally was laid out by premier British rally designers, and I had previously told her that I'd never run another British rally. "But it's in Europe," I'd said.

"You'll see," she said. She was right, of course. British rallies are way too much work. I recall that someone said at the end of the first Scottish Malts rally, "If I want to get in my classic car and swan about looking at lovely scenery, I don't have to pay a large entry fee to do that. A rally is supposed to be a *test*." There are oh so many reasons God put them on an island.

The London to Monte Carlo Run

Also early in this century we were moving my stepson Trace out of his apartment in England and coincidentally it was at the same time as the first *Cannonball 3000*. (I'm sure Brock Yates wanted to go after them for the use of the term, but the international law ramifications involved would have made the Natalie Holloway/Aruba case look like a parking meter violation in comparison).

We had a rented, two-liter diesel Peugeot station wagon. Other cars in this illegal road race from Chelsea stadium to Monaco were mostly 911 Turbos, Ferraris – stuff like that. We also carried a load of our luggage and Trace's apartment stuff.

We left London early on a Sunday morning in mid-September. We were the 18th car out. Trace did not have a car in London, though he'd lived there a year and a half. All the cars that started before we did turned left out of the parking lot. Trace told me to turn right, so I did. What the heck, we had the slowest car in the field.

About a half hour later we were the first car to catch the photo crew car, which had left an hour earlier. Soon enough the fast guys blew by us; we were running an easy 110mph. We all met at the channel ferry.

In France, we took off once again in our original starting order. As we sped down the *autoroute* toward Paris, Karen passed us in the Eurostar TGV train. She said she was holding up her glass of champagne and waving, but since the train was going about 75mph faster than we were, we couldn't pick her out. We got to Paris, and Trace gave me detailed routes down narrow streets and up quaint alleys. As I've mentioned, he'd lived there as well, for six months, while attending the *Sorbonne* and sharing a big apartment in the *Mouffetard* with three girls and dating Miss Turkey – and he didn't have a car there either. We were the third car to arrive at our hotel. It was a combination of Trace's excellent navigation and the fact that a lot of the French strolling the streets of Paris amused themselves by giving the English wrong directions.

The entire group dined in a huge beautiful private dining room in the hotel just off the *Place de la Concorde*, and when Trace and I got off the elevator, we heard what sounded to our untrained American ears like football-hooligan cheers coming from that area. The *rally* was partially sponsored by British *Penthouse* magazine and the early arrivals had talked the Pets in attendance into topless arm-wrestling after the *hors d'oeuvres* and before the soup. The Brits were cheering them on quite loudly, and the waiters and even a large proportion of the kitchen staff were standing around the edges of the room enjoying the spectacle. Trace and I did too.

The next day we departed third, as befitted our arrival in Paris. All competitors had to go through the Frejus tunnel; and knowing we didn't have speed, we elected to take some hilly back roads and hope the fast guys ran into a traffic jam on the *autostrada*. Oh, well. The organizers and other entrants gave me a nice party – it was my birthday – at Monaco, and all's well that ends well.

The girl who walked into the pre-event party and grabbed my stepson's buns as she went past showed up to greet him at the final party from which they disappeared. She was an F1 driver's girl, but I won't say whose. I was young once and in Europe, but somehow it wasn't quite the same. Dang!

La Vie en Rose

On another occasion, we had been invited to show the Bristol 407 Zagato at the Bagatelle concours in the park of the same name on the outskirts of Paris. We'd driven the car across France and so asked permission of the hotel to wash it in their basement garage.

Not only was permission granted, the management told us that since there was no water outlet in the garage we were free to use the cartons of Evian water stockpiled in a corner at no charge.

We did a decent *club concours* cleanup on the vehicle. The only problem was that there was only one light, bright but well off to one side. Every seven minutes the light went out. We got pretty good at navigating the garage in total blackness to find the button that turned the timer back on. Both sides of the car looked pretty good when we emerged into daylight to drive to the concours, but as we approached I started to get stage fright. Major concours. Foreign country. The entry form did say that patina was welcome. Americans generally over-restore their cars and the French over-restore their antique furniture. Honestly!

When we pulled into the registration line, I relaxed. In front of us was a sleek Panhard Dynamigue coupe with paint flaking off in patches as big as my hand. We'd definitely been *out-patinaed.*

The ambiance was wonderful, the sit-down lunch was exquisite, and the only folks who didn't seem to be having fun were the judges from the American Ferrari club. A French judge climbed out of my car. "Very nice," he said, "but your tachometer is wrong." I pulled out the owner's manual and showed him its photo of the dash; he was pleasantly surprised. He handed it back to me. "We are all crazy anyway," he said with a smile, as he strolled away.

The Bristol came in second to the Bertone *Jet* Aston Martin (which had lots of pigment missing from inside its tail lights and some paint missing from the bare rear license plate mount). At this juncture a gentleman came up, told me he had a Zagato Aston, and a Bristol-engined something or other, and invited us to the following weekend's French Ferrari Club meet at the Dijon-Prenois track. We should have gotten a clue that things were working against us when the car was charged and rammed by a wild boar en route. The damage was not too bad and some French shoe polish almost matched when Karen smoothed it on the scraped paint

We got to Dijon on Sunday, about noon. The car could not be admitted to the paddock, since it wasn't a Ferrari ("The Morgan people are much nicer in this respect," a gate guard told us). So we strolled over to the lunch tent. As we entered, we felt the chilly breeze created by a hundred pairs of French eyebrows rising in unison. Who were these strangers? A man came over to tell me this was a private function, and while I was explaining our informal invitation to him, a woman (that was no lady) approached Karen, inspected the Palm Springs Ferrari event pin on her lapel, and then flipped her lapel aside. "If she'd touched me again I was gonna deck her," said Karen later. I've previously mentioned not to trifle with an Indiana Basketball Queen if you know what's good for you.

As we were getting back into the Bristol some people trotted up to us, including the gentleman who had invited us back in Paris. He was crestfallen, chagrined, all that stuff. "We know when we're not wanted," said Karen. "No need to apologize. Toly writes for a vintage magazine in America and this will make a great story." We grinned at them cheerfully as they made their flustered retreat. Their public personas might have needed work, but by golly, none of the guys I saw were wearing gold chains.

Curtain Call

We've never attended the jewel of them all, the *Villa d'Este* concours, though. This magnificent villa hotel on the shore of Lake Como is something you should experience, period. Karen and I actually experienced it for a couple days awhile back. We had to leave a day earlier than planned, because the whole place was being taken over for a European financial conference. The day before, we saw armored personnel carriers of Italian SWAT-type people stationing themselves here and there; we felt very safe.

Anyway, I guess you could say that we got to see lots of *interesting* vehicles at *Villa d'Este*. We were safer than we thought. About 2:00 am, Karen decided to go out on the balcony and smoke a cigarette in the clear, starry night. All the lights in our suite were out, as she carefully crept between the furniture to the starlit balcony. She took out a cigarette. She took out her cigarette lighter. She lit her cigarette lighter and a spotlight instantly nailed her, from a frogman in the water two hundred feet away. About the time I'd responded to her, er, exclamation, and caromed off stuff as I staggered toward the balcony, I saw her wave both arms and take a bow. Reminded me of Judy Garland. She stood up, waved again, and the spotlight went off. So what is her true destiny – law enforcement or showbiz?

Ah Europe! You may think you have laid the best of plans but the surprises of traveling abroad have their own delightful flavor in memory even though at the time you would have preferred a little less *c'est la vie* and a whole lot more *Voila!*

Random Thoughts

W hy is it that whenever you have the garage door open, leaves and stuff blow in on the floor? It doesn't matter which direction the wind is coming from. If the wind's blowing toward the door, stuff blows in. If the wind's blowing from the opposite direction the eddies whip around the corners and deposit about the same amount of trash. If you have two doors and open them hoping for some kind of extractor effect more stuff will blow in than blows out. Must be a cosmic lesson here.

Setting: The *Escargot d'Or* (golden snail); a weeklong rally all over Europe. Our new friend: a guy who'd started as a gofer in a major food company and wound up owning a seventh of it well before age 50. He then retired and for fun, started a restoration company, which also made C-Jag replicas. He closed that company when he realized how his employees were taking advantage, shall we say.

I asked why gumdrops and jellybeans tasted and felt different nowadays. Simple. Around the Korean War era the candy companies started using aluminum molds instead of wood (!) for gumdrops, which needed a different temperature of the invert sugar mixture, etc. etc.

The reason Coke and Pepsi taste different from the way they used to in olden days: substitution of corn syrup for cane sugar. Heck, he said, his humongous company closed its test kitchen, because whenever there were several alternative recipes cooked up for a new product, test panels inevitably picked the concoction with the most sugar – and folks wonder why we're fat.

Of course all eras have their silly sides. *The Thought For The Current Semester* at some point was that driving a racing car was like making love to a woman. I swear I remember even such a rational personage as Jackie Stewart commenting agreeably on the idea.

I may have been dumb enough to have driven from Nashville to New Orleans to get a new speedometer cable for my '60 Alfa 2000 Spider. On the other hand, when it quit running somewhere in the wilds of Middle Tennessee, Bob Cameron and I discovered the carbon post in the center of the distributor cap had broken off. So, with pliers we pulled the center carbon post out of a flashlight battery, whittled it down with a pocketknife, took the spring out of a ballpoint pen, and put the contraption into the cap. It ran fine from then on, and it never occurred to me to ever get another distributor cap.

An unmuffled Ferrari V12 is definitely a musical sound. People have made recordings of songs using barking dogs and meowing cats. Why not use various engine notes to play some songs? Ought to be a cinch even to fake/duplicate all kinds of engine sounds. I recommend a selection of slowish ballads, to get full appreciation of the exhaust notes. Notes! Heck, there you are.

Earlier I wrote about lost stuff – places and, mysteriously, things. When I was five, my uncle was handing me a nickel, when it fell from his hand onto the concrete driveway. My eyes were a lot closer to the ground in those days, but the nickel just hit the pavement and disappeared. There was a wood filled seam in the concrete, so we figured it fell into a crack. But there were no cracks.

Many years later I asked Uncle if he had just been pulling a trick on me, but he swore he was as dumbfounded as I. Judge Crater must've needed the coin to make a phone call.

Loaned things get away too, including about three feet of hardcover fantasy and science fiction books, design books, ghost story books and at least a foot-thick stack of LPs. Then there's stolen stuff. This is sad for the thieves, as well as for the victims.

Then there are lost friends. Some involve cars and some don't. The biggest factor is just the passing of years. Some passings you hear about immediately and others, deaths you discover months or even years later. Treasure your friends, especially the far-away pals. Some people quit racing when they lose a friend in an accident. That's up to you. I could make a longish list but that would make us both unhappy.

If I could be sure that all of us wouldn't lose any more great guys from the car world until I was finished assembling this *opusette*, I'd keep scribbling the notebook equivalent of the Winchester Mystery House. People get old and then they're gone, so appreciate your elders while they're still around.

Doggone it! Let's have a film festival of just car movies! Various magazines have had people write in with names of racing movies; there are a few dozen at least. We need to do it centrally (i.e. close to where I live), and do a morning session, catered lunch break, afternoon session, catered dinner, evening session. It might carry over for a second or third day. It might go all night, with the well-known stuff scheduled late: *Two for the Road, Grand Prix, Le Mans*.

We want everybody to be able to see *Burn 'em Up Baxter* and *Speed* and that weird one filmed in Nassau with the real downer ending, where our cuckolded hero is blinded in a crash, but blackmails his despicable wife to take care of him for the rest of his life. Anybody remember the name of that one? Oh, yes, you're on your own regarding *Pit Stop Girls*.

Remember *safety* headlights that had a glowing orange filament, for when the regular one burned out? What about those radioactive AC sparkplugs with a genuine plutonium-tipped electrode. Heck, you even had a radioactive Dr. West's toothbrush in your bathroom. It emitted alpha particles that a sheet of paper would stop, but they killed germs on the toothbrush.

Is there a warehouse that has a dusty hidden stash of Firestone LXX tires on their special wheels? Available only on Buicks, I recall. Just think of it, a tire with an incredibly low, low 70 aspect ratio. "Gosh, Fred! It looks like somebody just wrapped a couple of layers of friction tape around those rims. Wieeerd!"

There was an incredibly neat item on the market in the early 1960s that showed how catching the motorsports virus was. Do you remember the refrigerator available with factory-decorated doors? There was the redwood forest, an ocean scene, maybe a lake view and flowers. There was also a front view of a shark-nose Ferrari '61 world champion car, steering to its right. Can anybody find one of those things in a junkyard? I mean the refrigerator!

The entire line was displayed in several full page ads in *Life*, *Look* and *Colliers* – it was no one-time thing. I never saw one in an appliance store, not that I often went appliance shopping. This fridge has disappeared into the memory hold along with the Dodges of 40 years ago with a daytime running light, off-center in the grill.

Motorsports and references to it are everywhere these days. It's something that's on TV, like golf or tennis or baseball or football. But sometimes it does stick its nose into inappropriate places. Karen and I were at the funeral for the 101-year-old grandmother of a friend in France. It was very traditional. The church, built in the twelfth century, was so narrow of door that there was minimal clearance to get the coffin in and out. A childrens' choir sang. We walked behind the Mercedes hearse to the cemetery; slowly up the hill, and all the cows in the field came over to the fence to watch the procession. And on the window in the rear door of the hearse, two feet across, was the decal *Mercedes Chooses Shell!*

You're familiar with Hemingway's statement that the only three sports are bull fighting, mountain climbing, and auto racing; all the others are simply games. Robert Morley furthered the philosophy when he said, "all games played with a round ball will damage the brain, except roulette."

They say in life, timing is everything. And that goes double for racing. Transponders have taken some of the fun of the unexpected out of the mix, though. Two cases in point, both hinging, I'm sure, on those stopwatches where the sweep hand went around once every 30 seconds, not every minute. You had to take a close look to see just where the teensy minute hand was: on a minute or the itsy-bitsy half-minute mark. Combine this with sincere but prejudicial attitudes on the part of timing personnel and you (well, me actually) get the following.

I felt really good with my qualifying laps at the Stuttgart, Arkansas airport course in the H Production Morgan, but there I was on the grid sheet, buried somewhere in the back of the nearly 40-car grid of all kinds of production and even some modified cars, timed about a half-minute slower than my crew had clocked me. I sought an audience with the timing chief. "That's where you belong," he told me brusquely, adding "I know how fast Morgans are."

He shouldn't have said that; or maybe it was good that he did. It was red mist city for yours truly. This was in the beloved days of standing starts, and Bill Pryor helped out. He went to the cars ahead of me on the grid. "Look," said Bill. "That Morgan comes off the line like a rocket, so spread out and give him room." Then he strolled back to the cars behind me. "The Mog really staggers off the line, so take it easy when the flag drops and don't run over him." The flag dropped and cars in front of me parted like that Red Sea thing. I won my class. Fun.

The flipside of this story was qualifying at Sebring in the Lancia Flaminia Zagato 3C, all 2700 pounds, 2½ liters, and 150 Italian horsepower of it, on those skinny 165x400 Michelin Xs. Oh how I wish we had't gotten cute and tried to rebuild the distributor the night before the race, because my official time was thirty seconds faster, to the tenth of a second, than I really had turned! We were way up toward the front of the grid, ahead of several GT Ferraris and some Corvettes and stuff like that, because I'm sure whoever was timing our car said to himself, "Swoopy Italian car, Zagato bodywork, didn't a Lancia win this race a few years back," and gave us the benefit of the doubt when he looked at those teeny little minute/halfminute marks on his watch. Dang distributor. We didn't even put the car on the freakin' grid.

I've already mentioned being disqualified in two racing associations and their resulting rules changes. So I decided, regarding the SCCA, to get in a little personal satisfaction. The year after my Runoffs victory/disqualification in the Morgan (when none of my competitors wanted to protest me, a steward, now gone to his reward, protested me) I took a teensy sip of fine cognac before every race. Actually, there are studies showing that a slight bit of alcohol improves motor skills performance in a noticeable percentage of people tested, so I figured it might even help.

What got to me was the phrase "willful and deliberate unsportsmanlike conduct" in the official disqualification document. I was so mad my emotional needle went off the dial and all the way around to a superior calm and so, I shook all the stewards' hands and told them they did what they felt was right and no hard feelings on my part – and I actually meant it. Gee, what a swell guy!

It reminds me now of old pal Ed Spurlock in Nashville, who, with his sons, rebuilt a wrecked Morgan and then a rusty, field-found Alfa sedan in his basement. As we walked through the paddock at a Road Atlanta runoffs, he remarked that he didn't want to join SCCA, because if he did, he thought he could file successful protests against the mechanical condition of about half the entire field. He knew the rulebook forward and backward and no, he wasn't the wrench who worked on my Mog and whose well-meaning efforts during the Targa Florio also got us disqualified there! Make that 3 major leagues: SCCA, IMSA, and FIA.

When racing dangers are discussed, first thing that pops to mind is a crash. Then fire – usually the result of a crash. Please add getting shot.

The track: Stuttgart, Arkansas airport. After a race, a Porsche Speedster driver pulls into the pits near us. "Man, somebody threw up a heckuva rock out there! Broke a chunk outta my windscreen and whacked me on the helmet." Then we saw the foot-long crease in his hood, pointing at the 3" triangle missing out of the top of his Plexiglas windscreen. Next we saw the gouge in the front of his helmet – an inch or so crater in the helmet with a teensy hole through to the inside that you could peek out of.

He'd caught a ricochet off the concrete runway, no doubt about it. No .22 could've done it. Maybe a .223 Hornet or such. We all said, "Wow!" and had a soft drink. No one reported it to a steward or anything. Just one of them racin' deals.

We used to have a rating scale for filthy restrooms on our race trips. You can still find cruddy places today, but our baseline was a Shell station northwest of Birmingham in the mid-sixties. Our shoes actually stuck to the floor there.

Cars and motorbikes, in all their wonderful and amusing variation, are about the most interesting moving things on the planet, but let's not forget trains. In an alternate universe, whose details I can provide if you were to request them, businessmen and sportsmen wouldn't have private planes, but private trains, two or three cars in length, with living quarters superior to the grandest motorhomes of today. Imagine the rail network at its densest, with totally integrated computer controls of block signals across the entire country. Very, very safe.

You would have the latest fuel-cell engines for the technophiles, while the family with two Morgans in the garage car might have a traditional steam locomotive, running on LPG with a carbon fiber boiler. The nicer trains would have proactive suspensions of course, reading the wobbles and waves in the track and instantly compensating to give a velvet ride.

There would be one or two household domestic servants taken along too, to cook and serve tasty meals from the ultra-ergonomic kitchen. These people would be going to the Super Bowl or to a sports car race – towing a garage car, remember? Or maybe on a business trip? Dad might drive the engine or hire an expert from the pool of professionals, like the corporate pilots of today.

Big railroad yards, appropriately located, would serve as overnight rest areas if the family wanted to see the most daylight scenery or didn't have a professional train crew. Dream on.

My friends and I conjured up this scenario with many more details long ago: most road races then were held on WWII training airfields and, of course, they had rail lines right to them. So, we thought it'd be really keen to get one of those Bugatti railcars or even their American equivalent, and have living quarters in it and, of course, room for the race car and go-to-town car in it, too.

Yeah, let those guys have those semis that were starting to appear here and there at the races. Just check out the looks on their faces when our self-powered railcar slowly lumbers and teeters down the rusty track to pull to a halt near the paddock. We could even put a wing on the roof and a spoiler on the front. Can't have too much downforce on a railroad car!

We embellished the idea once we got the mental momentum up: A nice big tent or awning in team colors with outdoor furniture in its shade. We'd race a pair of BMW 507s and have a few college girls in short-shorts uniforms as our pit crew. Maybe a mechanic too, but let's not stretch it.

There were other wonderful wacky ideas too, much cheaper. How about a London double-decker bus, with the racecar stored at the rear and the living quarters at the front? We'd put the driver up on the roof, so at night you would breeze down the Interstate with the lights on inside and as people passed they would look over at posh folks having cocktails and leaning their backs against the windshield and, "Omigawd Emily there's no freaking driver!"

Sex, Dogs and Rock and Roll

As previously mentioned, I've had occasional pleasant times with the ladies, but since I've had much more experience with dogs than with drugs, the heading seems appropriate. Drug-wise I've been under total anesthesia a half-dozen times. I once locked myself in a room with a ballerina and a joint. I have a feeling she knew more about weed than I did; but at any rate it just made me hungry and that's one stimulus I don't need.

It also struck me as such a cornball thing to do, like getting tattooed these days. I must admit, though, I nearly got a tattoo in 1975. At the first Long Beach Grand Prix the atmosphere, as you might know, was kind of the anti-Monaco as big time ocean-side races go: pool halls, seedy bars right out of central casting (Hollywood isn't that far away) and tattoo parlors.

That magnificent author and general intellect, Philip Finch, and I had a couple drinks in one of the aforementioned establishments and it occurred to me, that as one of the founders of the LBGP, it would be appropriate to have an LBGP pit pass tattooed on my upper arm. The closer I got to the parlor the idea, strong as it was, couldn't overcome the ambience of the shop. I got no tattoo.

Oh, yes, rock and roll – I have a few anthologies of the stuff up to about '73 to play as background music at parties. Since then, I think the vast majority of it sucks. Of course, rock and roll is much like country music; their latitudes are enormous. Almost anything contemporary can be called one, the other or both. My idea of rock and roll was formed when a rock band had a half-dozen wind instruments. Yes, Hannah, I'm old.

Now to that un-recommendable combo platter: drugs and cars. I did it once on the '75 *Cannonball Baker Sea to Sea Memorial Trophy Dash*. I figured in case of overwhelming fatigue, it would be nice to have some sort of backup; so after wheedling a long-gone-from-Tulsa acquaintance pharmacist, I was the proud owner of a Black Mariah, also known as an L.A. Turnaround: a black capsule of straight Benzedrine.

Never mind all the Cannonball stories. They're in Yates' wonderful book. Let's just say that somewhere, just west of Kingman, Arizona, with Bill Pryor snoring blissfully away in the passenger seat, I felt the real need for stimulation. I took out the capsule. I figured it was probably awfully strong, especially for the few hours remaining to the Portofino Inn. I pulled it apart, spilling most of it. I shook out maybe five teensy grains into my palm. That oughtta do it, I thought.

Boy did it ever! My Guardian Angel probably couldn't jostle me enough to spill it all, but I admit I didn't take all of the residue in the capsule, just a few of those little white spots. I woke right up, and about the time I'd decided I'd done the smart thing, I decided I really should kill that guy driving the green Pontiac ahead of me. I had nothing against him, the green Pontiac, itself, was the capital offense.

I kept myself under control, and eventually my higher brain functions were able to find amusing the fact that I hated every other car on the road. The crap wore off in an hour and from then on into the Portofino I was kept alert by the happy feeling that I hadn't taken any more of that stuff. Once was more than enough. At least I can spread the word about the experience along with the suggestion: Don't!

I do have dogs in my life, thanks to Karen. If any one had said a quarter century ago that I would be Uncle Toly (although Karen refers to me as Daddy) to an assortment of small, throw-away dogs we have rescued, I would have laughed and laughed and laughed. But I've been Uncle Toly to Spark Pug I, Spark Pug II, Mille Miglia, and Magneat-o; all Pugs. There was also Bizzarrini-Beany-Weany, a 17-year-old mostly blind crippled Chihuahua whose sole remaining tooth fell out as we brought her home from the shelter. Then there are Frou-Frou and Oui-Oui, the dumb but totally lovable blondes, one a Pekingese, the other a Japanese Chin and the one and only Loupy, the abandoned Schipperke. Talk about unconditional love! Karen says they like me because we all snore and kinda smell alike.

It just occurred to me: why do I ramble on so? It's a question I actually asked myself. The answer: it's not that I've been so active in all forms of motorsport recently, however you might care to define recently. Roger Penske I'm not. Carroll Shelby I'm not. Heck, Peter Giddings or Dean Buter I'm not. It's just that fewer and fewer people know much about things that used to happen as a matter of course in those past days. So a comment that might've taken a half-minute 40 years ago about a major event that had just taken place – well, today that comment rates minutes and paragraphs and pages, because the current crop of youngsters, no blame on them, knows zip/zero/nada about commonplace or annual events, yes, famous ones, of that era that even stay-at-home magazine reading car dweebs in those days could describe in detail - or in as much detail as Henry Manney, Bernard Cahier, John Bolster or Dean Batchelor had described to them.

So I try to fill in some details for Mr./Ms. Faithful Reader. Stories and history change, or at least the telling of them does. Take a modern encyclopedia (do they still print those things?). Look up, say, the Crimean War. Then look it up in the 1927 *Encyclopedia Brittanica*. Your jaw will drop. Can car tales be any different? Get your hands on ancient issues of *Autosport* or Gus Vignolle's *Motoracing* and you'll also be amazed how much political correctness has oozed its way into the current reporting of our beloved sport. These days you don't get much in the motoring press about who snuck off with who's mistress, while who or who's wife was doing something involving that handsome Latin ignition expert, and Heaven knows there's a lot more motoring press nowadays. TV and movie personalities have cornered the scandal market and it's just sleazy now. Not amusing at all.

Maybe a lot more things are wonderful when you're 20 than they would be at your present age. Twenty years old. No longer one of those annoying teens but you're not an authorized adult – at least in those days. After that first European trip I've told you about and a great boat ride back on the French Line's *Liberté*, I went home by train: first leg NYC to Chicago on the Broadway Limited. Not very far out of New York we ran along a river at sunset. The clouds were orange and pink in a pale blue sky. The train overtook a mahogany-bodied speedboat pulling a girl on an aquaplane – a slightly v-shaped platform itself towed by the boat, with the girl standing on it holding a loop of rope. Her one-piece swimsuit matched the sky. We rounded a gentle bend to the left and while she and the boat were still in view, far, far behind us, sunlit through through the mist of distance, a huge cantilever bridge glowed gold through the haze.

The scene was like an illustration that might have occupied the inside front cover and front page of a junior high school civics book. Are there still civics books? Do any schoolbooks at all these days have beautiful and evocative images of Americana?

Not long thereafter, the moon, high above the train and invisible, lit up little puffy white clouds like I've never seen since: glowing cotton balls glued to a dark blue dome thousands of feet overhead. Only a Divine Presence can create a few hours like this.

Thomas Wolfe said you can't go home again, but I sure have. Telling you so many semi-personal stories has let me simultaneously relive that part of my life. Just remember your eternal home is in the Kingdom of Heaven and it is within you. You can't take a date, though, and it's the best of the few great places you can't get to by car.

Epilogue

I'm human. I guess I've broken all the commandments. I've been redeemed by the shed blood of Jesus Christ, the Savior of the World. The easiest twinge of sin I ever get is when I read somebody's biography, where they say, "I wouldn't change a thing, if I had to live my life over." Lucky bastards! You wanna know what I'd change if I could? I mean things I did/didn't do that I'd do differently – things that were all my very own doing? Take out a piece of paper and number from one to twenty. Now crumple it up and throw it away, because I'm not going to tell you. I'm sure you can guess a few of them, though, from this stuff you've been reading.

Youth is wonderful, especially when you enjoy it all the time. I was going to say was *wonderful*, but then, of course, youth is just a state of mind. To you kids out there, being physically old is just feeling most of the time like being your age the day after your first football practice. Trouble is you won't look nearly as good and the feeling won't go away in 24 hours.

For some reason the world is divided into people who look almost the same as their yearbook pictures dozens of years later, and those who don't resemble their youthful selves in the least. A lot, but not all, of the difference is the loss of hair and the addition of fat; still, there are other particular changes. But you know if you take care of your car, it'll look just the same! Best Satchel Paige quote ever: "How old would you be, if you didn't know how old you were?"

I miss the good old days of my youth. Are there really people who don't? Even people who are continuously accomplishing this and that must have more than vaguely fond memories of a pleasant past, considered as a whole. I miss my parents.

You've heard a bit about mom. Car-wise, she used to really hustle down the road at 80 or so on that narrow rumbly concrete 2-lane between Bartlesville and Tulsa. You know, she talked to her cars, especially when driving fast. She called them "Honey," which she never called dad, at least within my earshot. She truly enjoyed a trip to Tulsa in the Porsche or Alfa, which always surprised me. Once she rolled a car, gently, into a ditch, when the road was icy. Mild concussion.

Mom's best *car story* didn't involve her driving. We were blasting across Mexico, going from Mexico City to Cuernavaca in a '53 Buick limousine. I've never seen another one. In Mexico City, my generous mother had learned not to give a dollar bill to a little kid, because in five seconds she'd be surrounded by about twenty kids of all ages with their hands out. A hundred bucks or so later, she decided that candy would be a much better little gift. She stocked up on shoebox-sized cellophane bags of individually wrapped peppermints and fruit sourballs.

And thus it was that as we were approaching, at undiminished velocity, a Mexican road repair crew, mom decided that those hard-working fellows should have some candy too. She launched two or three bags out the side window as we hurtled toward the workers – our driver, in his position of authority, wasn't about to slow down for those peons. He leaned on the horn about the time the bags of hard candy hit the road and exploded in a kind of glucose cluster-bomb attack. The workers cringed, ducked, doubled over. The cringing may have come from our roaring by, but the other behavior had to be due to that candy double-O buckshot. Mom never looked back, but we persuaded her to save the candy for the kids, one piece at a time.

Dad considered cars to be appliances. I guess his citizenship papers came with the general *American Automotive Attitude*. Once, I coaxed his feelings about an ideal car out of him. "Seating like a Model A Ford coupe, automatic transmission, air conditioning. As quiet as his '56 Caddy. Racing? Why would anyone want to drive around and around the same piece of road?" He more than tolerated my enjoyment, although he thought I might like it because it felt so good when it was over, like hitting yourself in the head with a hammer.

He was very pleased when Bryan Crow and I patented the idea of variable valve timing in 1965. We had the concept really covered. In our claim we provided adjustments for every part of the valve train. Conrero of Alfa Romeo race-tuning fame built a single cylinder motorcycle engine for us embodying our ideas and, of course, it put out more power everywhere on the curve. We heard rumors that GM then built something similar on an experimental version of their single-ohc Pontiac six – remember that neat engine? Remember the V6 and V12 (!) truck engines that International Harvester (I think) built in 1960? There's a nifty engine to put in a hotrod, instead of the ubiquitous crate motor. Find one and call me.

Besides v.v.t., we investigated patenting using engine exhaust for airflow management around a car and the concept of using air-conditioning during braking of a race car to chill the route of the intake charge. And then there were tire designs; so many fun things to think about regarding cars.

But I digress, again. My dad never went racing. He thought the idea of going around and around was a bit silly. Point-to-point races made more sense to him. Paris-Madrid, anyone?

He had an experience tangentially, but importantly involving a means of transport that went far beyond sports cars. The folks had finally made it out of Russia as the communists took over. I never heard the end of the stories; every time I brought another friend home from college there would be a new hour or two of tales I'd never heard. Traveling with bandits; miraculously, yes miraculously avoiding massacres; crossing a bombed bridge, that even soldiers were forbidden to try, while carrying my older brother between two big pillows. (Mom carried Sergei — she didn't trust dad).

So mom and brother were in Constantinople, and dad went to Berlin to meet with a bank about starting Reda Pump Company in Germany in about 1921, as I recall. Dad was 28 years old. From now-destroyed Russian connections and through tenuous communications from Constantinople, arrangements had been made. Dad had a small apartment and enough money for a few weeks until business financing came through. He was supposed to meet with a secretary to *Geheimrat* Deutsch. *Geheimrat* is a title and I don't know if it exists in modern German politics; let's just say this guy was Germany's Bernard Baruch or somewhat like the head of America's Federal Reserve. Dad wasn't going to meet him personally, just a secretary to formalize arrangements.

It was a winter evening, and a sleigh was sent to fetch pop: a couple of horses, driver, footman standing on the back – a real classy outfit. Dad got in, the footman covered him with a big bearskin robe, and off they went, from city streetlights into the country under a clear starry sky. Finally, they stopped at a pleasant house.

Hmmm, dad thought, I would've expected something a bit more grandiose. Dad was right: that was the estate gatekeeper's house. The gates opened and up they went along the long drive to the grand manor house. The footman runs to ring doorbell, as dad exits the sleigh, getting a small blob of pitch or wet paint or something on his right hand. There was nothing to wipe it on – certainly not that lovely bearskin lap robe.

The butler escorts dad in, and here comes the secretary's secretary. There was a curt little bow and heel clicking, as they shake hands. But dad doesn't want to get the stuff on the secretary's hand, so he gives him an odd grip. Secretary's eyebrows go up and dad thinks, swell, he thinks I'm a bit shall we say *twee*.

The secretary says, "Oh sir, excuse me a moment" and hustles off (dad was fluent in German, by the way – Good Czarist Polytechnic education). A few moments pass and another man tells dad, "The *Geheimrat* will see you now." This was totally unexpected, and dad was led upstairs to the great man's bedroom suite. Coffee, brandy, and Java-Sumatra cigars were brought in; remember, this was getting well on into the evening.

After introductions and traditional small talk, dad brings up the subject of financing for his new business. "Oh, that's nothing," says Herr Deutsch. "We have greater plans than that for you." Dad inquires as to exactly what it is they – whoever they are – have in mind. "Why, we want you to be the supreme trade representative from the German government to the new Soviet Socialist Republic," he is told. Dad is a bit stunned. He's been in Germany for less than two weeks.

He demurs, "No, really, all I am planning is a manufacturing plant," he says.

"Doktor Arutunoff, do not play at modesty! We are more than certain of your capabilities! We might say we know more about you than you know about yourself!"

Dad thinks, "It was that odd handshake! What else could it be?" He replies, "Sir, I thank you and I assure you that I am capable of such an assignment, but I can't take your most generous offer because of ethical reasons."

"Just what might these considerations be?" he is asked. Dad tells him of the atrocities he has seen as the commies take over little towns, big towns and cities. Killings for no reason at all; sadistic killings; counterproductive killings; killings for the sheer thrill of killing; bodies in the street, even bodies of families on park benches.

There is a moment of silence. "Doktor Arutunoff," says Deutsch. "We must be cosmopolitan about such things. In this world there are people who kill and people who get killed and you are far, far too intelligent not to know the difference." Dad thanks him again and tells him he simply won't accept this huge (and, he thought, monstrous) offer. He just would like to nail down his business financing. "Doktor, I'm sorry that you disappoint me," says Deutsch, and leaves the room. Dad is taken back to his hotel.

Next day, at the prearranged bank – oh, you guessed it already. No deal – and not at the next bank and the next. Many, many years after I first heard this story, I heard a tape dad made, and he said that as he was running out of money, he was going to commit his wife and son to the care of God and then go kill himself. There was only one man in the world who could help him, and this man was somewhere in Scandinavia.

The next morning after his decision, as he turned right instead of left to try another place for breakfast; guess who he met on the street? Of course, that's right. Another miracle. Went to Dresdener

Bank, got a loan, started the business, then brought mom and brother to Berlin. The story, like life, goes on and on, but this is enough to let you know why my dad was a conspiracy theorist all his life. Me too.

Dad invented, thank you Lord, the submergible oil well pump/motor combination. In 1922, in Germany, under contract to the government, he also built a pulsejet engine that was so powerful it tore out of its test bed (a long counterbalanced rotating arm), went through the roof of the building and landed a few blocks away. Late in his life he told me this story, apologizing for inventing the V-1's powerplant; although he said someone else would have figured it out soon enough, as the theoretical concept had been around for a year or two.

Dad never worked for anyone. In college, he had one of his professors working for him on various electrical projects. He wired the family home when he was twelve. He told me as an infant he had a word, which let him move things. He liked looking out the window from his baby bed, and so, when the nanny would move him away from the window to stay out of the draft, he would say the word and move the bed back to the window. "Who wants this child to die of a cold?" was the household question and blame briefly fell on one of his older brothers. When he was seven or eight, there was a good-sized rock with a cavity underneath that he wanted to investigate. "The Word!" he thought, but he'd forgotten it.

He always wanted to meet the man in Florida who mysteriously built that big coral castle and its surrounding sculptures – huge pieces – without a single tool on the property, but they never got together. He exchanged letters with Robert Goddard, the founder of American rocketry, but they never met.

Mom was psychic. Dad was psychic. Mom's advice saved dad's life a couple times, and hers too. When he died, he appeared to me in my bedroom 40 miles away, as the purest being I could ever see on earth, youthful and healthy, and when he hugged me goodbye, I didn't hear the word *son*, as I sort of expected, but *brother*. There was more, but this story's long enough. What wonderful parents I had.

L'Envoie

The months and years smoothly and quietly go by, like the numbers on your odometer on an all-day trip. I'd very much like to do some more *big time racing*, but when I can read things like a driver having car trouble at Le Mans can't take his helmet off to listen to advice from a helper on the scene, I just figure my team would be disqualified for something or other about the time we fired up for the first practice session. Freaking bureaucracy – every new "administration" thinks all the rules already in place simply form the bedrock for the new guys' edifice of ever more regulation. Pathetic. I am cheered when I read that a man won his class in a vintage race at the age of 93, in the car his father gave him around 1930. He died recently at 95. There's playtime left, it seems, with the proper blessings, of course.

Although it's inevitable, I don't eagerly anticipate leaving these lovely playing fields. But I'm not worried about Afterwards.

I've told you about dad. So, while I'm down here, Let's get together for a drink. It doesn't have to be real soon, but soon would be nice.

P. S. Never Forget: Never, ever forget: Wide Tires Ruined Racing

Gee whiz, saying goodbye sometimes involves standing by the front door or the car door for awhile. Did you ever know people who'd just commit themselves to "'bye now" and that was that? Graham Shaw was like that. Remember him? Tombstone Shaw. He bought a 2-seat P-51 Mustang right after he learned to fly in a Piper Cub. One time at the Chimney Rock Hillclimb, Graham got up real early and took his D-Jag.... well now, look at the time, Gotta split. Hope that old crate of yours can get you home.

Oh yes, one more thing; if you've liked this book enough to consider giving me a really nice Christmas present, let me suggest: BMW 507; the NASCAR Toronado that never raced (new right front tire every five laps); NSU Sport Prinz – one of the few with the 1100cc TT engine, instead of the teensy twin; a Hudson Italia -

if the designer had been a plastic surgeon instead, can you imagine what a girl might look like? John Passwater's USAC stocker Studebaker GT Hawk; 300SL Gullwing – yeah, yeah, just like everybody else; the Lambo 3500 Zagato; the Cadillac Eldorado Zagato; that OSI Alfa Scarabeo; a Berkeley B105; Packard Panther Daytona; what the heck, a Studebaker Golden Hawk; the twin-boom Pegaso Le Mans car; the Mac's Special; Yunick's Indy *Side-car*; that marvelous roadster that Luigi Colani is sitting on in his first design book; any Alfa Zagato old or new – now that I think about it, any Zagato, period; a Vincent anything; Scott Flying Squirrel; Ariel Square Four, or any Ariel (I like the name); the steam-powered motorcycle on the top floor of that castle in the Czech Republic; a Curtiss P40 to put in the back yard and climb in and out of and make airplane noises; a Doble and a Lozier.

How about this? Financing for my next six *art rod* designs – hey, we might even make a bit of money here.

I opened with a quote from George Carlin and I close with a quote from Elwood P. Dowd in the movie *Harvey*, about Elwood's closest friend, an invisible 6'3" rabbit.

Reality? Well, I've wrestled with reality for about 35 years, and I'm proud to say that I've finally won out over it!

Ignition off.

Track Appendix

Tracks I have graced with my presence: Courtland, Montgomery street course, Huntsville, Selma, Tuskegee, Dothan, Alabama. Stuttgart, the Eureka Springs and Mt. Nebo hillclimbs, Arkansas. Eloy, Arizona. Laguna Seca, Riverside, the vintage races at Palm Springs, Los Angeles and Coronado N.A.S., plus the Torrey Pines vintage hillclimb, California. Aspen, La Junta, Pueblo, Continental Divide, and the Steamboat Springs and Pike's Peak vintage hillclimb, Colorado. Daytona, Fernandina Beach, Sebring, West Palm Beach (Moroso), Miami, and Pensacola Beach, Florida. Road Atlanta and Savannah, Georgia. That nice track in East St. Louis, Illinois. Indianapolis Raceway Park, in Indiana. Greenwood, Iowa. Olathe, Lake Afton, Independence, Hutchinson, Heartland Park, and Coffeyville, Kansas. Mansfield, Bossier City, Lake Charles, and Opelousas, Louisiana. Tupelo, Mississippi. Mid-America, and the downtown Kansas City vintage race, Missouri. Alliance, Nebraska (big mistake). Vineland, New Jersey. Roswell and Las Cruces, New Mexico. Watkins Glen, New York. Charlotte and the Chimney Rock hillclimb, North Carolina. Mid-Ohio, Ohio. Muskogee, Okmulgee, Oklahoma City, Ponca City, and Hallett, Oklahoma. The Pittsburgh and Philadelphia vintage races, Pennsylvania. Chattanooga and Memphis, Tennessee. Big Spring, Green Valley, Dallas International, Austin, Texas Motor Speedway, New Braunfels, Victoria, and Texas International in, of course, Texas. VIR in Virginia. Elkhart Lake and Blackhawk Farms, Wisconsin. Nassau in the Bahamas. Silverstone and Brands Hatch, England. The Nurburgring in Germany. Orleans and another purpose-built circuit by a chateau in France. Monza, the Targa Florio, Vallelunga, Sirmione, and 3 other circuits in Italy. Spa in Belgium. The A1 Ring in Austria. I might've left out a few, and I won't mention the one-off races I missed, back then. This comes to 87 circuits, including hillclimbs (but not the fifteen hillclimbs in the *Coppa D'Italia*). If you guys had all been with me, we could have taken over a couple hotels and irritated everyone by demanding Coors beer.

My favorite club track of all: the one-time-only layout at Big Springs, Texas, on the airport. To make the course map, simply trace around a brick and make the four corners different from one another. The straights were a mile long. Great fun to just let 'er run and run and run. And much more recently, at Texas Motor Speedway in one of the small bore classes, although then we couldn't use the banking, you had almost a mile and a half wide open – you re-enter the NASCAR oval from the infield road course only about a hundred yards from where you left it.

Okay, now it really is bedtime. Just one more look in the garage.